Addictions Counseling

Addictions Counseling

A Competency-Based Approach

Cynthia A. Faulkner

and

Samuel S. Faulkner

OXFORD
UNIVERSITY PRESS

OXFORD
UNIVERSITY PRESS

Oxford University Press is a department of the University of Oxford. It furthers
the University's objective of excellence in research, scholarship, and education
by publishing worldwide. Oxford is a registered trade mark of Oxford University
Press in the UK and certain other countries.

Published in the United States of America by Oxford University Press
198 Madison Avenue, New York, NY 10016, United States of America.

Library of Congress Cataloging-in-Publication Data
Names: Faulkner, Cynthia A., author. |
Faulkner, Samuel S., editor.
Title: Addictions counseling : a competency-based approach /
Cynthia A. Faulkner, Samuel S. Faulkner.
Description: New York, NY : Oxford University Press, [2019] |
Includes bibliographical references and index.
Identifiers: LCCN 2018028251 (print) | LCCN 2018041079 (ebook) |
ISBN 9780190930417 (updf) | ISBN 9780190930424 (epub) |
ISBN 9780190926854 (pbk. : alk. paper)
Subjects: LCSH: Drug abuse counseling—Handbooks, manuals, etc.
Classification: LCC RC564 (ebook) | LCC RC564 .F38 2019 (print) |
DDC 362.29/186—dc23
LC record available at https://lccn.loc.gov/2018028251

CONTENTS

Competencies, Standards, and Case Scenario

INTRODUCTION

Whether you are an educator who is teaching this course or a student who is preparing for a career in the addictions field, we have designed this textbook for you. We, the authors, have almost four decades of practice experience in the field of substance abuse counseling. And we have years of experience as educators, researchers, and clinical supervisors with an expertise in behavioral health. It is through our teaching and practice experiences that we identified a need for a competency-based textbook to teach the practice of substance abuse counseling in the classroom. Within this first chapter, we explain how the text content is organized based on the most current competencies and standards for both the curricula and the practice of addiction counseling. We will end this chapter with the case scenario of Juanita. We include Juanita's psychosocial assessment and referral to treatment. We will follow Juanita throughout the text as we apply the various processes of addiction assessment and treatment to her case.

COMPETENCY-BASED PRACTICE

This text is designed to teach you the knowledge, skills, and values needed for competency-based substance abuse counseling practice, regardless of your discipline. Within each chapter, we have incorporated benchmark practice standards and educational standards aligned with certification and accreditations requirements. Throughout the text, we will be referring to these standards, also known as *competencies*. In addition, we will begin each chapter by identifying the competencies that are being addressed in that chapter and how they are applied.

SAMHSA's Addiction Counseling Competencies

In 1998, the Substance Abuse and Mental Health Services Administration (SAMHSA) and the Center for Substance Abuse Treatment (CSAT) published *Addiction Counseling Competencies: The Knowledge, Skills, and Attitudes of Professional Practice* as Technical Assistance Publication 21 (TAP 21), (SAMHSA, 2008*b*). These competencies were developed by the National Curriculum Committee of the Addiction Technology Transfer Center (ATTC) Network. They were an attempt to quantify and codify the 123 competencies that are essential to the effective practice of counseling for psychoactive substance use disorders. These competencies are believed to be the knowledge, skills and attitudes (KSAs) that counselors need to become fully proficient in each competency. These competencies have been widely accepted as benchmarks and are now incorporated into curriculum for substance abuse counseling programs. These competencies have even gained international acceptance and have been translated into several languages. Since their initial publication, the competencies have since been updated based on literature and research published in the expanding field of addiction.

TRANSDISCIPLINARY FOUNDATIONS AND PROFESSIONAL PRACTICE DIMENSIONS

SAMHSA's TAP 21 is a national model of competencies based on research findings and outcomes that are "essential to the effective practice of counseling for psychoactive substance use disorders" (Center for Substance Abuse Treatment, 2006, p. 1). The 123 educational competencies are benchmarks for developing curricula for the education and training of substance abuse counseling. These competencies are divided into two sections, Transdisciplinary Foundation and Professional Practice Dimensions. The Transdisciplinary Foundation section has four foundations, and the Professional Practice Dimensions section has eight practice dimensions. "The term 'transdisciplinary' was selected to describe the knowledge and skills needed by all disciplines (e.g., medicine, social work, pastoral guidance, corrections, social welfare) that deal directly with working with substance use disorders" (Center for Substance Abuse Treatment, 2006, p. 3). The practice dimensions section specifically addresses the competencies needed for professional practice as an addictions counselor.

Section I. Transdisciplinary Foundations
1. Understanding Addiction
2. Treatment Knowledge
3. Application to Practice
4. Professional Readiness

Section II. Professional Practice Dimensions
1. Clinical Evaluation
2. Treatment Planning
3. Referral
4. Service Coordination
5. Counseling
6. Client, Family, and Community Education
7. Documentation
8. Professional and Ethical Responsibilities

The majority (100 out of 123) of the competencies are located within the eight Practice Dimensions. In this text, we will identify the relevant competencies related to the content within each chapter.

KNOWLEDGE, SKILLS, AND ATTITUDES

Throughout TAP 21, you will find a reference to KSAs. The Foundation competencies require specific knowledge and attitudes but are not skill-based, as are the Practice Dimensions. Therefore, under the Transdisciplinary Foundations we see that Competency 7: "Understand the importance of research and outcome data and their application in clinical practice" requires *knowledge* of "Research methods in the social and behavioral sciences" and an *attitude* of "Openness to new information." Research is important to understand as a tool to help guide as well as evaluate counseling interventions.

Now, let's look at an example under Practice Dimension 1 covering Clinical Evaluation. Competency 24: "Establish rapport, including management of a crisis situation and determination of need for additional professional assistance" requires *knowledge* of "Rapport-building methods and issues," *skills* for "reflecting the client's feeling and message," and *attitudes* showing a "Willingness to establish rapport." The added skills in the Practice Dimensions relate to the performance of that specific competency.

Accreditation Standards

Accreditation standards were also important considerations for writing this text. We have included accreditation standards for two disciplines within this text: Addiction Counseling through the Council for Accreditation of Counseling and Related Educational Programs (CACREP) and Social Work through the Council on Social Work Education (CSWE) competencies addressed in the Educational Policies and Accreditation Standards (EPAS).

COUNCIL FOR ACCREDITATION OF COUNSELING
AND RELATED EDUCATIONAL PROGRAMS
Many of you who are reading this text may be students preparing to work as substance abuse counselors. Some of you are in a program accredited by CACREP which accredits specific school and university degree programs to assure that they meet a minimum level of standards in their education. Many states require a degree from a CACREP-accredited institution in order to sit for licensure such as a *Licensed Professional Counselor* in that state. Students who are preparing to specialize as addiction counselors are expected to possess the knowledge and skills necessary to practice within a wide range of issues in addiction counseling. In addition to common core curricula, addiction counseling education programs must also provide evidence of student proficiency in three domains: Foundations, Contextual Dimensions, and Practice in accordance with CACREP 2016 Standards in Section V: Entry-Level Specialty Areas—Addiction Counseling.

By including the CACREP standards for Addiction Counselors in this text, you will be in alignment with the educational coursework for your program. There are 27 individual standards located under these domains. Just as we will do with the SAMHSA TAP 21 competencies, we will include the relevant CACREP standards as they apply to each chapter. Listed here are the domains and standards for your reference.

I. Foundational
1. History and development of addiction counseling
2. Theories and models of addiction related to substance use as well as behavioral and process addictions
3. Principles and philosophies of addiction-related self-help
4. Principles, models, and documentation formats of biopsychosocial case conceptualization and treatment planning
5. Neurological, behavioral, psychological, physical, and social effects of psychoactive substances and addictive disorders on the user and significant others
6. Psychological tests and assessments in addiction counseling

II. Contextual Dimensions
7. Roles and settings of addiction counselors
8. Potential for addictive and substance use disorders to mimic and/or co-occur with a variety of medical and psychological disorders
9. Factors that increase the likelihood for a person, community, or group to be at risk for or resilient to psychoactive substance use disorders

10. Regulatory processes and substance abuse policy relative to service delivery opportunities in addiction counseling
11. Importance of vocation, family, social networks, and community systems in the addiction treatment and recovery process
12. Role of wellness and spirituality in the addiction recovery process
13. Culturally and developmentally relevant education programs that raise awareness and support addiction and substance abuse prevention and the recovery process
14. Classifications, indications, and contraindications of commonly prescribed psychopharmacological medications for appropriate medical referral and consultation
15. Diagnostic process, including differential diagnosis and the use of current diagnostic classification systems, including the *Diagnostic and Statistical Manual of Mental Disorders (DSM)* and the International Classification of Diseases (ICD)
16. Cultural factors relevant to addiction and addictive behavior
17. Professional organizations, preparation standards, and credentials relevant to the practice of addiction counseling
18. Legal and ethical considerations specific to addiction counseling
19. Record-keeping, third-party reimbursement, and other practice and management considerations in addiction counseling

III. Practice

20. Screening, assessment, and testing for addiction, including diagnostic interviews, mental status examination, symptom inventories, and psychoeducational and personality assessments
21. Assessment of biopsychosocial and spiritual history relevant to addiction
22. Assessment of symptoms of psychoactive substance toxicity, intoxication, and withdrawal symptoms
23. Techniques and interventions related to substance abuse and other addictions
24. Strategies for reducing the persisting negative effects of substance use, abuse, dependence, and addictive disorders
25. Strategies for helping clients identify the effects of addiction on life problems and the effects of continued harmful use or abuse, and the benefits of a life without addiction
26. Evaluating and identifying individualized strategies and treatment modalities relative to clients' stage of dependence, change, or recovery
27. Strategies for interfacing with the legal system and working with court-referred clients

COUNCIL ON SOCIAL WORK EDUCATION

Receiving a social work degree from a program accredited by CSWE is required by most state Social Work licensing boards. Individuals with a master's degree in social work and holding a clinical license are one of the few master's level clinicians approved to bill Medicare Part B. Social Work education is accredited by the CSWE and all programs under their accreditation must demonstrate that they adhere to a minimum set of standards for competent Social Work practice that " . . . integrate and apply social work knowledge, values, and skills to practice situations in a purposeful, intentional, and professional manner . . . " (Council on Social Work Education, Inc., 2015, p. 6). The CSWE competencies are located within the Educational Policy and Accreditation Standards (EPAS) manual. The 2015 revision was effective July 1, 2015, and is organized into 9 Competencies and 31 associated Practice Behaviors.

Competency 1: Demonstrate Ethical and Professional Behavior

Social workers:

1. make ethical decisions by applying the standards of the National Association of Social Workers (NASW) Code of Ethics, relevant laws and regulations, models for ethical decision-making, ethical conduct of research, and additional codes of ethics as appropriate to context;
2. use reflection and self-regulation to manage personal values and maintain professionalism in practice situations;
3. demonstrate professional demeanor in behavior; appearance; and oral, written, and electronic communication;
4. use technology ethically and appropriately to facilitate practice outcomes; and
5. use supervision and consultation to guide professional judgment and behavior.

Competency 2: Engage Diversity and Difference in Practice

Social workers:

6. apply and communicate understanding of the importance of diversity and difference in shaping life experiences in practice at the micro, mezzo, and macro levels;
7. present themselves as learners and engage clients and constituencies as experts of their own experiences; and
8. apply self-awareness and self-regulation to manage the influence of personal biases and values in working with diverse clients and constituencies.

Competency 3: Advance Human Rights and Social, Economic, and Environmental Justice

Social workers:

9. apply their understanding of social, economic, and environmental justice to advocate for human rights at the individual and system levels; and

10. engage in practices that advance social, economic, and environmental justice.

Competency 4: Engage in Practice-Informed Research and Research-Informed Practice

Social workers:

11. use practice experience and theory to inform scientific inquiry and research;

12. apply critical thinking to engage in analysis of quantitative and qualitative research methods and research findings; and

13. use and translate research evidence to inform and improve practice, policy, and service delivery.

Competency 5: Engage in Policy Practice

Social workers:

14. identify social policy at the local, state, and federal level that impacts well-being, service delivery, and access to social services;

15. assess how social welfare and economic policies impact the delivery of and access to social services;

16. apply critical thinking to analyze, formulate, and advocate for policies that advance human rights and social, economic, and environmental justice.

Competency 6: Engage with Individuals, Families, Groups, Organizations, and Communities

Social workers:

17. apply knowledge of human behavior and the social environment, person-in-environment, and other multidisciplinary theoretical frameworks to engage with clients and constituencies; and

18. use empathy, reflection, and interpersonal skills to effectively engage diverse clients and constituencies.

Competency 7: Assess Individuals, Families, Groups, Organizations, and Communities
Social workers:
19. collect and organize data and apply critical thinking to interpret information from clients and constituencies;
20. apply knowledge of human behavior and the social environment, person-in-environment, and other multidisciplinary theoretical frameworks in the analysis of assessment data from clients and constituencies;
21. develop mutually agreed-on intervention goals and objectives based on the critical assessment of strengths, needs, and challenges within clients and constituencies; and
22. select appropriate intervention strategies based on the assessment, research knowledge, and values and preferences of clients and constituencies.

Competency 8: Intervene with Individuals, Families, Groups, Organizations, and Communities
Social workers:
23. critically choose and implement interventions to achieve practice goals and enhance capacities of clients and constituencies;
24. apply knowledge of human behavior and the social environment, person-in-environment, and other multidisciplinary theoretical frameworks in interventions with clients and constituencies;
25. use interprofessional collaboration as appropriate to achieve beneficial practice outcomes;
26. negotiate, mediate, and advocate with and on behalf of clients and constituencies; and
27. facilitate effective transitions and endings that advance mutually agreed-on goals.

Competency 9: Evaluate Practice with Individuals, Families, Groups, Organizations, and Communities
Social workers:
28. select and use appropriate methods for evaluation of outcomes;
29. apply knowledge of human behavior and the social environment, person-in-environment, and other multidisciplinary theoretical frameworks in the evaluation of outcomes;
30. critically analyze, monitor, and evaluate intervention and program processes and outcomes; and
31. apply evaluation findings to improve practice effectiveness at the micro, mezzo, and macro levels.

Certification

IC&RC ALCOHOL AND DRUG COUNSELOR JOB ANALYSIS

A long-standing practice for certification readiness has been to use the International Certification & Reciprocity Consortium's (IC&RC) original 12 Core Functions with their corresponding Global Criteria, developed in the 1980s to delineate essential criteria for the day-to-day practice activities of a substance abuse counselor. In 2015, these 12 Core Functions were replaced to reflect the updated Alcohol and Drug Counselor Job Analysis (JA). This also modifies the examination for certification as an Alcohol and Drug Counselor through IC&RC. In this Job Analysis, there are four Domains and each Domain has specific Tasks. These tasks also have associated knowledge and skills that are required to achieve each specific task. Here, we have listed only the Domains and Tasks. However, you can locate the complete document at: http://www.internationalcredentialing.org/Resources/Documents/ADC_JA_Finished_Announcement.pdf.

Domain I: Screening, Assessment, and Engagement

Task 1: Demonstrate verbal and nonverbal communication to establish rapport and promote engagement.

Task 2: Discuss with the client the rationale, purpose, and procedures associated with the screening and assessment process to facilitate client understanding and cooperation.

Task 3: Assess client's immediate needs by evaluating observed behavior and other relevant information, including signs and symptoms of intoxication and withdrawal.

Task 4: Administer appropriate evidence-based screening and assessment instruments specific to clients to determine their strengths and needs.

Task 5: Obtain relevant history and related information from the client and other pertinent sources to establish eligibility and appropriateness of services.

Task 6: Screen for physical needs, medical conditions, and co-occurring mental health disorders that might require additional assessment and referral.

Task 7: Interpret results of screening and assessment and integrate all available information to formulate a diagnostic impression and determine an appropriate course of action.

Task 8: Develop a written summary of the results of the screening and assessment to document and support the diagnostic impressions and treatment recommendations.

Domain II: Treatment Planning, Collaboration, and Referral

Task 1: Formulate and discuss diagnostic assessment and recommendations with the client and concerned others to initiate an individualized treatment plan that incorporates client's strengths, needs, abilities, and preferences.

Task 2: Use ongoing assessment and collaboration with the client and concerned others to review and modify the treatment plan to address treatment needs.

Task 3: Match client needs with community resources to facilitate positive client outcomes.

Task 4: Discuss rationale for a referral with the client.

Task 5: Communicate with community resources regarding needs of the client.

Task 6: Advocate for the client in areas of identified needs to facilitate continuity of care.

Task 7: Evaluate the effectiveness of case management activities to ensure quality service coordination.

Task 8: Develop a plan with the client to strengthen ongoing recovery outside of primary treatment.

Task 9: Document treatment progress, outcomes, and continuing care plans.

Task 10: Utilize multiple pathways of recovery in treatment planning and referral.

Domain III: Counseling

Task 1: Develop a therapeutic relationship with clients, families, and concerned others to facilitate transition into the recovery process.

Task 2: Provide information to the client regarding the structure, expectations, and purpose of the counseling process.

Task 3: Continually evaluate the client's safety, relapse potential, and the need for crisis intervention.

Task 4: Apply evidence-based, culturally competent counseling strategies and modalities to facilitate progress toward completion of treatment objectives.

Task 5: Assist families and concerned others in understanding substance use disorders and engage them in the recovery process.

Task 6: Document counseling activity and progress toward treatment goals and objectives.

Task 7: Provide information on issues of identity, ethnic background, age, sexual orientation, and gender as it relates to substance use, prevention, and recovery.

Task 8: Provide information about the disease of addiction and the related health and psychosocial consequences.

Domain IV: Professional and Ethical Responsibilities

Task 1: Adhere to established professional codes of ethics and standards of practice to uphold client rights while promoting best interests of the client and profession.

Task 2: Recognize diversity and client demographics, culture, and other factors influencing behavior to provide services that are sensitive to the uniqueness of the individual.

Task 3: Continue professional development through education, self-evaluation, clinical supervision, and consultation to maintain competence and enhance professional effectiveness.

Task 4: Identify and evaluate client needs that are outside of the counselor's ethical scope of practice and refer to other professionals as appropriate.

Task 5: Uphold client's rights to privacy and confidentiality according to best practices in preparation and handling of records.

Task 6: Obtain written consent to release information from the client and/or legal guardian, according to best practices.

Task 7: Prepare concise, clinically accurate, and objective reports and records.

CASE SCENARIO

Another way that this text diverges from many others is in the way that each chapter demonstrates one or more knowledge, skills and values discussed using a client case that we will follow throughout the treatment process. For this, we present Juanita, a 34-year-old, single, Hispanic woman with two children and a long history of substance abuse. We will follow Juanita through the counseling process, paying attention to the TAP 21 Competencies and the Accreditation Standards from CACREP and CSWE. Presented here is Juanita's psychosocial history.

Case Study: Juanita

Descriptive Information

Juanita is a 34-year-old, single, Hispanic woman. She is the mother of two children; her son Jorge (George) is age 15 and her daughter Lucinda (Lucy) is age 8. Juanita lives with her two children and raises them as a single mom. She has never married the father of her children, though he lives across the street from them and is actively involved in the children's lives.

Client Systems
Person System
Juanita identifies with her role as a mother and describes this as the most
important role in her life. Juanita is proud of her children and feels that she
is responsible for the things they have accomplished. As a single mother
raising two children on her own with little or no support from others, she
has had to rely on her own strengths and abilities. As a result, Juanita is
slow to trust others, feels an overdeveloped sense of responsibility, and is
perceived by others as somewhat of a "control freak." On the other hand,
Juanita only believes that she is doing what she needs to do for herself and
her children.

Juanita works as a nurse's aide. In the past, she has been employed at
various low-skill jobs including working as a school custodian, an exotic dancer, and a bartender. She has maintained steady employment
throughout most of her adult life. Juanita supplements her income by the
sale of marijuana and other drugs. Though she is aware that her son, Jorge,
has experimented with marijuana, she believes that her children are una-
ware of her sale of illegal drugs.

Family and Household System
As stated, Juanita is a single mother who is raising two children on her
own. The father of her two children, Paco, is a Mexican immigrant who
lives across the street from Juanita and her kids. Paco and Juanita met
when they were both employed at a local hospital. Juanita was working
as a nurse's aide, and Paco was employed as a custodian. While Paco is a
Mexican citizen, he is a permanent resident and has a "green card" to work
in the United States.

Paco, who is 65 years of age, is 30 years older than Juanita. He speaks
very little English, and he and Juanita communicate in Spanish. Paco is a
widower. His wife died when she was in her early 30s, before any children
could be born to them. Juanita selected Paco as the father for her children
for several reasons. She states, "I could tell Paco would be a good father for
my kids. He is very kind, and he will love them very much." She has always
been straightforward with Paco, telling him that she does not wish to be
married and only wants a father for her children. In spite of Juanita's desire
to remain single, Paco has managed to stay involved in his children's lives.
He lives in a house across the street from Juanita and the children, and
Paco sees his children daily. During the school year, he walks his daughter
to school (wheeling his bicycle along as they walk to school). When they
reach the school, he drops her off and then rides his bike home. Paco is

also faithfully there in the afternoon to meet his daughter when she gets out of school. Juanita has never tried to hide the identity of their father from her children. They are aware of their parents' unique arrangement and seem to accept it with equanimity.

Over the course of her children's lives, Juanita has dated several other men and has had at least two relationships that lasted almost a year. During this time, she has not found anyone that she cares enough about to ask to move in with her. She prefers living as a single mother with her children and having the children's father involved in their lives on an ongoing basis.

Community System
Juanita has several close friends and socializes with them on a regular basis. She and her friends go out to eat, enjoy parties at each other's houses, and occasionally take short trips together. All of her socialization involves getting high and the use of drugs. Other than spending time with her friends, Juanita has little or no ties to her community. She is not involved in any clubs or civic organizations, she does not belong to any church groups, and she does little with any organizations at her children's schools such as the Parent-Teacher Association (PTA) or fund-raising activities.

Developmental History
Juanita is the only child born to her parents, Roberto and Concerta. Concerta was 25 years of age when she conceived and delivered Juanita. Juanita states that, as far as she knows, she reached developmental milestones such as walking and talking at appropriate ages. She says that "My mother used to tell me I was a really easy baby. She never had any trouble with me." Juanita's earliest memory is from around 4 years of age. "My dad had been away for quite a while and I remember him coming home. He had a big box that was a present for me. I opened it up and it was a doll from Japan. I remember that doll because of the way her eyes looked and the way she was dressed was so different. I know now that she was a Geisha."

Personal and Familial
Juanita lived with her parents for the first 8 years of her life. Her father was a Merchant Marine, and he was gone most of the year. He would return home and spend up to 2 months with Juanita and her mother before leaving to go out to sea again. Her mother was a housewife who doted on Juanita. Juanita reports that those early childhood years were the happiest times of her life. She had many cousins, aunts, and uncles, and the entire

family would get together on weekends and holidays for barbecues and celebrations.

Juanita's mother died suddenly of a heart attack when Juanita was 8 years old. Her father was away at sea at the time, and it took almost a week for him to return home. She remembers little of this time except that "I was very afraid. I really didn't understand what was happening—just that my mother was no longer there and I was taken to stay with one of my aunts." Shortly after her father returned, it was decided that he could not adequately care for Juanita because he was gone for a large percentage of the time. Her father made the decision to legally give custody to Juanita's aunt and uncle (her mother's sister and brother-in-law). They had already been caring for Juanita while waiting for her father to return. This made the decision to care for her a legal one.

Juanita knew her aunt and uncle well since they were regular attendees at family functions. She was also well acquainted with her three cousins (twin boys who were 2 years older than her and a male cousin who was 3 years younger than her).

Critical Events
Shortly after she was sent to live with her aunt and uncle, her uncle began to sexually abuse Juanita. The abuse started with her uncle coming into her bedroom at night after everyone else had gone to bed. "I would lie awake and listen for the sound of his footsteps," she said, "Often I would try to pretend to be asleep hoping he would leave me alone, but it never worked." Juanita experienced sexual molestation by her uncle for the next 5 years. Eventually, at the age of 13, Juanita ran away from home and never returned.

Sexual Development and Maturity
Juanita self-reports that she began puberty at the age of 11. It was around this time that she began her menses. Because her uncle had been raping her, she lived in fear that she would become pregnant. However, she did not become pregnant until years later when she had her first child with Paco. She reports that she developed breasts at a very young age (11) and that she looked much older than her chronological age. This helped her to survive when she made the decision to run away from home at age 13.

At the age of 13, Juanita left a note for her adoptive family and walked the 3 miles to the Houston bus station. She took a bus from Houston to San Antonio, Texas, where she lived for the next 12 years of her life. Shortly after arriving in San Antonio, she met a woman who was working as a dancer in a strip club. Her friend gave Juanita a place to stay and helped her get a job as a dancer in the club (the woman thought that Juanita was 18 years old). It was shortly after this that Juanita began using alcohol and other drugs. Juanita's adoptive family tried to make her move back home, but Juanita confronted her aunt and uncle with the sexual abuse and threatened to expose her uncle. "I told my Tio—either you back off and leave me alone or I go to the police and social services and tell them what you have been doing to me. . . . By then, I was 14, going on 15 years old, so they chose to leave me alone." It wasn't too long afterward that she was able to legally drop out of school and become an emancipated minor.

Alcohol and/or Drug Use

Juanita is a poly-drug abuser. Her primary drugs of choice are alcohol and cocaine, but she also uses marijuana, amphetamines, and hallucinogens on a regular basis. At various times, Juanita has experimented with many other drugs, including opioids such as hydromorphone (Dilaudid) and oxycodone (OxyContin) and antianxiety medications such as alprazolam (Xanax) and diazepam (Valium). In the past, Juanita has struggled with an addiction to heroin. She self-reports that, after she became pregnant with her first child, she quit using heroin. She reports that she has not used heroine since then (a period of more than 15 years).

Juanita's first exposure to alcohol was at the age of 13. She drank three beers, and she self-reports that the first time she drank alcohol she "felt normal." At first, Juanita only drank alcohol occasionally (mainly on weekends). Her tolerance was very low, and it would only take a few beers for her to get drunk. However, within a few months, Juanita was drinking almost daily. Within a year, Juanita experienced her first blackout. Over the course of the next few years, Juanita had developed a tolerance for alcohol. She self-reports that she could drink up to a fifth of whiskey without passing out by the time she was 20 years old. Juanita has been abusing alcohol for more than 20 years. She self-reports that she experiences blackouts on a regular basis. Her longest period of sobriety was during her two pregnancies. She managed to abstain from alcohol for several months at a time (at one point she went for almost 5 months without drinking). However, she admits that "once I start I can't stop. . . . I am fortunate that my babies were born healthy and didn't have anything wrong with them."

Juanita began experimenting with cocaine at the age of 18. She reports that once she started using coke, everything else paled in comparison. "I would use coke to get high and then drink Jack Daniels to take the edge off. I found with coke that I could dance and stay up for days—nothing seemed to matter or to bother me."

Juanita soon began using cocaine and alcohol together and on a regular basis. Her longest period of abstinence from cocaine coincided with her two pregnancies. "I really wanted my babies to be healthy, so I did everything I could to stay clean and sober," she states.

Juanita first used heroin around the age of 15. She was dating a man who both used and sold heroin on a regular basis. Juanita tried heroin by inhaling (snorting) it. "It kind of made me sick to my stomach the first time I tried it. However, then the high kicked in and it was great." She kept snorting, but found it was harder and harder to get a buzz. "My boyfriend tried firing it [injecting] but I have always been a little afraid of needles." She started running up quite a habit, snorting about $100–150 a day. "Once I became pregnant, though, I quit and I haven't touched any since."

Juanita has experimented with other drugs including marijuana and various synthetic narcotics including OxyContin and Dilaudid. She self-reports at various times using amphetamines (speed) and hallucinogens including LSD, mescaline, and 3,4-methylenedioxymethamphetamine (MDMA, Ecstasy). She also reports using marijuana on a regular basis since age 15. "I don't really consider pot to be a drug," she states. "It is everywhere, and it just mellows me out. It isn't like it is really harmful or anything."

Psychosocial History
Medical/Physical
Juanita self-reports that she is in good health other than the occasional cold or the flu. She states that she has had no major illnesses in her lifetime. There is a history of diabetes (her mother's side), but Juanita has had no symptoms of being diabetic. She self-reports that she had a broken arm in childhood when she fell out of a tree, and she had an emergency appendectomy at age 6.

Legal
Juanita was arrested for possession of cocaine (less than 1 g) and possession of marijuana (less than 4 g) while stopped for a traffic violation (she failed to stop at a stop sign). The judge ordered Juanita to undergo an assessment for substance abuse and to comply with the recommendations of the counselor. Juanita has no other prior arrests or convictions.

Educational
Juanita reports that she was a good student in elementary and grade school and did well until she dropped out of school. She eventually went back

and acquired her General Educational Diploma (GED) and has since completed her Nurse's Aide Certification and a Red Cross CPR Course (necessary to maintain her Nurse's Aide Certificate). Other than that, she has no formal schooling, although Juanita expresses a desire to one day return to school and become a Registered Nurse.

Employment

Juanita is currently employed as a Nurse's Aide at a local hospital, a position she has held for the past 3 years. She also supplements her income by selling marijuana to friends and people she knows and trusts. She briefly worked as a waitress but didn't like it because the work was hard and the tips were too small. In the past, she was employed as a custodian in an office building. However, most of her prior working career has been as an exotic dancer. Juanita reports that the "money was good." However, she reports that it was a hard job being that close to so many men without wearing clothes. "But, where else can I make that kind of money?" she asks.

Recreational

Juanita admits that most of her recreational activities center on getting high with her friends. She states that, "Most of what we do, we do it when we're high. . . . It just seems to be more fun when I have a buzz on." Juanita's interest range from listening to music, playing cards, hanging out/socializing with friends, and going out to clubs. "I am not much into sports, and I don't like to dance because I got enough of that when I worked. . . . I just like to hang out and chill when I am not working."

Religious/Spiritual

Juanita was raised as a Roman Catholic. She was baptized as a Catholic as an infant and self-reports that she attended Mass on a fairly regular basis while growing up. She remembers her mother taking her to church when she was a small girl and has fond memories of the place of worship that she and her mother attended. "I can recall the smell of the incense in the church," she states, "It always reminded me of a combination of cinnamon and burning leaves."

Today, Juanita reports that she has not attended Mass or confessional in several years, although she still considers herself to be a Catholic and self-reports that she has strong spiritual beliefs. "I pray often," she states. "Just because I don't go to church doesn't mean I don't believe." At other times, Juanita admits that she is angry with God. "Why would a God who is supposed to love me let me go through all of that abuse I had as a child? What kind of God does that?" For this reason, she has mixed feelings about religion and her spirituality.

Prior Psychological or Social Services
Juanita reports that she has had no prior involvement with Child Protective Services or any other social service agency. Being referred for an alcohol and drug assessment is her first involvement with the legal or any social service system.

CONCLUSION

In conclusion, this text will be walking you through the practice of substance abuse counseling using competencies and standards for best practices that are recognized by educational accreditation organizations and practice (licensing and credentialing) boards. We have provided you with a case study of our client Juanita. We encourage you to read this over carefully because we will be following her case throughout the remainder of this book.

In addition, we have introduced both the SAMHSA's TAP 21 competencies and accreditation standards for CSWE and CACREP. Throughout this text, we will be providing you with the relevant competencies and standards as they apply to that particular section of the book.

2

Intake

INTRODUCTION

This chapter describes evidenced-based and common practices related to the intake process. We are using a case scenario to demonstrate some of the competencies we will be covering. *Intake* is mostly an administrative function that occurs before an assessment and entails the point of inquiry or referral, verification of benefits, and informed consent to treatment. The *informed consent* is the most critical part of the intake process because it involves protecting the rights of clients by informing them of the mechanisms related to the delivery of services before they engage in the assessment process. The informed consent consist of notifying and discussing with clients payment and reimbursement expectations, risks and benefits of treatment, program/agency policies, alternative treatments, freedom to refuse services, confidentiality and the release of information, and mandatory reporting. Listed here are the Council for Accreditation of Counseling and Related Educational Programs (CACREP), Council on Social Work Education (CSWE), International Certification & Reciprocity Consortium (IC&RC), and Substance Abuse and Mental Health Services Administration (SAMHSA) standards associated with intake processing.

CHAPTER COMPETENCIES AND STANDARDS

CACREP: Standards 7, 10, 18, 19, 25
CSWE: Competencies 6 and 7
IC&RC: Domain IIII: Tasks 2, Domain IV: Tasks 5, 6
SAMHSA: Competencies 1, 5, 10, 15

Case Scenario

Another way that this text diverges from many others is in the way that each chapter applies knowledge, skills, and attitudes (KSAs) to a client case that we will follow throughout the treatment process. For this, we present again Juanita, a 34 year-old, single Hispanic woman with two children and a long history of substance abuse.

Referral Information

Juanita is a 36-year-old, single, Latina woman who was arrested for possession of cocaine (<1 g) and possession of marijuana (<4 g) while stopped for a traffic violation for failing to stop at a stop sign. Juanita has no other prior arrests or convictions other than traffic tickets, one for speeding and one a parking fine. When Juanita appeared before the judge for sentencing for her possession charges, the judge ordered that she obtain an alcohol and drug evaluation by a certified alcohol and drug counselor and that she comply with the recommendations of that counselor. If she fails to comply with any of the recommendations she would be required to reappear before the court and show just cause. Failure to comply and follow through with the counselor's recommendations could result in her being sent to a state correctional facility. As long as she complies with the recommendations of the counselor and agency where she is being evaluated, she can remain on probation and out of jail.

Juanita's license was revoked, and she was given 90 days to obtain an assessment/evaluation and have a copy sent to the judge. After leaving court, Juanita was provided a list of treatment agencies approved by the court system for conducting an alcohol and drug assessment. Juanita selected one of the agencies on that list—New Beginnings. Juanita chose this particular agency for several reasons: it was near her home, she knew others who had also been court-ordered to go there (and, for the most part, their reports had been positive), and they had a sliding fee scale based on annual income.

Agency Setting

New Beginnings is a nonprofit agency that operates under a contract with the state. New Beginnings offers both mental health counseling and substance abuse treatment. New Beginnings started as a small, outpatient clinic offering mental health counseling in the early 1970s. Since that time, it has grown into a comprehensive treatment facility. The mental health unit has inpatient treatment, complete with a crisis stabilization unit for those mental health patients who need a secured environment. The facility provides day treatment (partial hospitalization), outpatient treatment (including both individual and group therapy), intensive outpatient therapy (IOP), and family therapy, and is the area's only facility which offers play therapy for children with a certified play therapist on staff.

The substance abuse treatment program provides residential treatment (including detoxification), day treatment, outpatient services, IOP (a minimum of three group, family, and/or individual sessions per week), and aftercare. Because the agency works with clients who have both substance abuse and mental health issues (co-occurring disorders), the agency has staff who are trained to deal with dual diagnosis.

New Beginnings also strives to incorporate "best practices," as identified by SAMHSA and others who are leaders in the field of addiction counseling. New Beginnings evaluates their programs' effectiveness as well as their client's progress within each program. We will be exploring this issue further in other chapters.

There are some considerations to explore when preparing for this case. Let's look at one that is agency related and one that is client-related.

Agency-Related Considerations
Many facilities are backlogged with appointments, and the waiting list can be long. Juanita has 90 days to obtain a thorough assessment. A thorough assessment may take two to three visits to collect enough information for a diagnosis and to determine the treatment recommendations, including the appropriate level of care. It is important to be aware of how far out the wait will be for a client making a new appointment. Some larger organizations have a centralized intake system, while individual businesses may use a receptionist. Some agencies have a walk-in day designated for court-ordered clients or some other process for ensuring clients are seen in a reasonable time frame. Some private practitioners even make their own appointments. The larger the organization, the less visible the waiting list will be to individual counselors.

There is very little information about Juanita in the referral. Prior to or when a client is making the initial appointment, an *Intake* form is completed. Sometimes this is conducted over the phone when the client calls for an appointment, sometimes it is on a website or sent to a client to complete and bring to the first appointment, and it is sometimes completed on the day of the first appointment. Usually a client is asked to come early to complete paperwork before seeing the counselor. The intake form should include all agency policies (e.g., what to do if you have a crisis; how no-show appointments are handled, etc.) and address methods of payment by collecting insurance information or have a fee-based pay scale for self-pay clients. It should also ask for demographic information about the client such as address, date of birth, and family status. It should also request contact and emergency information.

Client-Related Considerations

Juanita has a lot at stake to be compliant with the judge's orders. This could be important to remember when conducting the assessment. Minimizing drug use might be seen as a way to substantiate a need for only minimal treatment recommendations. Collecting a thorough *alcohol and drug use history* is important and may take more than one visit and might even include collateral information (i.e., law enforcement, family members).

Juanita may also have considerations related to her culture, gender, physical health, age, and family and social support. This is information you will want to make sure you collect during the first interview. For instance, Juanita cannot drive without a license—does she has the social support to rely on others for transportation? Do others rely on Juanita for income or care? Does she have any health issues that will impede treatment?

Finally, there may be others who need to be involved in treatment or have access to treatment information. For Juanita, you will need to at least get a Consent to Release Information for the court. This will be described and demonstrated later in this chapter.

THE INTAKE PROCESS

Intakes are a critical component of establishing treatment services. Intakes involve the legal and administrative part of an admission to treatment and must always be completed prior to any services being rendered. When working in an agency, a counselor may not even be aware of some of the intake paperwork and processes that occur, especially when there is a *centralized intake* department and a separate or coordinated function for *utilization review*.

Point of Inquiry or Referral

Intakes start at the point of inquiry from a potential referral. This could be when the client calls, emails, or messages a request to learn about the treatment services. It could also be a brokering agency (i.e., protective services or court order) or person (i.e., family member or supervisor) that is making contact on behalf of the client. Either way, the inquiry is funneled through to an intake coordinator or on-call/crisis counselor. So, what are the items that need to be covered in an intake? First, the presenting problem must be determined. The presenting problem will help identify if the agency offers the appropriate services for the concerns that the client describes. Examples of when the identified problem does not match the services offered are varied. For instance, if the client is having withdrawal symptoms and the agency does not offer detox services, then a referral should be made to a hospital emergency room or arrangements made to admit the client to a detox facility. A client who is suicidal should be immediately referred to crisis services, local law enforcement, or an emergency room before an admission is considered. Another example occurs when the client has a severe and persistent mental illness (SPMI) that is not stabilized and would interfere with treatment attempts.

Verification of Benefits

Another part of an intake is determining how treatment services will be paid. State-funded *community mental health centers* (CMHCs) are usually required to see a client whether or not they have the ability to pay, and, therefore, insurance information may not be required at the point of inquiry or referral. CMHC services are usually comprehensive (multiple levels of care, crisis services, etc.) and can be available 24/7. There are also agencies that are *nonprofit* and therefore accept donations and may receive grants to help supplement their costs. However, many agencies/organizations and private outpatient clinicians are *for-profit* and depend on insurance reimbursement and/or cash payments to remain viable. Nearly all agencies address the ability to pay as part of the intake process.

Clients are usually asked to provide their insurance information before an appointment is established, and a *verification of benefits* (VOB) is usually completed at intake, which means that the coverage is verified to ensure that it is current and applicable. It is also important to inquire whether the agency is a provider covered by the insurance carrier and if the agency is in-network or out-of-network. Being in or out of network is based on a contractual agreement between the agency and the insurance carrier and affects co-payment, deductibles, what services are covered, and limitations of service (annual, lifetime, etc.). Therefore, verifying insurance should also include inquiring about the co-payments, deductibles, and limitations for services. Many individuals only have a structural understanding of what services are covered by their insurance and what deductibles or co-payments are required, so the information revealed by the VOB is critically important to a client when making decisions regarding financial expectations for the various treatment services that are available to him or her. This will be addressed under the section "Informed Consent to Treatment."

Juanita's Intake

When Juanita called to schedule her appointment, she was asked to provide her health insurance information to verify benefits. She was also asked to describe her reason for seeking an appointment so that she could be matched with the appropriate program and counselor. Her appointment was scheduled for the following week with "Steve."

On the day of Juanita's appointment, she shows up at the appointed time. When she is greeted by the receptionist, she is asked to produce a copy of her medical insurance card, which is copied and returned, and she is told that her co-payment is $20 for this visit, for which she immediately pays. She is then given a form to complete and return that includes her disclosing some basic information about herself such as name, age, residence, contact information, marital status, and emergency contact person. It also asks her reason for this visit, details about any prior substance abuse or mental health treatment, and medications that she is taking, and it asks her to list any known medical conditions. When Juanita completes the paperwork (it takes approximately 15 minutes) she returns it to the receptionist who then gives her a copy of an Informed Consent to Treatment, and she is asked to read it while waiting to see the counselor.

As stated previously, in an agency setting, the point of inquiry or referral and verification of benefits usually occurs "behind the scenes," conducted by administrative staff prior to the client being seen by a counselor. However, the *informed consent* is best discussed in a clinical setting with the counselor to ensure that (1) a client fully understands the information, (2) the client has the capacity to understand the information, and (3) the client is given opportunities to ask questions or clarify the information.

Informed Consent to Treatment

The most critical part of the intake process is protecting the rights of clients by informing them of the mechanisms related to the delivery of services. This helps ensure that clients are fully aware of what to expect as a result of their involvement with treatment before consenting to participate and that they can refuse treatment at any time during their involvement. A standard informed consent includes (1) the financial costs of the treatment services, (2) the risks and benefits of treatment, (3) program policies and procedures, (4) alternative services that are available, (5) the freedom to choose or refuse treatment, (6) confidentiality, and (7) treatment recommendations.

PAYMENT AND REIMBURSEMENT

As stated earlier, the client's ability to pay is an important part of the intake process, and discussing the cost of treatment ensures that the client is fully informed before engaging in services. There are generally two forms of payments; insurance reimbursement and cash. When discussing insurance coverage, clients are usually asked to present an insurance card. This is copied and placed in or scanned into the medical record. Insurance coverage changes for many reasons such as loss of job/cancelled insurance, change in plan coverage, covered dependent ages out of insurance coverage, divorce from insurance holder, change in policy choice, and more. Just because a person presents an insurance card that has active dates does not mean he or she is covered. As explained earlier, a VOB is usually performed at intake to ensure that the coverage is current. Sometimes VOBs can be completed online, and sometimes they must be verified by calling the insurance carrier directly. Verifying insurance can also include determining deductibles, co-payments, and limitations for services. Because many individuals are not sure what services are covered by their insurance, the information revealed by the VOB is sometimes surprising and maybe even distressing. Therefore, many agencies offer payment plans to help spread out the financial burden of large deductibles.

There are three primary reasons that cash payments would be discussed: insurance deductibles, insurance co-payments, and self-pay. Most agencies collect outpatient co-payments at the time of service, either before the start of counseling or upon leaving a counseling session. These are generally manageable amounts, whereas deductibles can be large depending on the type of policy. For individuals with large deductibles, payment plans are sometimes made available. There are several reasons for individuals paying cash for services. For instance, paying cash allows greater confidentiality and anonymity because information is not shared with an insurance company. Other reasons could be a limitation of benefits (a particular service is not covered), exhaustion of an annual benefit cap (client has reached the maximum amount allowed for a service), or an individual wants to continue in a level of care that his or her insurance company has denied meeting criteria and therefore will not be covered. Some agencies and individual counselors have a set fee-for-service that requires the full amount be paid at the time of service; the agency also may help clients obtain reimbursement from their medical plans or will offer a sliding fee scale to clients who either do not want to file through their insurance or do not have coverage. In these case, payment is established on their *ability to pay*—usually based of the combined household income. Payment agreements may also be used for more costly treatment, such as residential or intensive outpatient services. One of the most recent uses of self-pay has been seen with medically assisted treatment (MAT), such as methadone and buprenorphine. This is a very controversial approach due to the opportunity for exploitation by prescribers denying the client his or her maintenance medication until a cash payment is received or providing maintenance medication for cash without treatment. This issue will be explored more in a later chapter.

RISKS AND BENEFITS OF TREATMENT

Most of the risks from participating in substance abuse treatment involve confidentiality problems. The phrase that sometimes "it has to get worse before it can get better" can be true in counseling. Substance abuse treatment involves talking about and expressing intense and possibly painful emotions such as guilt, resentment, anger, and despair. It also involves facing and dealing with difficult issues in the present, such as damaged relationships, job loss, and criminal behavior. Additionally, it also involves recalling frightening or challenging parts of a person's personal history, such as maltreatment and other trauma.

Conversely, counseling may result in feeling better about oneself and others. Effective substance abuse counseling can improve the ability to handle or cope with marital, family, and other interpersonal concerns that affect recovery. It can help strengthen coping skills needed to identify triggers, manage withdrawal symptoms, and increase problem-solving skills to avoid relapse. Some other benefits of counseling may include, but are not limited to, increased maturity, improved self-esteem, and increased personal happiness.

PROGRAM/AGENCY POLICIES AND PROCEDURES

Counselors should also cover any data collection procedures, attendance compliance requirements, cancellation notices, policies regarding no-show or failure-to-attend (FTA), and the procedure to follow if the client has an emergency/crisis. These business items should be carefully explained before clients enter treatment so that their decisions are made with a clear understanding of compliance issues. In addition, many residential programs have extensive rules and regulations about client behavior (such as nonsmoking facilities), constraints on privacy (sharing bedrooms), limitations on communication with friends and family (set visitation and phone hours), and other behavioral rules while the client is in treatment. These should be discussed fully before clients enter the program. This is also important for faith-based organizations, where activities may have religious aspects associated with them (e.g., reading religious material, worship groups, spiritual education classes).

ALTERNATIVE TREATMENTS

An important but seldom practiced element of fully informed consent is the *description of alternative treatments* so that clients can make an informed choice. Providers who are locked into standardized models of care, such as some residential programs that require client adherence to a 12-step program, may not be able to offer alternative treatments within their own facility. In these cases, providers are ethically required to offer information about alternative providers. This includes public, nonprofit, faith-based organizations (FBOs) that receive federal financial assistance or are governed by state or private funding contracts and/or accreditation regulations. Executive Order 13279 of December 12, 2002 (Equal Protection of the Laws for Faith-Based and Community Organizations) amended during the Obama administration, has mandated that a referral be provided to an alternative provider for a "beneficiary or prospective beneficiary" when the beneficiary "objects to the religious character of an organization" (The White House, 2010). Offering alternative treatments can be a challenge for providers in closed treatment networks or rural communities; however, choices can include different modalities of care or alternative clinicians within the same network or organization.

FREEDOM TO REFUSE SERVICES

The principles of autonomy and self-determination are identified in the Code of Ethics of most behavioral health licensing boards. US courts have repeatedly confirmed Americans' right to autonomy, especially in making medical decisions for themselves. An adult with "decisional capacity" has the right to decide which treatment he or she will accept or to refuse treatment altogether. Clients also have the right to withdraw consent to treatment after having given it. Clients who have been coerced into treatment by an external authority (e.g., court ordered) still have the right to refuse or discontinue treatment. However, the program has the obligation to inform them of the possible consequences of that decision. Client refusals to participate in treatment should be met with respect and not with punitive responses. Leaving the offer open for clients to revisit engaging in treatment services can remove a barrier to accessing services at a later date.

CONFIDENTIALITY AND THE RELEASE OF INFORMATION

One of the challenges, especially for new counselors, is understanding the limitations of releasing medical information. This is especially true when it comes to addiction services. This is such an important issue that the federal government enacted regulations that codify what a substance abuse counselor can and can't disclose and regulations for how information can be shared. The Code of Federal Regulations (CFR) Title 42, Part 2 (also known as 42 CFR—Part 2) titled *Confidentiality of Substance Use Disorder Patient Records* and the *Health Insurance Portability and Accountability Act* (HIPAA) of 1996 (P.L. 104-191) both address release of medical information.

The 42 CFR—Part 2 addresses five subparts: (Subpart A) Introduction— including criminal penalties for violations; (Subpart B) General Provisions— including minor patients, incompetent or deceased patients, informants and restrictions on patient access; (Subpart C) Disclosures with Patient Consent; (Subpart D) Disclosures without Patient Consent—such as medical emergencies, research and evaluation, and; (Subpart E) Court Orders Authorizing Disclosure and Use—including criminal investigations and confidential communications (Code of Federal Regulation, Title 42, Part 2, 2017).

Providing information to a third party is generally referred to as a *release of information* (ROI). We realize that the regulations surrounding the ROI contain a great deal of "legalese" so here we will attempt to paraphrase them into something that is easier to understand.

Basically, you are prohibited from disclosing anything about the client without his or her written permission unless mandated (such as reporting child maltreatment) or ordered to do so by law (such as a subpoena). This written permission as set forth in 42 CFR—Part 2 (located in §2.31(a) except where indicated) must include the following items:

- Name or general description of the individual or program(s) making the disclosure
- Name or title of the individual or organization that will receive the disclosure
- Name of the client who is the subject of the disclosure
- Purpose of or need for the disclosure
- How much and what kind of information will be disclosed
- A statement that the client may revoke the consent at any time, except to the extent that the program has already acted in reliance on it
- Date, event, or condition upon which the consent expires, if not previously revoked
- Signature of the client
- Date on which the consent is signed
- Signature of minor in some states, and/or his or her parent (§2.14)
- Notice against redisclosure of information (§2.32)

(Code of Federal Regulation, Title 42, Part 2, (2017))

Let's examine specific parts of a release of information.

What information is to be disclosed: For example, the client may only want to have a copy of his or her assessment and/or treatment plan released, and then the release of information will state that only this information is to be released.

The time frame that the release of information is to remain in effect: Releases of information must have an end date. They are not legal if they are open-ended.

Examples of this could be a specific calendar date (month/day/year) or a date based on an "event or condition." Examples of these might be "Within one year of this date," "Upon receipt of the requested record," or "Upon discharge from treatment." The ROI can be revoked at any time by the client regardless of the date placed on the document—and this should be stated clearly on the form.

Signatures of minors and parental consent: To release information about a minor, even to a parent or guardian, the minor must have signed a consent form. In the event that state law requires parental consent for treatment of a minor, the parent (or legal guardian) must also provide written consent to release information.

Required notice against redisclosing information:

The following statement should be given and explained to the recipient at or before the time of disclosure. This protects the client from having the information re-released except as permitted by the regulations or unless the client signs a consent form authorizing such a redisclosure.

"Any consent for release of information must be accompanied by a written statement that the information disclosed is protected by Federal law and that the recipient may not make any further disclosure unless permitted by the regulations," (Code of Federal Regulation, Title 42, Part 2, (2017), §2.32).

One of the most confusing areas for new counselors is the question of what can and can't be discussed outside of the counseling session without written consent. Most counselors assume that when a record is subpoenaed that a client's right to provide consent is waived. However, keep in mind that even *if* the client has signed a consent this does not force a program to make the proposed disclosure, unless the program has also received a subpoena or court order, (Code of Federal Regulation, Title 42, Part 2, (2017), §2.61). If you are subpoenaed and you do not have a release of information, you must comply with the subpoena and appear in court at the stated time. However, without a release of information, you cannot be compelled to state that you either know or do not know the client in question.

MANDATORY REPORTING

As we stated earlier, for the most part, whatever the client shares with you during the assessment and process is privileged information. This means that you are bound by law to not disclose their information to anyone else unless the person specifically gives you written consent. However, there are some cases where you are mandated by law to report information, and these need to be stated clearly on the Informed Consent form.

Self-Directed Violence, Suicide

Both the Center for Disease Control (CDC) and the World Health Organization (WHO) list "drug or alcohol abuse" as a risk factor for suicide (US Public Health Service, 1999; World Health Organization, 2002). While the exact definition of what is reportable varies by state, if a client tells you that he is thinking or planning to harm himself, the need to intervene supersedes any pact of confidentiality you may have with him. This will be discussed more in Chapter 3, the "Assessment."

Duty to Warn or Protect

Some states mandate warning or protecting a potential victim if a client discloses that he or she planning on harming them. However, the statues vary from state to state on whom to make the report (the victim and the police, only the victim, etc.). In addition, there are conflicting protections for the counselor due to variations in invoking the law; little or no statutory or common law guidelines on what constitutes a clear threat to justify the report; variations within states in interpreting their own law; and ambiguity in the threshold for the risk assessment that determines imminent risk of harm (Johnson, Persad, & Sisti, 2014). To locate for state-specific information regarding mental health professional's duty to warn or protect go to http://www.ncsl.org/research/health/mental-health-professionals-duty-to-warn.aspx.

Child Maltreatment

If you suspect or someone discloses to you that a child is being harmed, then you have a legal and ethical responsibility to report that abuse. All states have principal agencies (i.e., Child Protective Services and law enforcement) that are responsible for investigating and intervening on behalf of child maltreatment reports. To search for state-specific information regarding mandatory reporting laws for child maltreatment go to https://www.childwelfare.gov/topics/systemwide/laws-policies/state/.

Elder and Vulnerable Adult Abuse

Almost every state has regulations mandating healthcare professionals to report abuse of older persons and/or vulnerable adults. Specific conditions vary by state. To search for state-specific information regarding mandatory reporting laws for abuse of older persons and vulnerable adults as of 2013, download the PDF at http://www.napsa-now.org/wp-content/uploads/2014/11/Mandatory-Reporting-Chart-Updated-FINAL.pdf.

Domestic Violence

Most states have regulations mandating healthcare professionals to report domestic violence. However, the conditions of reporting vary by state, including the type of injury and even the relationship of the victim to the perpetrator. To search for state-specific information regarding mandatory reporting laws for domestic violence as of 2010, download the PDF at http://www.acf.hhs.gov/sites/default/files/fysb/state_compendium.pdf

Every counselor should be knowledgeable about the mandatory reporting laws within the state where he or she practices. Let's look at how Steve discusses this with Juanita.

Steve Reviews Confidentiality and Informed Consent with Juanita

It is only a couple of minutes before a white man in his early 40s comes out and calls Juanita's name. Standing up, he introduces himself: "Hi, I'm Steve and I will be meeting with you today." While shaking hands, he asks her what she would like to be called, to which she replies, "Juanita is fine." He leads her back to his office, which has a desk and workstation at one end. Near the door, there is a small couch and two chairs (one facing the couch and one at a right angle to the couch). Steve indicates that Juanita should sit where she likes, and he takes a seat across from her.

Before beginning the assessment, Steve explains to Juanita the laws governing substance abuse counselors and patient rights surrounding confidentiality. He reviews with her the consent to disclose to the judge the results of her assessment. He also reviews the state mandatory reporting requirements if she discloses harm to a child or vulnerable/elderly adult, or if she discloses intent to harm herself or someone else. Other than those exceptions, what she says in their sessions is confidential. He asks her if she can repeat back to him in her own words what he has told her about her rights and limitation of confidentially to ensure that she heard correctly. He also asks her if she has any questions about the items on the informed consent, to provide an opportunity for her to clarify anything she finds confusing. Steve asks Juanita to sign the Informed Consent and a release of information to the Judge to share the following information: assessment, diagnostic impressions, treatment recommendations, summary of progress in treatment, and discharge summary. Now that the formalities have been dispatched, Steve and Juanita can begin the assessment.

CONCLUSION

The intake process is the initial—and a critical—component of service delivery. Although counselors may not be involved in some of the administrative processes that occur "behind the scenes," such as insurance verification, there are several competencies and standards for substance abuse counselors that pertain to the elements of intake. The Informed Consent protects the client by providing information to the client regarding the structure, expectations, policies, and purpose of the counseling process. These include payment and reimbursement expectations, risks and benefits of treatment, program/agency policies, alternative treatments, freedom to refuse services, confidentiality and the release of information, and mandatory reporting. Informed Consent also benefits the agency and counselors in that the client is made fully aware of what to expect during the course of the treatment process (risks and benefits), thus creating some protection against claims of malpractice.

Assessment

INTRODUCTION

This chapter describes evidenced-based and common practices related to the assessment process. The *initial assessment* is a comprehensive, holistic, and multifaceted system of engaging with the client while collecting the information needed to make treatment decisions. This chapter presents a framework for the initial assessment (also known as a *comprehensive assessment*). Listed here are the Council for Accreditation of Counseling and Related Educational Programs (CACREP), Council on Social Work Education (CSWE), International Certification & Reciprocity Consortium (IC&RC), and Substance Abuse and Mental Health Services Administration (SAMHSA) standards associated with assessment.

CHAPTER COMPETENCIES AND STANDARDS

CACREP—Standards 4, 6, 9, 12, 20–23
CSWE—Competencies 6 and 7
IC&RC—Domain I: Tasks 1–6
SAMHSA—Competencies 11, 16, 24–36, 28, 33, 75–76, 111

SEVEN ELEMENTS OF ASSESSMENT

Assessments are generally thought to be both an event and a process. The event entails the initial meeting with the client for the collection of information. However, the process of an initial assessment has multiple parts that together create a comprehensive picture of the client. In fact, the assessment is ongoing throughout the treatment process, accommodating dynamic

changes that occur in the client's situation over time. We have divided the
initial assessment into seven elements: (1) rapport building and engagement,
(2) drug use inventory, (3) readiness for change, (4) biopsychosocial assessment, (5) assessing for suicide, (6) screening tools, and (7) mental status
impressions.

Element 1: Rapport Building and Engagement

During the first sessions, two simultaneous events occur: rapport building and
engagement. *Rapport* is the relationship that is developed between the counselor and the client, and this occurs when the counselor utilizes various skills to
engage the client. The intensity, or closeness, of the rapport increases when concern and understanding of the client's feelings or ideas are well communicated.
Engagement is the ability to join with the client. Yatchmenoff (2005) talks about
engagement as an investment that is needed to develop a working relationship. Skills for building rapport and obtaining engagement entail many core
counseling skills such as genuineness (being open and authentic), reflective
listening to convey empathy and understanding, remaining nonjudgmental,
demonstrating warmth (being inviting), and focusing on strengths using
affirmations to build a positive relationship. Engagement requires counselors
to use their "professional self" to help build trust. The *professional self* is the
combining of knowledge, skills, and attitudes/values gained in education with
aspects of the counselor's personality traits, belief systems, life experiences, and
cultural heritage (Dewane, 2006). The culmination of this blend of the personal with the professional is what the client experiences during the assessment and will affect the development of the therapeutic alliance and the level
of participation.

Building Rapport and Engagement

Steve begins the assessment by asking Juanita: "What brings you here
today?" She responds that she has been court-ordered to seek an assessment and is simply complying with the judge's orders.

Steve explains to Juanita what his role will entail and what she can expect of their time together: "My job is to listen and to gather information.
Usually an initial assessment takes about an hour—occasionally it can take
longer. Based on what the assessment reveals, you may need to come back
for additional visits."

Steve takes the opportunity to acknowledge her compliance with the court order: "You have done your part by complying with the judge's order to come for the assessment." Juanita thanks him for the acknowledgment.

He then moves into what he expects from her during this session: "I ask that that you be as truthful as you can." And he reassures her with, "I am not here to convince you whether you do, or don't, have a drug problem." Juanita responds affirmatively.

Steve completes his explanation of what she can expect from this session with: "After the assessment, we will discuss the results and what the next step should be. That next step can range from no further services to needing residential treatment. I will tell you exactly what I am going to recommend to the judge so that there are no surprises. Is that fair?" Juanita responds that she supposes that is about as fair as she can expect.

It is important to note that when Juanita walked into the door of the agency, she was feeling several emotions. She was apprehensive, anxious, and nervous, and also a bit afraid. At the same time, she was feeling just a bit hopeful that maybe someone would be able to help her deal with all of the sadness, anger, confusion, and hurt she is experiencing (though she had no words to articulate this desire for help).

Element 2: Drug Use Inventory

There are many commonalities about what to include in collecting a history of drug use. Most agencies have a standardized form (either paper or electronic) that may incorporate items from various screening tools, assessment criteria from best-practice literature (such as ASAM), or suggested competency skills such as those published by SAMHSA or IR&RC. Remember, that collecting drug use information is essentially a "fact finding" mission. Therefore, when evaluating the pattern of drug use can begin with asking the client to list all of the drugs that s/he has used. Then starting with the client's drug of choice and work through each drug history using the categories below. This is a systematic way to help ensures that a thorough drug history is attempted. Here are the key collection items that help ensure a thorough drug use history:

- drugs used (examples; alcohol, marijuana, cocaine, oxycodone)
- age when started each drug use
- patterns of use for each drug (i.e. only weekend, during lunch, etc.)
- frequency, amount, method of use for each drug (e.g. daily, 2grams, intravenously)

- stimuli and events that trigger use (fight with spouse, hanging out with friends, cravings)
- family history of drug/alcohol use (specifically any known abuse or dependency)
- consequences of drug use behavior:
  - legal involvement (i.e. DUI)
  - trouble at work, home, in social settings, or with friends
  - financial consequences
  - physical health consequences ("meth mouth", liver disease)
  - mental health consequences (depression, anxiety)
  - cognitive consequences (i.e. blackouts, episodes of paranoia)
- history of withdrawals
- current prescribed medications (list all including amount, how often, how long)
- length of time, over the last six months they have gone without using
- prior attempts at treatment/recovery
- substance use disorder criteria as defined by the DSM 5

By the time you have completed the drug inventory, a fairly complete picture of the client's drug usage and consequences will emerge, keeping in mind that some clients may deny, minimize or exaggerate their information, either on purpose or due to impaired memory.

Element 3: Readiness to Change

It is helpful for counselors to have a way to measure a client's readiness to change. The personal motivation must be strong enough to overcome denial about the problem, and counselors will face a real challenge until the client is ready. Different tools have been created to measure a client's readiness to change, and we present two of them here. The first is a simple subjective tool that can easily and quickly be used with a client to measure readiness at one point in time or over multiple times. It is called the Readiness Ruler (Zimmerman et al., 2000). The second is an assessment of readiness based on Stages of Change (Prochaska et al., 1992).

READINESS RULER
The Readiness Ruler is a subjective tool that uses a scale from 0 to 10. The client is asked to place a mark on the scale where 0 indicates that they are not prepared to change and 10 indicates that they are already changing. A score

greater than 5 shows that the person is willing to consider change and should be supported and encouraged (Zimmerman et al., 2000).

Readiness Ruler

Below, mark where you are now on this line that measures your change in

_____.

Are you not prepared to change, already changing or somewhere in the middle?

```
0   1   2   3   4   5   6   7   8   9   10
I__ I__ I__ I__ I__ I__ I__ I__ I__ I__ I
```

Not prepared to change   Already changing

STAGES OF CHANGE

The "stages of change" is a transtheoretical framework for understanding the process by which people overcome addiction. It was developed from research looking at how change occurs in "natural recovery" from addictions, and it has been embraced by the move away from confrontational and pathological approaches toward motivational and person-centered approaches, such as motivational interviewing (Prochaska et al., 1992). There are five main stages: precontemplation, contemplation, preparation, action, and maintenance. Some models also include a sixth stage titled "relapse."

1. *Precontemplation*: In this stage, the client is not ready or willing to engage in change. For instance, they may not recognize that a problem exists, or they are aware that they have a problem but have not experienced enough adverse consequences or crises to consider their pattern of use to be problematic or risky.
2. *Contemplation*: Individuals who have some awareness that a problem exists may still be ambivalent to change. They recognize that there are benefits to making a change but are unsure if they are ready to commit to what change will entail. Often they are considering the possibility of stopping or cutting back in the future. Some will have brief periods

where they will seek support, educational material, and even reach out for professional help. This vacillation may continue for extended periods, often for years.

3. *Preparation*: Once an individual sees that the benefits of change outweighs any positive aspects of continuing to use, they are in the preparation stage. Although the individual is still using substances, they are also planning for change, such as making choices about whether treatment is needed and, if so, what kind. They may have already attempted to reduce or stop using on their own. They begin to set goals for themselves and make plans to stop using.

4. *Action*: In the action stage, individuals choose a strategy for change and begin to pursue it by modifying their habits and making changes to their environment. They are making drastic lifestyle changes and may be faced with particularly challenging situations as well as the effects of withdrawal. The action stage can typically last from 3 to 6 months following termination or reduction of substance use. For some, it is a honeymoon period before they face more difficult recovery challenges.

5. *Maintenance*: Maintenance is the stage at which people work to sustain sobriety and prevent relapse. Individuals learn how to detect triggers that may cause them to use substances again. In most cases, individuals attempting long-term behavioral change do return to use at least once and revert to an earlier stage. Relapse can be viewed as part of the learning process. Maintenance requires prolonged behavioral change—by remaining abstinent or moderating consumption to acceptable, targeted levels—and continued vigilance for a minimum of 6 months to several years, depending on the target behavior.

6. *Lapse/Relapse*: This stage is sometimes included in the change model in recognition that a person might have lapses (events of using, then a return to abstinence) or a relapse (when the addictive behavior is taken up again).

It is important to view these stages as a cycle in which people jump between stages, forward and backward, and can be in more than one stage at a time. As Figure 3.1 indicates, individuals start at the precontemplation stage and stabilize at the maintenance stage. However, a client could be at any of these stages of change at the point of assessment.

SAMPLE INDIVIDUAL TREATMENT PLAN

Name of Client: _____

Date: _____

Date	Goal	Objectives	Steps/Methods	Date for Review
	1. Comply with court-ordered requirements for drug screens	No positive drug screens	Submit a urinalysis specimen for examination upon request (random)	Ongoing, upon receiving drug screen results
	2. Develop a network of sober, supportive people	1. Participate in a recovery group/community 2. Secure one or more recovering individuals as a sponsor/mentor/friend	1. Select and attend one or more support groups weekly 2. Engage individually with one or more recovering persons during before or after four support group meetings.	Weekly Six weeks
	3. Comply with court-ordered requirements for counseling	Attend weekly counseling sessions	Meet with counselor every Tuesday at 3:00pm for individual counseling	Four weeks
	4. Improve relationship with children	1. Identify three strategies for increasing positive interactions. 2. Attend six-week parenting education course.	1. Review strengths and past successful strategies. 2. Identify new strategies learned in parenting education classes.	Four weeks Upon completion of parenting education course

Client Signature: _____ Date: _____

Counselor Signature: _____ Date: _____

Figure 3.1 Sample Individual Treatment Plan

Element 4: Biopsychosocial Assessment

The biopsychosocial assessment is a holistic tool used to collect information about the major biological, psychological, and social issues that a client is experiencing. Substance use disorders can affect physical functioning, health, and social interaction and create psychological instability; each client has his or her own unique experiences. Many risks and protective factors will be identified through the biopsychosocial assessment. *Protective factors* include skills, strengths, resources, supports, or coping strategies that are utilized by, or available to, the client. For instance, when asking about a client's living situation, examples of risk factors would be living with "using" friends or family members or being on the verge of eviction. Examples of protective factors would be owning a home and living with supportive family members.

There are several interview forms/tools in the public domain that are used to collect biopsychosocial information. Some are created or modified within an agency to encompass specific information related to the services that agency provides. However, there are others that have been well researched and proved to be standards for best practice, such as the Addiction Severity Index (ASI) and the ASAM assessment tool. We will present an overview of both. Keep in mind that a barrier to using either the ASI or the ASAM assessment is that both require some training. And while the ASI is open to public domain, the ASAM assessment tool is copyrighted and has costs associated with its use.

The ASI, 5th ed. (McLellan et al., 1980) has been well researched and is highly regarded among professionals. The ASI is a semi-structured interview designed to address seven potential problem areas in substance-abusing patients: Mental Status, Employment/Support Status, Alcohol/Drugs, Legal Status, Family History, Family/Social Status, and Psychiatric Status. Over the course of an hour-long session, a skilled interviewer can gather information on recent (past 30 days) and lifetime problems in all of these areas. In addition, it has easy to use checkboxes as well as sections for written comments, and it covers drug use history. To review the scale go to http://www.bu.edu/igsw/online-courses/substanceabuse/AddictionSeverityIndex,5thedition.pdf.

The ASI has a Severity Ratings scale that is both subjective and objective:

Interviewer Rating Scale		Patient Rating Scale
0–1	No real problem, treatment not indicated.	0 None, Not at all
2–3	Slight problem, treatment probably not indicated.	1 Slightly
4–5	Moderate problem, some treatment indicated.	2 Moderately
6–7	Considerable problem, treatment necessary	3 Considerably
8–9	Extreme problem, treatment <u>absolutely</u> necessary	4 Extremely

While the ASI scale can indicate the level of problem severity, its lacks the ability to place a client within a specific level of care (outpatient, intensive outpatient, residential, etc.), which is one of the benefits of the ASAM assessment tool.

The ASAM developed an assessment tool using criteria located under six dimensions to create a comprehensive biopsychosocial assessment of an individual. This assessment can then be used for treatment recommendations and planning, including level of care and placement criteria. In fact, ASAM has the most widely used placement criteria for clients with substance abuse disorders in the nation (this is discussed further in the next chapter). Listed here are the six ASAM dimensions along with questions associated with each dimension.

Dimension 1. Acute Intoxication and/or Withdrawal Potential: Exploring an individual's past and current experiences of substance use and withdrawal.

Explanation: Assessment for intoxication or withdrawal management in a variety of levels of care and preparation for continued addiction services.

Questions:
What risk is associated with the patient's current level of acute intoxication?

Is there significant risk of severe withdrawal symptoms or seizures based on the patient's previous withdrawal history, amount, frequency, chronicity, and recency of discontinuation or significant reduction of alcohol or other drug use?

Are there current signs of withdrawal?

Does the patient have supports to assist in ambulatory detoxification, if medically safe?

Dimension 2. Biomedical Conditions and Complications: Exploring an individual's health history and current physical condition.

Explanation: Assess and treat co-occurring physical health conditions or complications. Treatment provided within the level of care or through coordination of physical health services.

Questions:
Are there current physical illnesses, other than withdrawal, that need to be addressed or that may complicate treatment?

Are there chronic conditions that affect treatment?

Dimension 3. Emotional, Behavioral, or Cognitive Conditions And Complications: Exploring an individual's thoughts, emotions, and mental health issues.

Explanation: Assess and treat co-occurring diagnostic or subdiagnostic mental health conditions or complications. Treatment provided within the level of care or through coordination of mental health services.

Questions:
Are there current psychiatric illnesses or psychological, behavioral, emotional, or cognitive problems that need to be addressed because they create risk or complicate treatment?

Are there chronic conditions that affect treatment?

Do any emotional, behavioral, or cognitive problems appear to be an expected part of the addictive disorder, or do they appear to be autonomous?

Even if connected to the addiction, are they severe enough to warrant specific mental health treatment?

Is the patient able to manage the activities of daily living?

Can he or she cope with any emotional, behavioral or cognitive problems?

Dimension 4. Readiness to Change: Exploring an individual's readiness and interest in changing.

Explanation: Assess stage of readiness to change. If not ready to commit to full recovery, engage into treatment using motivational enhancement strategies. If ready for recovery, consolidate and expand action for change.

Questions:
What is the individual's emotional and cognitive awareness of the need to change?

What is his or her level of commitment to and readiness for change?

What is or has been his or her degree of cooperation with treatment?

What is his or her awareness of the relationship of alcohol of other drug use to negative consequences?

Dimension 5. Relapse, Continued Use, or Continued Problem Potential: Exploring an individual's unique relationship with relapse or continued use or problems.

Explanation: Assess readiness for relapse prevention services and teach where appropriate. If still at early stages of change, focus on raising consciousness of consequences of continued use or problems with motivational strategies.

Questions:

Is the patient in immediate danger of continued severe mental health distress and/or alcohol or drug use?

Does the patient have any recognition of, understanding of, or skills with which to cope with his or her addictive or mental disorder in order to prevent relapse, continued use, or continued problems such as suicidal behavior?

How severe are the problems and further distress that may continue or reappear if the patient is not successfully engaged in treatment at this time?

How aware is the patient of relapse triggers, ways to cope with cravings to use, and skills to control impulses to use or impulses to harm self or others?

Dimension 6. Recovery/Living Environment: Exploring an individual's recovery or living situation and the surrounding people, places, and things.

Explanation: Assess need for specific individualized family or significant other, housing, financial, vocational, educational, legal, transportation, childcare services.

Questions:

Do any family members, significant others, living situations, or school or work situations pose a threat to the patient's safety or engagement in treatment?

Does the patient have supportive friendships, financial resources, or educational/ vocational resources that can increase the likelihood of successful treatment?

Are there legal, vocational, social service agency or criminal justice mandates that may enhance the patient's motivation for engagement in treatment?

Are there transportation, child care, housing, or employment issues that need to be clarified and addressed?

Collecting Assessment Information

Steve reviews and collects additional information on some of the basic information about Juanita that she provided at intake, such as where she was born, including whether she was adopted or raised by her biological parents; her relationship with her parents; whether her parents are alive or deceased; her current relationship status; number of children and their ages; brief employment history; and her hobbies. Steve then moves the conversation into her history of alcohol and drug use. He begins by asking Juanita to explain the circumstances that caused her to be referred for this assessment. When Juanita mentions that she was arrested for possession of cocaine and marijuana, Steve uses this opportunity to ask her to identify her drug of choice.

Element 5: Assessing for Suicide

Suicide risk is a clinical judgment based on a systematic collection of evidenced-based information relevant to suicide factors that is gathered through the assessment process with a client. There is a national initiative called Zero Suicide that is "a commitment to suicide prevention in health and behavioral health systems" and is a key concept in the *2012 National Strategy for Suicide Prevention: Goals and Objectives for Action* (US Dept. of Health and Human Services, 2012). The Toolkit for Zero Suicide requires counselors to "identify every person at risk for suicide" by having counselors "screen and assess every new and existing patient for suicidal thoughts or behaviors."

This initiative includes using SAMHSA's Suicide Assessment Five-Step Evaluation and Triage (SAFE-T) assessment protocol (SMH & SPRC, 2009). The five steps of the suicide assessment are outlined here and details of the steps are modified with additional information located on the Suicide Prevention Resource Center website (http://www.sprc.org/):

1. *Identify risk factors*: The strongest predictor of suicide is one or more previous attempts; however, most people who die by suicide die on their first attempt. Therefore, it is important to identify the following risk factors for suicide:
   - *Suicidal behavior*: history of prior suicide attempts, aborted suicide attempts or self-injurious behavior.
   - *Family history*: of suicide, attempts, or psychiatric diagnoses, especially those requiring hospitalization.
   - *Current/past psychiatric disorders*: especially mood disorders (e.g., depression, bipolar disorder), psychotic disorders, alcohol/substance abuse, traumatic brain injury (TBI), posttraumatic stress disorder (PTSD), personality disorders (e.g., borderline personality disorder). Comorbidity with other psychiatric and/or substance abuse disorders and recent onset of illness increase risk.

- *Key symptoms*: anhedonia, impulsivity, hopelessness, anxiety/panic, insomnia, command hallucinations, intoxication. For children and adolescents: oppositionality and conduct problems.
- *Precipitants/stressors*: triggering events leading to humiliation, shame or despair (i.e., loss of relationship, financial, or health status—real or anticipated).
- *Chronic medical illness* (esp. central nervous system disorders, pain).
- *History of or current abuse or neglect.*
- *Access to firearms*

2. *Identify protective factors*: Keep in mind that protective factors alone may not counteract the risks of suicide; however, listed here are some internal and external protective factors to assess:
   - *Internal factors*: ability to cope with stress, religious beliefs, frustration tolerance, life satisfaction, coping skills, problem-solving skills.
   - *External factors*: responsibility to family members or pets, positive therapeutic relationships, social supports, connections/memberships/involvement with social groups.

3. *Conduct a suicide inquiry*: It is common for new counselors to wonder, "If I bring up the issue of suicide won't that cause them to start thinking about it, even if they currently are not?" The answer is, "No." It is far better to raise the issue and deal with the possibility of self-harm than to ignore it and hope that the client is not in some way planning to self-harm. Some sample indirect (passive) questions to begin the inquiry are:
   - "Sometimes, people in your situation (describe the situation) lose hope; I'm wondering if you may have lost hope, too?"
   - "Have you ever thought things would be better if you were dead?"
   - "With this much stress (or hopelessness) in your life, have you thought of hurting yourself?"
   - "Have you ever thought about killing yourself?"
   - *For youths*: Ask parent/guardian about evidence of suicidal thoughts, plans, or behaviors, and changes in mood, behaviors, or disposition.

     However, as stated earlier, also ask directly "Are you having thoughts of hurting yourself?" If there is an acknowledgment of suicidal ideation, you should then collect the following information:
   - *Ideation*: frequency, intensity, duration—in past 48 hours, past month, and worst ever

- *Plan:* timing, location, lethality, availability, preparatory acts
- *Behaviors:* past attempts, aborted attempts, rehearsals (tying noose, loading gun) versus nonsuicidal self-injurious actions
- *Intent:* extent to which the patient (1) expects to carry out the plan and (2) believes the plan/act to be lethal versus self-injurious. Explore ambivalence: reasons to die versus reasons to live

4. *Determine the risk level and intervention*: The Suicide Prevention Resource Center identifies some behaviors that may indicate immediate and severe risk for suicide.

Immediate or high risk: There are three warning signs that carry the highest likelihood of short-term onset of suicidal behaviors and require immediate attention (Jacob, Rudd et al., 2006):

- Threatening to hurt or kill self
- Looking for ways to kill self: seeking access to pills, weapons, or other means
- Talking or writing about death, dying, or suicide

Possible interventions: Hospital admission is generally indicated unless a significant change reduces risk. Suicide precautions (e.g., 24-hour observation).

Serious or moderate risk: Suicidal ideation with plan, but no intent or behavior:

- Talking about feeling trapped or in unbearable pain
- Talking about being a burden to others
- Increasing the use of alcohol or drugs
- Acting anxious or agitated; behaving recklessly
- Sleeping too little or too much
- Withdrawing or feeling isolated
- Showing rage or talking about seeking revenge
- Displaying extreme mood swings

Interventions: Admission may be necessary depending on risk factors. A referral for a mental health evaluation and/or medication evaluation may also be indicated depending on the presence of a mental health issue. Many times, a client will agree to a *commitment to treatment statement* (CTS). This involves working with them to develop a suicide safety plan with emergency and/or crisis numbers. Prior practice for suicide prevention was asking a client to sign or agree to a "no-harm contract." However, this focused on what the client would not do as opposed to what the client would do to prevent his or her suicide (Joiner Van Orden et al., 2009)

The following Suicide Safety Plan is adapted from the Safety Plan Template by Stanley and Brown (2008).

SUICIDE SAFETY PLAN

Step 1: Warning signs:

1. _____
2. _____
3. _____

Step 2: Internal coping strategies—Things I can do to take my mind off my problems without contacting another person:

1. _____
2. _____
3. _____

Step 3: People and social settings that provide distraction:

1. Name_____ Phone_____ _____
2. Name_____ Phone_____ _____
3. Place_____ 4. Place _____

Step 4: People whom I can ask for help:

1. Name_____ Phone_____
2. Name_____ Phone_____
3. Name_____ Phone_____

Step 5: Professionals or agencies I can contact during a crisis:

1. Clinician Name_____ Phone_____

   Clinician Pager or Emergency Contact #_____

2. Local Urgent Care/ER Services _____

   Urgent Care Services/ER Address_____

   Urgent Care Services/ER Phone # _____

3. National Suicide Prevention Hotline (1 (800) 273-8255)

4. Local Community Mental Health Center _____

   Local Mobile Crisis Unit Phone # _____

Step 6: Making the environment safe:

1. _____
2. _____

Low Risk: Thoughts of death, no plan, intent, or behavior.
- Modifiable risk factors
- Strong protective factors

Possible interventions: Outpatient referral for symptom reduction. Referral for mental health evaluation and/or medication evaluation may be indicated depending on the presence of mental health issue. Give emergency/crisis numbers.

5. *Document the assessment of risk, intervention, and follow-up*. For more information and a digital copy of SAFE-T go to http://store.samhsa.gov/product/Suicide-Assessment-Five-Step-Evaluation-and-Triage-SAFE-T-Pocket-Card-for-Clinicians/SMA09-4432

Element 6: Screening Tools

To avoid having to construct a formal assessment based solely on the client's self-report, it is important to incorporate some formal screening instruments into the assessment process. While a standardized screening tool does not provide a diagnosis, it can add to or lend support to the clinical impressions you have garnered from the assessment with the client. This can be particularly helpful when writing your assessment results and recommendations, especially if this report will be shared with a third party such as a judge or an attorney. A screening tool can also be useful when sharing the results with a client, particularly if the results do not line up with the client's self-report. For instance, a client who is not ready to acknowledge the need for help may be surprised to learn that the AUDIT screener (described later) indicates a possible abuse problem based on their reported information. Also screening tools can be used over time to show changes in symptoms or problems from a starting point or Baseline (A) and then after treatment intervention (B). This AB design "is the most common and least complicated of the measurement designs because there is one baseline measure and one intervention," (Faulkner & Faulkner, 2018, p. 144).

The difference between a substance abuse screening tool and a diagnostic tool is that a diagnostic tool is a definitive measure for providing a clinical diagnosis, whereas the screening tool simply identifies criteria associated with a disorder that can help substantiate a diagnosis when added to the rest of the assessment. There is a plethora of screening tools on the market; therefore, the following will be a brief overview of strengths and limitations of some of the most commonly used screening instruments. As a practicing professional, you will soon become familiar with these and many more and will develop a comfort level with your own personal favorites.

The following is a quote from the National Institute of Health's National Institute on Alcohol, Abuse and Alcoholism (NIAAA) regarding screening.

> Screening is not the same as diagnostic testing, which establishes a *definite* diagnosis of a disorder. Instead, screening is used to identify people who are *likely* to have a disorder, as determined by their responses to certain key questions. People with positive screening results may be advised to undergo more detailed diagnostic testing to definitively confirm or rule out the disorder. A clinician might initiate further assessment, provide a brief intervention, and/or arrange for clinical follow up when a screening test indicates that a patient may have a problem. (NIAAA, 2005)

CAGE

Screening tools do not have to be lengthy or difficult to administer. For example, a short (but effective) tool is the CAGE (a mnemonic device based on the four questions to be asked):

C Have you ever felt you should cut down on your drinking?
A Have people annoyed you by criticizing your drinking?
G Have you ever felt bad or guilty about your drinking?
E Eye opener: Have you ever had a drink first thing in the morning to steady your nerves or to get rid of a hangover?

CAGE-AID

A modification to the CAGE uses four conjoint questions to include drug use as well as alcohol use (Brown & Rounds, 1995).

1. In the past three months, have you felt you should cut down or stop drinking or using drugs?
2. In the past three months, has anyone annoyed you or gotten on your nerves by telling you to cut down or stop drinking or using drugs?
3. In the past three months, have you felt guilty or bad about how much you drink or use drugs?
4. In the past three months, have you been waking up wanting to have an alcoholic drink or use drugs?

Strengths: The CAGE can identify alcohol problems over the course of a patient's lifetime (Mayfield et al., 1974). The CAGE-AID limits the answer to the past three months but includes all drug use. A client would simply respond with a "yes" or "no" answer to each question. Two positive responses in the CAGE is considered a positive test and indicates further assessment is needed. One "yes" answer to any item in CAGE-AID indicates a need for further testing.

Weaknesses: Again, as with many psychometric tools, clients can always "fake good" by responding in a way that would indicate they do not have a problem. This is an inherent problem with many behavioral health instruments. The only way to combat this lack of validity is to develop a solid therapeutic relationship with the client so they feel more secure in being honest with the therapist.

MICHIGAN ALCOHOLISM SCREENING TEST
The Michigan Alcoholism Screening Test (MAST; Selzer, 1971) focuses mainly on alcohol (though the questions are easily adapted to almost any drug of choice). The long form of the MAST has 24 questions that range from "Do others ever complain about your drinking" to such questions as "Have you ever been arrested for drinking or alcohol related behavior?"

Strengths: There are many positive aspects to the MAST including the fact that it is easy to administer. Many counselors incorporate the questions into their interviews with the client without formally filling out the screening tool. Another positive aspect is that a counselor needs no special training to administer or score the questionnaire.

Weakness: One criticism of the MAST is that it is overly sensitive, tending to identify problems with alcohol and other drugs where none exists.

DRUG ABUSE SCREENING TEST
The Drug Abuse Screening Test (DAST-10; Skinner, 1982) is a 10-item brief screening tool that can be administered by a clinician or self-administered. Each question requires a yes or no response, and the tool can be completed in less than 8 minutes.

Strengths: It is very similar to the MAST in that it can be self-administered and is easy to interpret with little to no training required.
Weaknesses: This tool does not assess for alcohol or tobacco use.

SUBSTANCE ABUSE SUBTLE SCREENING INVENTORY
The next screening tool we have chosen is the Substance Abuse Subtle Screening Inventory (SASSI; Miller, 1985). This is another instrument that has been used for decades and is widely accepted.

Strength: One of main advantages of the SASSI is that it has an internal validity scale that gives an indication of how truthful the client is being. This helps to alleviate some of the issue of "faking good" that we mentioned earlier.

Weakness: The downside to this questionnaire is that it does require training in order to interpret. Anyone interested in being trained to interpret the SASSI can learn more at the SASSI website (http://www.sassi.com).

ALCOHOL USE DISORDER IDENTIFICATION TEST

The Alcohol Use Disorder Identification Test (AUDIT; Babor & Grant, 1989) is a short 10-item test developed by the World Health Organization to be used internationally. As its name implies, it is designed to identify people who have problematic drinking. A score of 8 or more in men (7 in women) indicates a strong likelihood of hazardous or harmful alcohol consumption. A score of 20 or more is suggestive of alcohol dependence. A copy of the AUDIT in its entirety is available from the National Institute of Health's National Institute on Alcohol Abuse and Alcoholism (http://pubs.niaaa.nih.gov/publications/Audit.pdf).

Strength: One of the strengths of the AUDIT is that it is a rapid assessment instrument (only 10 items), and it can be given to clients to fill out themselves.

Weakness: The negative is that it focuses solely on alcohol and no other drugs—a minor limitation, to be sure.

We would like to note here that these screening tools represent only a smattering of the various instruments available to practitioners. We have selected these because they are widely used and generally accepted by substance abuse counselors and mental health professionals in a variety of clinical settings. This is in no way an endorsement nor is it meant to rule out/exclude many other valuable tools currently available. There are literally hundreds of screening and assessment tools on the market today. Our objective is only to give you a brief introduction to screening tools commonly used in behavioral health settings. It should also be mentioned here that there are other more specific screening instruments for select populations. For instance, a counselor working with an adolescent population may want to choose a screening tool designed especially for teens. As part of its Treatment Improvement Protocol (TIP) publication series, SAMHSA has some excellent resources on assessment and referral of substance abuse disorders with young people (SAMHSA, 2009*a*).

There are also multiple screening tools for suicide risk. A systematic review of 86 articles representing 56 studies concludes that screening instruments may be able to identify adults at increased risk of suicide but are unable to predict who will die from suicide (O'Conner et al., 2013). Therefore, as with other screening tools, a thorough suicide assessment is also required.

Columbia–Suicide Severity Rating Scale

The Columbia–Suicide Severity Rating Scale (C–SSRS) is part of a national and international public health initiative involving the assessment of suicidality. The C–SSRS was found to reliably predict a potential suicide attempt in those who had previously attempted suicide (Posner et al., 2011). It also was able to determine clinically meaningful points at which a person may be at risk for an impending suicide attempt, something that other scales have been unable to consistently determine. The C–SSRS shows successful suicide attempt prediction in suicidal adolescents and in nonsuicidal adults. It is the only screening tool that assesses the full range of evidence-based ideation and behavior items, with criteria for next steps (e.g., referral to mental health professionals); thus, the C–SSRS can be exceptionally useful in initial screenings. There are also versions of the screener for military/veterans, with triage points, since last visit, pediatric versions, and others. No mental health training is required to administer it, although there is free online training available. To access the scales, trainings, and general information, go to http://cssrs.columbia.edu/clinical_practice.html.

There are also multiple screening tools for so many social issues that it is impossible to list here. However, a sampling includes mental health issues (i.e., anxiety, depression, psychosis), mental status evaluations, relationship issues (i.e., interaction, connectedness), emotional problems (i.e., anger, impulsivity), and health issues (i.e., dementia), and many are targeted for specific populations (i.e., adolescents, couples).

Element 7: Mental Status Impressions

Clinical impressions are an important part of an assessment. We can not only learn information from what a client says (verbal), but we can also learn information from what a client does (behavioral), and we can develop overall impressions from both. Many assessments include a mental status component that can capture clinical impression. There are several mental status examination (MSE) screeners available in the public domain. However, many counselors use orientation as a simple indicator of the client's cognitive ability to understand what is occurring during the assessment. *Orientation* involves the awareness of four dimensions: person, place, time, and situation.

Orientation to person: "What is your full name?" "What is your daughter's name?"
Orientation to place: "What city and state are we in?"
Orientation to time: "What is today's date?" "What year is it?"
Orientation to situation: "Can you explain why you came here today?"

Another simple examination is *recall*, which is used to test for memory issues. You give a client three words to remember (such as book, ball, and pencil) and tell the client that you will later ask him or her to repeat these back to you. Then you move on to a different task, such as asking the orientation questions just listed. After a few minutes, ask the client to repeat the three words you said earlier.

If the client struggles with any of these examinations, you should review the other findings from the assessment (such as an indication of depressed mood, a traumatic brain injury, or medication/drug effects) that might explain these struggles. A referral to a physician to rule out a medical condition may be indicated.

Here, we have listed groupings of common categories that are often used to capture mental status impressions for describing a client's mood, affect, and attitude as well as their insight, judgment, and thought content. We have included terminology that you can use to best describe these impressions.

Mood: Mood is a temporary state of mind. An individual's mood will change based on internal and external triggers.

- *Anhedonia*: the inability to experience any pleasure
- *Angry*: feeling or showing anger or strong resentment
- *Annoyed*: irritated, bothered
- *Anxious*: mental distress or uneasiness due to fear or danger, real or imagined
- *Bored*: not having or showing interest, weary
- *Depressed*: sad, hopeless, discouraged, an inability to experience pleasure
- *Elevated*: elated feeling or mood, high-spirited
- *Euthymic*: normal or neutral mood in which the range of emotions is neither depressed nor highly elevated (absence of a depressive or manic cycle)
- *Grandiose*: an inflated appraisal of one's worth, power, knowledge, importance, or identity
- *Irritable*: easily irritated or annoyed; readily excited to impatience or anger
- *Raging*: to act or speak with fury; show or feel violent anger

Affect: Affect is a set of observable manifestations of emotion conveyed by the person's nonverbal behavior (body movement, facial expressions, and gestures).

- *Aggressive*: vigorously energetic, especially in the use of initiative and forcefulness

- *Appropriate*: suitable or fitting affect for a particular purpose, person, occasion, etc.
- *Bright affect*: Positive; pleasant expression, often accompanied by smiles, even laughter
- *Congruent with mood*: a person's affect matches their thought content
- *Incongruent with mood*: a person's affect does not match their mood
- *Congruent with thought content*: a person's affect does matches their thought content
- *Incongruent with thought content*: a person's affect does not match their thought content
- *Irritable*: easily irritated or annoyed; readily excited to impatience or anger
- *Constrict*: to hold in or limit expression of feelings
- *Exaggerated*: unrealistically magnified
- *Passive*: not reacting visibly to something that might be expected to produce an emotion or feeling.
- *Passive aggressive*: denoting or pertaining to a personality type or behavior marked by the expression of negative emotions in passive, indirect ways, as through manipulation or noncooperation
- *Sad*: affected by unhappiness or grief; sorrowful or mournful

Attitude: Refers to the patient's approach (manner, disposition, feeling, position) to the interview process and the quality of information obtained during the assessment.

- *Ambivalent*: relating to the coexistence within an individual of positive and negative feelings toward the same person, object, or action, simultaneously drawing him or her in opposite directions
- *Cooperative*: working or acting together willingly for a common purpose or benefit
- *Guarded*: cautious, careful, prudent
- *Hostile*: opposed in feeling, action, or character; antagonistic
- *Indifferent*: a lack of interest, concern, or sympathy
- *Resistant*: opposed to something; wanting to prevent something from happening
- *Suspicious*: having or showing cautious distrust of someone or something
- *Uncooperative*: unwillingness to cooperate

Insight: An understanding of the motivational forces behind one's actions, thoughts, or behavior; the recognition of sources of emotional difficulty and an understanding of relationships that sheds light on or helps to solve a problem.

- *Intellectualizing*: to ignore the emotional or psychological significance of an action, feeling, behavior by an excessively intellectual or abstract explanation
- *Impaired*: weakened, diminished, or damaged; functioning poorly or inadequately; deficient or incompetent
- *Improved*: to make improvement through change
- *Good*: satisfactory understanding of motivation behind one's actions, thoughts, or behavior
- *Poor*: unsatisfactory understanding of one's thoughts, actions, or behavior

Judgment: Used in reference to the quality of cognitive faculties and capabilities and refers to the patient's capacity to make sound, reasoned, and responsible decisions. For instance, forming of an opinion, estimate, notion, or conclusion from circumstances presented to the mind.

- *Good*: satisfactory ability to form opinions and conclusions
- *Impaired*: weakened, diminished, or damaged; functioning poorly or inadequately; deficient or incompetent
- *Improved*: to make improvement through change
- *Impulsive*: rash, quick, hasty
- *Irrational*: without faculty of reason; without or deprived of mental clarity
- *Poor*: inability to form satisfactory conclusions and opinions
- *Rational*: endowed with the faculty of reason; lucid, sane

Thought content: Abnormalities of thought content are established by exploring individuals' thoughts in an open-ended conversational manner with regard to their intensity, salience, the emotions associated with the thoughts, the extent to which the thoughts are experienced as one's own and under one's control, and the degree of belief or conviction associated with the thoughts.

- *Congruent*: the feeling or the emotion that a person is experiencing matches the affect they display or express
- *Delusional*: maintaining fixed false beliefs even when confronted with facts

- *Fearful*: the unpleasant emotional state consisting of psychological and psychophysiological responses to a real external threat or danger
- *Grandiose*: an inflated appraisal of one's worth, power, knowledge, importance, or identity
- *Homicidal ideations*: having an inclination to kill
- *Intrusive*: unwelcome involuntary thoughts, images, or unpleasant ideas that may become obsessions and can be difficult to manage or eliminate
- *Obsessive*: an all-consuming compulsive fixation
- *Paranoid*: having or showing an unreasonable feeling that people are trying to harm or do not like the individual
- *Persecutory*: to exterminate or subjugate people based on their membership in a religious, ethnic, social, or racial group
- *Phobia*: a dread of an object or situation that does not in reality pose any threat; this is distinct from a *delusion* in that the patient is aware that the fear is irrational
- *Preoccupation*: thoughts that are not fixed, false, or intrusive but that have an undue prominence in the person's mind
- *Projecting*: to ascribe one's own feelings, thoughts, or attitudes to others
- *Suicidal ideation*: recurring thoughts of or preoccupation with suicide
- *Suspicious*: having or showing cautious distrust of someone or something

There are other observations that can be included in the assessment, such as appearance. Appearance should focus on what is not common or what is unique to the client that can provide insight or support to the assessment impressions. For instance, poor hygiene may be an indication of self-neglect due to depression, a product of a physical limitation or disability, or related to financial problems (i.e., water turned off). It is especially important to notice changes in appearance (improvements or deterioration) over time. Appearance can also be an indicator of substance abuse, such as malnutrition, bloating or distended stomach (possible liver disease), dental erosion (smoking meth), rash around the mouth (inhalant abuse), needle marks (intravenous drug abuse), and appearing older than the chronological age.

CONCLUSION

As a counselor, it is imperative that you continually assess what you know about your client. As the therapeutic relationship develops over time, clients will reveal more and more information, making it necessary to re-evaluate your initial assessment. This process will carry on throughout the time the client is in counseling with you.

There is one obvious flaw in the assessment process—the fact that this is all predicated on the client's self-report. Many times, clients are hampered by "social desirability" (the need to present themselves in a positive light so that others will not think badly of them) or are simply not ready for change. Therefore, they may minimize or even deny the amount of their usage or the negative impacts that drug use has had on them and/or their family. It is important to accept what the client says at that time unless there are facts that state otherwise. Remember that you, as a counselor, are trying to build a positive, therapeutic relationship with them, and the quickest way to put impediments into the counseling process is to begin by challenging what the client tells you. It is far better to accept what they say, without judging, and then use the ongoing relationship to re-evaluate and assess the client as they feel more comfortable and become increasingly open and honest.

4

Diagnosis, Placement,
and Treatment Planning

INTRODUCTION

In this chapter, we will discuss and demonstrate best practice for developing a *diagnostic impression* of a substance abuse problems utilizing *diagnostic tools* such as the *Diagnostic and Statistical Manual of Mental Disorders* (DSM). We will also discuss various placement decisions such as the *levels of care* (LOC) and criteria for placement as outlined by the American Society of Addiction Medicine (ASAM). Finally, we will discuss how to develop a treatment plan, also called a service plan. Listed here are the Council for Accreditation of Counseling and Related Educational Programs (CACREP), Council on Social Work Education (CSWE), International Certification & Reciprocity Consortium (IC&RC), and Substance Abuse and Mental Health Services Administration (SAMHSA) standards associated with diagnosis, placement, and treatment planning.

CHAPTER COMPETENCIES AND STANDARDS

CACREP—Standards 3, 23–27
CSWE—Competencies 6 and 7
IC&RC—Domain I: Tasks 7–8, Domain II: Tasks 1–10
SAMHSA—Competencies 9, 13, 37–48, 56–61

DIAGNOSTIC IMPRESSION

Addiction is often characterized by the ABCDE mnemonic:

a. Inability to consistently Abstain;
b. Impairment in Behavioral control;
c. Craving; or increased "hunger" for drugs or rewarding experiences;
d. Diminished recognition of significant problems with one's behaviors and interpersonal relationships; and
e. A dysfunctional Emotional response. (ASAM, 2011)

This is an example of a simple and broad way to define addiction, but it is not a diagnostic tool. The difference between a screening tool (as discussed in Chapter 2) and a diagnostic tool is that the latter utilizes recognized standardized criteria for providing a clinical diagnosis, whereas the screening tool simply indicates a possible problem that requires further investigation. For example, the Triage Assessment for Addictive Disorders-5 (TAAD-5) published by The Change Companies, is a brief structured interview designed to identify current alcohol and drug problems. This 31-question interview takes approximately 10 minutes to administer and 2–5 minutes to score and interpret. It offers high internal reliability to produce diagnostic indications for a DSM-5 substance use disorder with four criteria for abuse and seven for dependence. For ordering information, go to https://www.changecompanies.net/products/?id=TA-T.

Another example of a screening tool that is widely used among psychologists and other mental health professionals is the MacAndrews Alcoholism Scale of the Minnesota Multiphasic Personality Inventory (MMPI). In fact, several supplementary scales have been developed for the MMPI including the MacAndrews Alcoholism Scale, MacAndrews Alcoholism Scale Revised, Addictions Potential Scale, and the Addictions Acknowledgement Scale. All subscales and the MMPI itself can only be interpreted by a person with specialized training (master's level or above).

Diagnostic and Statistical Manual

The primary and most widely recognized behavioral health diagnostic tool is the DSM, currently in its fifth edition (American Psychiatric Association,

2013). In this manual, substance use disorders are assigned codes used to justify reimbursement by third-party payers using the same process as seen with medical conditions. In the newest edition of the DSM, abuse and dependence for substance use are placed on a continuum as opposed to in separate categories (use, abuse, dependency) and are measured for level of severity from mild to severe based on the number of criteria present within a 12-month period.

Substance use criteria within the past 12 months include:

1. Substance taken in larger amounts over a longer period than intended.
2. Persistent desire to cut down or control usage.
3. Significant time spent obtaining, using, and recovering from substance use.
4. Use resulting in failure to fulfill major role obligations.
5. Continued use despite recurrent social or interpersonal problems.
6. Social, occupational, or recreational activities given up or reduced.
7. Use in situations that are physically hazardous.
8. Continued use despite known recurrent physical or psychological problems likely caused by use.
9. *Tolerance*: Using more produces the same effect and/or effects are diminished with same amount.
10. Withdrawal symptoms.
11. Craving or strong desire or urge to use.

For instance, when looking at these 11 criteria, individuals with 0–1 criterion would not receive a diagnosis for substance use disorder. However, someone with 2–3 criteria would be considered to have a mild substance use disorder, 4–5 criteria a moderate substance use disorder, and 6 + criteria a severe substance use disorder.

Specify current severity is based on the following guidelines:
    Mild: Presence of 2 or 3 symptoms
    Moderate: Presence of 4 or 5 symptoms
    Severe: Presence of 6 or more symptoms

The DSM-5 also recognizes that vulnerability to addiction varies due to multiple conditions such as lower levels of self-control and genetic predisposition, which all may be brain-based. Because of these difference, DSM-5 has two groups of substance-related disorders: *substance use disorders* (just described) and *substance-induced disorders*. Examples of substance-induced disorders include substance-induced mental disorders, substance-induced sleep disorders, substance-induced sexual dysfunctions, substance-induced delirium, and substance-induced neurocognitive disorders.

DSM and ICD Coding

The DSM is the recognized behavioral health diagnostic tool for insurance re-imbursement. Up until the newest fifth edition, the DSM had a numeric coding system. Now it follows the medical coding of the International Classification of Diseases (ICD). All substance use disorders are listed under the F1 codes and are divided by substance type starting with F10—Alcohol use and ending with F19—Multiple drug use, as seen here.

✓ F10—Disorders due to use of alcohol
✓ F11—Disorders due to use of opioids
✓ F12—Disorders due to use of cannabinoids
✓ F13—Disorders due to use of sedatives or hypnotics
✓ F14—Disorders due to use of cocaine
✓ F15—Disorders due to use of other stimulants, including caffeine
✓ F16—Disorders due to use of hallucinogens
✓ F17—Disorders due to use of tobacco
✓ F18—Disorders due to use of volatile solvents
✓ F19—Disorders due to multiple drug use and use of other psychoactive substances

There are also nine coding specifiers with each substance abuse F1 code.

✓ .0—Acute Intoxication
✓ .1—Harmful Use
✓ .2—Dependence syndrome
✓ .3—Withdrawal state
✓ .4—Withdrawal state with delirium
✓ .5—Psychotic disorder
✓ .6—Amnesic syndrome
✓ .7—Residual and late-onset psychotic disorder
✓ .8—Other mental and behavioral disorders
✓ .9—Unspecified mental and behavioral disorder

These specifiers are additionally expanded to be more descriptive. For instance, in Table 4.1, you will see that F10 (Disorder due to alcohol use) is specified with .2—Dependence Syndrome. For DSM, this would fall on the continuum of Alcohol Use, Moderate or Severe, depending on the number of criteria identified. There are additional coding specifiers to identify whether the client was intoxicated at the time of the assessment (F10.220–F10.229) or whether the client is in recovery (F10.21). However, a diagnosis for a client who is not intoxicated at the time of assessment and meets the criteria for alcohol dependence (six or more criteria items within the past 12 months) would be coded as F10.20.

Table 4.1 EXPANDED SPECIFIERS

ICD-10 CODE	ICD-10 CODE DESCRIPTION
F10.20	Alcohol dependence, uncomplicated
F10.21	Alcohol dependence, in remission
F10.220	Alcohol dependence with intoxication, uncomplicated
F10.221	Alcohol dependence with intoxication delirium
F10.229	Alcohol dependence with intoxication, unspecified

Diagnostic Finding for Juanita

Assessment findings revealed that the following diagnostic criteria were met within the past 12 months, indicating Severe Use:

1. *Substance taken in larger amounts over a longer period than intended.* Juanita would find herself binging on cocaine for longer periods of time, sometimes overnight, despite her intent to return home.
2. *Persistent desire to cut down or control usage.* Juanita reports that she had promised herself multiple times that she would reduce how much cocaine she was using but was unable to control her binges once she started.
3. *Significant time spent obtaining, using, and recovering from substance use.* Juanita states that her life revolves around getting high. She states that she was constantly preoccupied with seeking and using drugs (specifically cocaine or other stimulants and marijuana).
4. *Use resulting in failure to fulfill major role obligations.* Juanita expressed tremendous guilt and remorse for being a "bad mother." She frequently lied to her children to cover her drug use and would go into debt to purchase drugs while denying her children payment for school activities.
5. *Continued use despite recurrent social or interpersonal problems.* Juanita reports the unwanted breakup of a male friend who discovered her extensive drug use. "He was the best thing that happened to me and was wonderful to the kids."

6. *Tolerance: Using more produces the same effect and/or effects are diminished with same amount.* Juanita recently found herself needing more cocaine to achieve the effect she desired.

7. *Craving or strong desire or urge to use.* Juanita reports significant craving to continue to use cocaine. She feels "normal" when she is high, as evidenced by more energy, increased sociability, increased productiveness at work and home, and lack of depressive symptoms.

Juanita is also experiencing some mild generalized paranoia and significant symptoms of depression, as evidenced by feeling overwhelming guilt and remorse, tearfulness, lack of energy and motivation, and difficulty both falling and staying asleep. She reports continued daily use of marijuana to "take the edge off" and to help her sleep.

F14.20—Cocaine use disorder, severe

F14.24—Cocaine-induced depressive disorder. With severe use disorder

F12.240—Cannabis Use Moderate: Currently using, without physical features

LEVELS OF CARE AND PLACEMENT CRITERIA

There are many LOCs available and multiple versions of placement criteria (see Table 4.2). First, will examine the most common LOCs in a hierarchical fashion from least restrictive to most restrictive.

Levels of Care: ASAM Criteria

The ASAM criteria also describe four levels of care, but they are more descriptive of the specific services provided. Levels are assigned a number based on the information collected in the six dimensions of the ASAM biopsychosocial assessment (see Element 4 in Chapter 2).

Table 4.2 ASAM CRITERIA AND LEVELS OF CARE

Level of Care, Description, and Examples
0.5   Early Intervention, for at-risk patients who do not meet criteria for addiction; e.g., DUI/DWI programs
1   Outpatient Services, less than 9 hours of service per week; e.g., medication management visits
2.1   Intensive Outpatient Services, 9 or more hours of service per week; e.g., outpatient treatment programs
2.5   Partial Hospitalization Services, 20 or more hours of service per week but not requiring 24-hour care; e.g., partial hospitalization programs
3.1   Clinically Managed Low-Intensity Residential Services, 24-hour structure with trained personnel available; e.g., half-way houses
3.3   Clinically Managed Population-Specific High-Intensity Residential Services, 24-hour care with trained counselors with less intense milieu and group treatment; e.g., residential treatment for patients with cognitive difficulties
3.5   Clinically Managed High-Intensity Residential Services, 24-hour care with trained counselors with more intense milieu and group treatment; e.g., residential treatment for patients with normal cognitive abilities
3.7   Medically Monitored Intensive Inpatient Services, 24-hour nursing care with physicians available for significant problems; e.g., residential treatment for patients with significant problems with addiction, mental health, and/or general medical conditions
4   Medically Managed Intensive Inpatient Services, 24-hour nursing care and daily physician care for severe, unstable problems; e.g., hospital-based care
OTP Opioid Treatment Program, administration of methadone or buprenorphine in conjunction with counseling for those with severe opioid addiction, e.g., methadone clinic

Source: The ASAM Criteria, CATR, 2014;2(7), Risk and Reimbursement.

LEVEL 1: OUTPATIENT COUNSELING

The first level is outpatient counseling. As the name implies, this method takes advantage of the client's ability to maintain employment, live at home, and carry on a normal daily routine. The patient would normally see the counselor one time a week for about an hour (usually for 8–12 weeks for the initial portion of treatment). After that, depending on how the client is doing, a graduated step-down may occur (the client would be seen once every 2 weeks for a month or so, and then once a month until discharge).

LEVEL 2.1: INTENSIVE OUTPATIENT

Intensive outpatient (IOP) services require more time commitment on the part of the client. Many states have regulations that specify how many hours a week a client must be seen (usually 9 or more) to be considered as participating in an IOP program. IOP programs often combine the use of group therapy, family therapy, and individual therapy. For example, an IOP program may require clients to attend group 3 nights per week for 3 hours each night augmented by a 1-hour individual counseling session. Another program is structured for clients to attend a 2-hour treatment group every evening Monday through Friday, with Friday being "Family Group."

LEVEL 2.5: DAY TREATMENT/PARTIAL HOSPITALIZATION PROGRAMS

Day treatment programs, also commonly called partial hospitalization programs (PHPs), typically provide all of the services that a person would receive if he or she was admitted to an inpatient (residential) treatment facility but with the benefit of being able to go home at night and on weekends. Day treatment programs commonly run from around 8 A.M. until sometime around 4 or 5 P.M. People who are in day treatment typically attend 20 hours or more a week of group counseling sessions, individual counseling sessions, family counseling, and psychoeducational groups, and may participate in supportive services such a case management, peer support, and support groups (like Alcoholics Anonymous [AA] and Narcotics Anonymous [NA]).

LEVEL 3.1: RESIDENTIAL TREATMENT

Residential treatment centers (RTC) are secure, 24/7, nonmedical facilities that provide structured programming throughout the day and evening hours. Clients in residential treatment might stay for a few days to several months. Residential placement can help stabilize the patient whose drug use is unmanageable in an outpatient setting.

LEVEL 3.7: INPATIENT TREATMENT

Inpatient services typically reside in a hospital setting where there is 24-hour medical oversight and services. This level of care is necessary to provide medically managed detoxification services for a patient with acute withdrawal symptoms from alcohol due to the effects of the drug on the central nervous system. Another example is a patient who has taken an overdose of cocaine and is experiencing cardiovascular problems. Many hospitals have a detox unit specifically for these patients.

Client with a substance use disorder may also have a comorbid mental health condition that requires stabilization before engaging in substance abuse treatment. Crisis stabilization may be available on a medically managed mental health unit at a hospital. However, some behavioral health crises can also be stabilized in a 24-hour, medically monitored setting that is located in the community. The risk factors associated with a crisis may need to be evaluated by a physician to determine whether a client can be medically monitored safety outside a hospital setting. For instance, a client who is psychotic would need medical management, including monitoring and adjustments to psychotropic medications, whereas a client who has suicidal ideations with intent might be medically monitored successfully in a non-hospital setting that provides a safe and supportive environment.

Levels of Care Utilization System

The Level of Care Utilization System (LOCUS) (AACP, 2009) is a tool used for mental health and substance abuse assessments. It has three objectives:

1. *Provide a system for assessment based on six dimensions*: (1) risk of harm; (2) functional status; (3) medical, addictive, and psychiatric comorbidity; (4) recovery environment; (5) treatment and recovery history; and (6) engagement and recovery status.
2. *Describe a continuum of care under four categories of services*: care environment, clinical services, supportive services, crisis stabilization and prevention services. The continuum of care entails six LOC dimensions (see later discussion).
3. *Create a method for quantifying (scoring) the assessment* to determine placement recommendation.

As with the ASAM, a numeric rating is given to each of the six dimensions. LOCUS specifies six dimension criteria that are rated from least to most acute using a 5-point scale.

✓ Dimension 1: Risk of Harm—(1) minimum, (2) low, (3) moderate, (4) severe, (5) extreme *risk of harm*
✓ Dimension II: Functional Status—(1) minimal, (2) mild, (3) moderate, (4) serious, (5) severe *impairment*

✓ Dimension III: (1) none, (2) minor, (3) significant, (4) major, (5) severe *comorbidity*

✓ Dimension IV: Recovery Environment—(A) *Stress*: (1) low, (2) mild, (3) moderate, (4) high, (5) extreme (B) *Support*: (1) high, (2) supportive, (3) limited, (4) minimal, (5) none

✓ Dimension V: Treatment and Recovery History (*Responsive to Treatment*)—(1) fully, (2) significant, (3) moderate/equivocal, (4) poor, (5) negligible

✓ Dimension VI: *Engagement* and Recovery Status—(1) optimal, (2) positive, (3) limited, (4) minimal, (5) unengaged

In the example scoring sheet seen here, the shaded areas indicate independent criteria that require admission to that level regardless of the composite score. An asterisk indicates special consideration in scoring. The counselor, based on information from the client, completes the assessment and sums the individual dimension ratings to generate the composite scores. Independent placement criteria supersede the composite scores for placement decisions.

						Score
1. Calculation of LOCUS Composite Score						
Dimension	**Dimension Rating (circle score)**					**Rating**
I. Risk of Harm	1	2	3	4*	5	
II. Functional Status	1	2	3	4*	5	
III. Medical, Addictive and Psychiatric Co-Morbidity	1	2	3	4*	5	
IV. Recovery Environment						
Level of Stress	1	2	3	4	5	
Level of Support	1	2	3	4	5	
V. Treatment and Recovery History	1	2	3	4	5	
VI. Attitude and Engagement	1	2	3	4	5	
Composite LOCUS Score (Add member in right column)						
2. LOCUS—Derived Level of Care Recommendation: (consult Determination Grid)						

For younger populations, there is the Child and Adolescent Service Intensity Instrument (CASII), formerly called Child and Adolescent Level OF Care Utilization System (CALOCUS; AACAP, 2001). It is a tool to determine the appropriate level of care placement for a child or adolescent, and it draws from the following resources: CASSP/Guiding Principles for Systems of Care (Stroul & Friedman, 1986), developmental theory, family empowerment, cultural competence, wraparound services, and clinical expertise. For more information, visit http://www.aacap.org/App_Themes/AACAP/docs/member_resources/practice_information/casii/CASII_infor_and_data.pdf.

Placement Criteria

Most counselors operate on the principle of "least restrictive environment." This means that the counselor will refer the client to the level of care that causes the minimum amount of disruption to his or her life but that still matches the level of care determined by the assessment. The added benefit of a least restrictive environment is that if a client fails to respond to treatment at one level, the counselor can always refer him or her to a higher (more intensive) level of treatment. Two placement criteria are used universally by insurance providers for utilization review purposes: the ASAM Criteria and the LOCUS.

ASAM PLACEMENT CRITERIA
ASAM has the most widely used placement criteria for clients with substance abuse disorders in the nation (ASAM, 2011). A 2006 survey of all 50 US state authorities conducted for National Association of State Alcohol and Drug Abuse Directors (NASADAD) found that 43 states (84%) required the use of standard patient placement criteria. Among those 43 states, approximately two-thirds (66%) require providers to use The ASAM Criteria.

Under the section on "Biopsychosocial Assessment" in Chapter 3, we described the six dimensions of the ASAM assessment tools and some associated question. Based on the responses to these questions, you would evaluate the risks for each dimension and determine a level of care for each dimension. For instance, you may find that the Dimension 1 risks are moderate to severe due to acute withdrawal from opiates, but not in need of medical intervention (Level 2.5). However, Dimension 6 is a severe risk due to using family members in the home creating an unsafe recovery environment (Level 3.1). Residential treatment might be the best option for the client who has a history of relapse (Dimension 5—Level 2.5) and poor impulse control coupled with a mental health diagnosis of generalized anxiety (Dimension 3—Level 3.3). You also want to make sure that the client does not have any health conditions that can become serious due to acute withdrawal (Dimension 2). For instance, if you discover that the client has an unstable medical condition that creates a serious risk for a life-threatening event during withdrawal, you would assign a Level 3.5. Based on this dimension alone, the appropriate LOC would be medically monitored inpatient services. Keep in mind that the numbers associated with the levels of care for each dimension are *not* cumulative (added together), nor are they averaged to come up with a single score. The level of risk and protective factors within each dimension must be taken into consideration and weighed against each other to determine the most appropriate treatment recommendation.

Placement Recommendation for Juanita

Steve starts this session with Juanita by reviewing her assessment findings. In addition to a clinical interview, he also administered the ASI and the DAST. Based on the results of the assessment (her ASAM score was 2.3, which falls between IOP and partial hospitalization) and her scores on these two instruments, Steve recommends that Juanita be admitted to an intensive outpatient program (IOP). Steve believes that Juanita may have developed a dependency on cocaine and is not sure if IOP will be structured enough for her to remain clean; however, his recommendation is based on several factors: (1) Juanita was fairly honest, open, and unguarded; (2) Juanita has no prior attempts at treatment; (3) Juanita is still employed; (4) Juanita expressed a (vague) desire to get help and make some changes in her life during her interview with Steve, and; (5) the IOP program will provide Juanita with some psychoeducational groups to teach her more about the effect of her drug abuse on her body, her mind, and her relationships with her children and others. Additionally, recommending IOP is adhering to the principle of "least restrictive environment" and will allow her to continue to work. If Juanita is unable to stay clean in IOP, Steve will reevaluate her for a more structured environment such as partial hospitalization or residential treatment. Juanita agrees to this recommendation, and, when she returns for her next session scheduled for the next week, he will share a copy of the report that he will send to the court.

LOCUS PLACEMENT CRITERIA

LOCUS identifies six LOC dimensions for placement:

✓ Level One—Recovery Maintenance and Health Management
(Composite Rating 10–13)
✓ Level Two—Low-Intensity Community Based Services (Composite
Rating 14–16)
✓ Level Three—High-Intensity Community Based Services (Composite
Rating 17–19)
✓ Level Four—Medically Monitored Nonresidential Services (Composite
Rating 20–22)
✓ Level Five—Medically Monitored Residential Services (Composite
Rating 23–27)
✓ Level Six—Medically Managed Residential Services (Composite
Rating 28 or more)

The Determination Grid shown here outlines how the composite scores are determined for the LOC based on the assessment scores.

Start by identifying any independent placement criteria. If there are independent placement criteria, assign the level accordingly. If no independent placement criteria, locate the composite score in the bottom row. Review the column above. If most items are consistent with the dimension scores, assign the client to that level. If most items are inconsistent, move to the column where most items are consistent with the client's dimension scores, and apply that level.

TREATMENT PLANNING

While the actual mechanics of treatment planning will differ depending on where you are employed, agencies generally have a standard format that they use to record treatment planning that adheres to their particular practices and philosophies. The "old school" way of developing a treatment plan was a one-size fit all model. Treatment plans looked nearly identical, using a "menu" of preprinted goals and interventions. Individual needs were often overlooked in the plan—even if they were addressed during the treatment process. Little training was offered on developing good treatment plans, so the treatment libraries outlining a selection of goals and interventions for various problem statements became the standard practice.

Level of Care / Dimensions	Recovery Maintenance Health Management — Level 1	Low-Intensity Community Based Services — Level 2	High-Intensity Community Based Services — Level 3	Medically Monitored Nonresidential Services — Level 4	Medically Monitored Residential Services — Level 5	Medically Managed Residential Services — Level 6
I. Risk of Harm	2 or less	2 or less	3 or less	3 or less	④ / 3	⑤ / 4
II. Functional Status	2 or less	2 or less	3 or less	3 or less	④ / 3	⑤ / 4
III. Comorbidity	2 or less	2 or less	3 or less	3 or less	④ / 3	⑤ / 4
IV. A. Recovery Environment "Stress"	Sum of IV A + IV B is 4 or Less	Sum of IV A + IV B is 5 or Less	Sum of IV A + IV B is 5 or Less	3 or 4	4 or more	4 or more
IV. B. Recovery Environment "Support"	2 or Less	2 or Less	3 or Less	3 or Less	4 or more	4 or more
V. Treatment & Recovery History	2 or Less	2 or Less	3 or Less	3 or 4	3 or more	4 or more
VI. Engagement	2 or Less	2 or Less	3 or Less	3 or 4	3 or more	4 or more
Composite Rating	10 to 13	14 to 16	17 to 19	20 to 22	23 to 27	28 or more

o Indicates independent criteria requires admission to this level regardless of composite score

Now treatment plans are in the spotlight of best-practice approaches. For example, a treatment plan can sometimes be called a *service plan* or *recovery plan* and can include specifiers such as *individualized* or *person-centered* in the description. As a new counselor, you will be introduced to your agency's methods for developing and keeping records, and it is sometimes a daunting process to adapt to a new system. Some agencies record treatment plans, intake assessments, progress notes, discharge summaries, and entire case files entirely on a computer program (electronic medical records). Others use individual hard copies, stored in a locked filing cabinet within a locked room or office.

But regardless of how a client plan is created and maintained, it is virtually worthless unless clients feel that they have a voice in creating the goals and objectives that will shape their treatment. In essence, this needs to be the client's treatment, not the counselor's. Think of the treatment plan as the blueprint for outcomes that the client strives to achieve.

The individualized treatment plan (ITP) focuses on the individual's vision of recovery, his or her priority treatment goals and objectives, and the interventions that will help meet those goals and objectives. The plan must be written in a way that gives the individual and/or family a clear understanding of the services being offered and specifically how the plan will address their concerns. Consequently, the individual must take part in the process of developing the plan to make sure the treatment is relevant to his or her priorities and incorporates strengths as well as barriers to treatment.

In some cases, a *treatment team* is involved in the ITP. This occurs routinely in residential and inpatient settings were a multidisciplinary team is involved in the client's care. It can also occur in an outpatient center where multiple services are offered, such as medication, case management, peer support, supportive housing, and the like. The treatment team always includes the client and any of the client's significant others involved in the client's recovery plan. Many agencies require documentation of family involvement (or attempts to involve family) as a best practice. The treatment team can also include a physician; an occupational, vocational, and/or activity therapist; a peer support specialist; a case manager; an agency supervisor; and other treatment providers involved with the clients care and recovery.

Universally, treatment plans have a common format that includes *goals* (for instance, a long-term recovery vision and 2–3 short-term treatment goals), *objectives* (steps the individual will take to achieve the short-term goals), *interventions* (what the counselor or treatment team will do/provide to help the client achieve goals), *signature* boxes for the treatment team (including client), and a *review date* for when the plan will be reviewed and revised (e.g., 30–90 days) and/or a *target date* for when a goal is expected to be achieved.

Treatment Planning with Juanita

Juanita identified four initial goals: to stay clean and sober, to find nonusing friends, to complete court-mandated treatment, and to improve her relationship with her children. Steve and Juanita created the treatment plan together, using these four goals. The plan is designed to be reviewed monthly during individual counseling sessions. You may notice that these goals are a mixture of external goals (to satisfy the requirements of the court system) and internal goals (to be a better parent). Table 4.3 shows a sample treatment plan for you to review. Notice that the treatment goals are *person-centered* with associated objectives and interventions. It also includes the *evidence*—or how everyone knows that the goal is being met—and the *date for review*.

We would also like to take a moment to discuss objectives. This is one of the most difficult areas for new counselors, but it is also one of the most vital to learn to do well. Goals, by definition, do not have to be measurable. Goals are a broad-based view of what the client wants/needs to accomplish. On the other hand, objectives need to be measurable. One way to think about objectives when you are creating/writing them is to make sure that they comply with the acronym MOST. Objectives need to be:

M—Measurable
O—Observable
S—Specific
T—Time-lined

Returning to our sample treatment plan, we can examine each of the objectives and submit them to the acronym test. Are they measurable, observable, specific, time-lined? If not, then they need to be rewritten to meet these criteria. Writing treatment plans that are measurable and specific helps both you and the client. If both of you have a clear understanding of what is to be worked on while in treatment, then the treatment plan becomes a road map that directs the counseling sessions. It is also important to point out that treatment plans are dynamic—not static. This means that they are meant to be used—to be reviewed and changed, with new goals and objectives added as old ones are completed.

Table 4.3 Juanita's Individualized Treatment Plan

Date	Person-Centered Goals	Objectives	Interventions	Evidence	Review/Target Date
m/d/year	"I want to stop using drugs"	Juanita will identify using at least one recovery and/or relapse prevention strategy daily.	IOP will provide Psycho-educational groups on recovery and relapse prevention strategies.	1. Journal entries of strategies. 2. Negative urinalysis drug screens.	Review once a week during IOP
m/d/year	"All my friends are users. I need some new friends."	1. Juanita will attend one meetings of her choice per week. 2. Juanita will identify one or more persons as potential mentor or sponsor within 30 days.	Counselor will provide a schedule of local support group meetings	1. Attendance sheets signed by person chairing each meeting. 2. Name and contact information of one support person.	1. Review once a month during individual counseling 2. Target Date: Next individual appointment
m/d/year	"The judge says that I need to come to counseling or I will go to jail. She will want a report that I completed treatment."	1. Juanita will arrange for childcare on the evenings she attends IOP. 2. Juanita will attend all counseling appointments as scheduled.	1. Evening IOP 3 × week 2. Individual counseling 1xmonth	1. Attendance compliance at IOP 2. Monthly documentation of treatment compliance sent to Judge	Review once a month during individual counseling
m/d/year	"I want to be a better mom."	Juanita will work with counselor to identify primary parenting concerns during next individual appointment.	Individual Counseling 1xmonth	Attendance at scheduled appointment	Target Date: Next individual appointment

Strengths: Strong bond with children, desire to complete court recommendations, highly motivated to remain sober, stable employment.
Barriers to treatment: Strong urges, lack of sober support system, feelings of guilt and remorse, symptoms of depression, using cocaine to feel "normal."

CONCLUSION

The diagnosis, placement recommendation, and treatment planning become the foundation of what will occur in treatment. The DSM diagnosis is generated from the information gathered in the assessment. While the primary diagnoses for treatment of a SUD will be F1-codes, this diagnosis section should also include significant/relevant diagnoses that may affect treatment delivery and/or outcomes. A few examples are comorbid mental health issues such as major depressive disorder, significant physical health issues such as diabetes, developmental delays such as mental retardation, and social communication disorders such as autism spectrum. Placement recommendations should be drawn directly from the assessment findings. Insurance providers generally require specific justification as a part of the utilization review process to authorize services. By using recognized criteria such as the ASAM assessment or LOCUS, you increase the likelihood of precertification for services. Similarly, the ITP should be related to the presenting problems and DSM diagnoses. Helping the client understand expectations of a specific level of care, such as IOP, will prevent confusion and mistrust as treatment progresses. The treatment plan is individualized to account for the clients' strengths and limitations and lays out the outcomes (goals) that the client desires and the action steps (objectives) that the client commits to achieve change. All interventions should be based on best practices related to helping clients achieve their goals. There may also be significant issues discovered during the assessment that require referrals to other providers. For instance, the client may request or agree to a medication evaluation by a prescriber, or the client may need a physician appointment to rule out a medical condition that could be impacting recovery. These referrals can also be included in the ITP as short-term goals and objectives.

5

Addiction Theory and Treatment Approaches

INTRODUCTION

In this chapter, we address theories and approaches to addiction counseling focusing on best practices. We will begin with an overview of the most common addiction theories (moral, disease, social learning, and genetic). We will also discuss some of the most widely used approaches in addiction counseling with a focus on current approaches that have been identified as being highly effective. These include cognitive behavioral, behavioral, motivational interviewing, ego-psychology, and some Internet-based counseling tools. After reviewing these approaches, we apply a theoretical perspective to our case study of Juanita. Listed here are the Council for Accreditation of Counseling and Related Educational Programs (CACREP), Council on Social Work Education (CSWE), International Certification & Reciprocity Consortium (IC&RC), and Substance Abuse and Mental Health Services Administration (SAMHSA) standards associated with addiction theory and treatment.

CHAPTER COMPETENCIES AND STANDARDS

CACREP—Standard 2
CSWE—Competencies 4, 8
IC&RC—Domain III: Tasks 4
SAMHSA—Competencies 10, 117, 118

CASE SCENARIO UPDATE

Juanita will be attending her weekly session with Steve to begin addressing issues that they mapped out in last week's session as part of the process of developing a treatment plan. One of Juanita's agreed upon treatment goals was for her to remain clean and sober. As part of this goal (and to facilitate her developing a network of clean and sober friends), Steve has made it a part of Juanita's treatment plan that she participates in a 12-step support group such as Alcoholics Anonymous or Narcotics Anonymous. These meetings are not meant to replace counseling but to augment her treatment. Research has demonstrated a positive link between self-help support groups and positive outcomes in treatment (Donovan et al., 2013; Kelly et al., 2010). The conventional wisdom among substance abuse counselors has been to recommend that clients attend a minimum of one meeting per day (30 meetings in 30 days) when initially beginning recovery. One of the things Steve will do when he meets with Juanita today is to review her participation at meetings, what she liked, didn't like, how she felt about attending, and more. Steve will also spend time discussing the role of the 12-step program in recovery, the definition of a "sponsor" (someone with long-term sobriety who agrees to act as a mentor to the newcomer), and the importance of a support group. Steve will also use his time with Juanita to further develop the therapeutic relationship and check his initial assumptions obtained during the assessment interview.

Steve opens the counseling session by "checking-in" with Juanita. He asks about her week, how things are going? How has she done in maintaining sobriety? What have been the challenges of staying sober? He also is alert for any crises or other immediate problems that need to be dealt with before moving on.

THEORIES OF ADDICTION

Before we delve into a discussion of theories of addiction, we need to add a caveat. A quick search of any library's database with the keywords "theories of addiction" will result in literally thousands of articles. This is a very controversial and complex subject, with new information being added daily. Obviously, there is no possible way that in a few pages we can in any way cover all the possible theories. Our goal here is to situate substance addiction (such as alcoholism) within a historical and theoretical context so that you, the clinician, can have a better understanding of how these theories have evolved. With that said, the first theory we will review is the moral model.

Moral Theory

This theory uses a psychosocial approach to explain addiction. In its simplest form, the moral model views addiction as a character flaw. People who are addicted, they would say, are simply "weak-willed." The phrase "can't handle his liquor" was born out of the moral model. Addiction is viewed as more of a result of poor choices (or a series of bad choices) that result in an addiction to a drug. Proponents of this model believe that drug addiction can be overcome with willpower, and people who use drugs should be punished (often this means imprisonment). The moral model was the prevailing model of explaining addiction well into the early twentieth century, and it is not difficult to see vestiges of this model throughout our justice system today.

Disease Theory

It was not until Dr. E. Morton Jellinek began to systematically examine alcoholics and later publish his landmark book *The Disease Concept of Alcoholism* (1960) that psychiatrists, psychologists, and medical professionals began to change their concept about addiction. For the first time, a well-respected researcher, author, and academician was advocating that alcoholics, specifically, and drug addicts, in general, were not necessarily morally weak—but they suffered from an inability to control their drinking much like a diabetic cannot control his or her ability to process sugar. He postulated that people who were addicted had a physiological deficit making it impossible for them to drink normally. Jellinek postulated three phases of alcoholism (early, middle, and late). The early stage was characterized by blackouts, and using to alleviate anxiety or pain are the most common characteristics of this stage. The middle stage was characterized by problems with family, work, finances, and changes in moral behavior. In the last or late stage, the alcoholic experiences decreased tolerance and deterioration of the body and the brain, and it is not unusual for the alcoholic to struggle with hospitalizations due to alcohol complications.

There are both strengths and limitations to viewing addiction as a disease. If an addiction is a disease, then addicts will be treated with dignity and not stigmatized for being an addict. Relieving the guilt and shame of addiction may help some addicts to be more amenable to treatment. One of the advantages to viewing addiction as a disease (as opposed to a character flaw) was that it then opened up the field of addiction to scientific research—placing addiction on a level playing field with other illnesses. However, the limitations/weaknesses are that, in claiming to have a disease, some addicts will deny responsibility for their behavior, instead blaming their behavior on the disease.

Social Learning Theory

Social learning theory was developed, in part, as a reaction to psychodynamic theory and behavior theory. Albert Bandura believed that humans learn more from what they witness around them than from the impulses and inner drives postulated by Freud several decades earlier (Bandura, 1971). Bandura's work (initially started by his research on children's behavior after witnessing several different adults model both passive and aggressive behavior) has become legendary in the field of social psychology (Bandura et al., 1961). At least one study has identified a link between social learning theory and adolescent tobacco use (Akers et al., 1979). This study, conducted over a 5-year period, tracked the tobacco use of teenagers. The authors state that tobacco usage is increased based on the smokers' proximity to peers who smoke (the more that others around them smoked, the greater the usage of tobacco). Social learning theory has been used as the theoretical basis for other social problems, too. In another study, Tomlinson and Brown (2012) found a correlation between expectations and predictors of amount and frequency of adolescent drinking. Today, much of the research on multigenerational family violence uses this theory as a framework for explaining domestic abuse (Mihalic & Elliott, 1997).

One of the drawbacks to social learning theory is the fact that there is little consensus among social scientists on how to define (and measure) social learning theory. One study (Reed et al., 2010) raises the question of the researcher's ability to assess whether learning has occurred and how much of the learning is attributed to social learning and how much is assigned to individual learning. On the other hand, social learning theory, at least as an explanation for behavior, has applicability for explaining the behavior of adolescent smoking (and perhaps even consuming alcohol). Using this theory to explain addiction raises more questions. For example, social learning theory would predict that children who grow up in a home where one or more of the parents are addicted to alcohol (or another drug) would learn (by witnessing their behavior) to use drugs themselves. However, this theory does not explain people who are reared in a home with addiction and choose for themselves to refrain from all drug usage.

Genetic Theory

Genetic theory, as the name implies, posits a link between biological/genetic markers and addiction. For decades, counselors in the field have known, via practice wisdom, that not all people have the same reaction to alcohol and other drugs. For example, one client may begin to drink alcohol in her teen years and drink for years before experiencing any negative effects of the drug. Another individual may begin to drink as a teenager and, within a few months, be experiencing blackouts and other behaviors associated with alcohol addiction. The only common factor between the two clients may be that the client who started drinking alcohol at a young age had a history of alcohol addiction in her family while the former client did not.

Back in the early 1980s, a landmark book, *Under the Influence: A Guide to the Myths and Realities of Alcoholism* (Milam & Ketcham, 1984), appeared. This text was the first to establish that alcoholics process alcohol differently than social drinkers. Using detailed methods to explain the biochemical processes that happen in the liver and brain, the authors were the first to demonstrate what others had been speculating on for years.

Using their research as a basis for future study, scientists are moving closer to identifying the biological markers within the liver that will positively identify those people who are at risk for alcoholism. One study, conducted in Sweden (Kendler et al., 2012), was one of the first to use a larger population to examine the effects of genetics on addiction. The researchers found that both familial environmental factors and genetics were important predictors in determining an outcome of addiction. One study proposed a typology for classifying alcoholic drinkers (noted as type A and type B) (Babor et al., 1992). Later, this was expanded to be generally referred to as type I and type II drinkers. Both are known to have different characteristics in their personalities and their drinking behaviors, and there is a strong link to genetics. Type I drinkers tend to be able to drink for many years without developing the symptomatology of alcoholism (blackouts, for example), while type II drinkers tend to experience blackouts early on in their drinking. Type I, it is now thought, inherit the genetics of alcohol addiction cross-gender. This means a mother who is alcoholic may not have a daughter who is addicted but may have a son who is an alcoholic. The opposite is true for type II alcoholics. A type II alcoholic is more vulnerable to genetic influences from the same-gender parent. A father who is addicted to alcohol is more likely to have a son who will be an alcoholic. Sometimes, the addiction skips a generation so that we would see a grandfather being addicted to alcohol, no addiction in his son, and then a grandson who displays type II alcoholism characteristics.

Genetics alone, however, cannot fully explain the complex issue of addiction. Scientist are increasingly focusing research on the human brain and the changes in brain chemistry that occur when a person gets high. The authors in one study (Kreek et al., 2012) point out that while genetics contribute to the initial vulnerability to being addicted, brain chemistry also plays a part.

Without going into a detailed analysis of the role of neurobiology and brain function, it is important to note that drug abuse has both short-term and long-term effects on brain chemistry. It is now understood that the brain's reaction to drug abuse lasts sometimes far beyond periods of abstinence, which is now thought to be a factor in the relapse process.

Like all theories, genetic theory has both strengths and weaknesses. The strength of this theory is that research into genetic and biological factors for addiction leads to further research. Intergenerational studies are useful for locating patterns of occurrence in substance abuse. Intergenerational studies give a broad overview of the conditions, including areas where further research should be conducted. Weaknesses also exist. Intergenerational studies are not effective in discerning the effects of genetics versus environment.

Studies are inconclusive and can be used to prove both sides of an argument. For example, if a study shows that one-third of a certain group became alcoholic, the same figures could demonstrate that two-thirds did not become alcoholic. One other weakness to this theory is its inability to account for other addictions including gambling, sexual, and eating disorders.

COUNSELING APPROACHES

There are a multitude of practice approaches in counseling. The approaches presented here are known as *best practices* because they have substantial evidence of good outcomes for clients: centered therapy, cognitive behavioral therapy, behavioral therapy, and motivational interviewing. In addition, we also include some counseling tools from ego-psychology and technology.

Client-Centered Therapy

Client-centered therapy (sometimes referred to as *Rogerian therapy*) is most effective for establishing a therapeutic relationship with the client (Lambert & Barley, 2001; Ponzo, 1976). Client-centered therapy essentially seeks to create a safe environment for the client to work in—to change. Part of the creation of this safe environment requires a counselor who accepts the client as he or she is—something Carl Rogers referred to as "unconditional positive regard" (Rogers, 1957). Rogerian therapy utilizes the technique of *active listening* or focusing on the client's verbal and nonverbal cues and then reflecting those through paraphrasing and parroting. Active listening, to be effective, requires the therapist to set aside preconceived notions about the client and fully engage with the client by giving the speaker their undivided attention (Rogers & Farson, 1957; Lang et al., 2000). However, after the therapeutic relationship has been firmly established and the client knows without hesitation that the counselor has their best interest at heart, it is often advantageous to combine client-centered therapy with other techniques. One positive aspect to this is that client-centered therapy is not a "stand-alone therapy." The concepts and procedures can be employed throughout the counseling process and then over-laid with other techniques.

Cognitive Behavioral Therapy

The second counseling theory we will examine is that of *cognitive behavioral therapy*. Cognitive behavioral therapy emerged (and is closely associated with) rational emotive behavior therapy. However, there are other antecedents to this therapy including those proposed by Albert Bandura, B. F. Skinner, and Jean Piaget. Rational emotive behavior therapy was first developed by Albert Ellis in what he then referred to as rational therapy (RT) and later to rational emotive therapy (RET). Today, RET has been expanded and Ellis has now added a behavioral component, calling his system of therapy rational emotive behavior therapy (REBT) (Ellis, 1995). The basic tenets of RET are that thoughts drive emotions and emotions drive behavior. If we can change our thoughts, we can change our behavior. Rational emotive therapy focuses on events, our thoughts related to the event, and our emotional response. For example, let us imagine a young man who wants to ask someone out on a date. Normally, this young man is self-confident, gregarious, and never at a loss for words, but when he tries to ask someone for a date, he suddenly feels shy and tongue-tied. Upon further analysis, he realizes that this is a direct result of his own inner dialogue or self-talk. He is giving himself negative messages even before he asks someone out. Thoughts like, "she will never go out with me" lead to him feeling shy and inadequate. If he can change his thinking, he can change his shy and nervous behavior. Thoughts like, "she will never go out with me" and "I will never get a date" are generalizations. A more rational thought might be, "she may not go out with me, but there are plenty of other people to date." By extension, cognitive behavioral therapy focuses on maladaptive beliefs or mistaken thoughts that drive an individual's behavior. The therapist works with the client to challenge and change these ways of thinking.

Therapist who utilize cognitive behavioral therapy techniques often use tools like journaling (asking a client to keep track of their thoughts and self-talk) and visualization (asking the client to imagine that they are in a situation that may ordinarily cause them to feel distress). Visualization is commonly used for patients who have mild phobias and panic attacks associated with a situation. For example, we once had an adolescent client who was paralyzed by the fear of having to get an inoculation at the doctor's office. The client needed an injection to participate in a sport. By using the technique of visualizing the situation and continually imagining themselves coping with the situation in incremental methods (for example, the counselor would say "imagine yourself walking up to the door of the doctor's office," and then later "imagine yourself opening the door," etc.), the client was eventually able to conquer his fear and anxiety.

Behavioral Therapy

Behavioral therapy, on the other hand, is less interested in the client's thoughts and perceptions and more interested in their behavior. The primary goal of behavior therapy is to change behaviors—to emphasize and focus on positive behaviors and to diminish and eliminate negative behavior. The nature of behavior therapy becomes, then, highly focused—paying attention to the behavior and ignoring everything else. Behavior therapy is rooted in two basic principles. The first is the idea of *classical conditioning* (the belief that organisms respond to specific stimuli in their environment). For example, if you are hungry and someone sets a plate of food in front of you, your mouth may begin to water. The second principle is that of *operant conditioning*—reinforcement and punishment can be used to increase or decrease a behavior. An example is the child who is in line with his mother at the grocery store. Standing in line at the check-out aisle, the child spies a candy bar and begins to beg and plead for the candy. If the mother (at last feeling exasperated and tired of the begging) gives in and gives the child the candy, guess what happens the next time they are at the grocery store? You are correct: the child will again beg and plead because she has learned that this type of behavior leads to a reward. A second example is that of the seat belt in your car. If your car sounds a chime when you fail to buckle your seat belt (and you buckle your belt in order to silence the chime), you are responding to operant conditioning—exhibiting a behavior to remove a stimulus (the chime). But, you may be asking, "how can behavioral therapy be utilized with clients?"

It is very common to use behavioral models with certain populations, especially adolescents. Many residential treatment programs utilize a "token economy" system. A token economy works on the principle that pro-social behaviors are rewarded, and negative behaviors are punished. When a person attends group on time, participates in group, completes homework assignments given by the counselor, and exhibits other acceptable behaviors, then the client receives points or other tokens. Later, these can be exchanged for privileges—a chance to view a movie, extra recreational time, or perhaps a pass away from the facility for a few hours. Loss of points or tokens can result in punishment (loss of privileges, time-outs, etc.). The downside to the token economy system, however, is that it only works if the rewards are intrinsically motivating for the client. If the client has no interest in the potential reward, then there exists no incentive to participate.

Residential and outpatient treatment program utilizes the behavioral technique of *counterconditioning* (the idea of substituting the pleasurable response from the use of a drug with a negative association). For alcohol, one way of doing this is by giving the patient a drug that is known to make a person sick if they drink while taking the drug (e.g., disulfiram, marketed under the trade name Antabuse). When a person takes Antabuse, nothing happens unless they consume alcohol. When a person drinks while taking Antabuse, then they become violently ill. Adverse conditioning uses this model of behavioral therapy, pairing negative associations (being sick while drinking) to replace the former positive associations of alcohol.

Motivational Interviewing

Motivational interviewing is a counseling approach that has been identified by SAMHSA as one of their best-practices models for addiction counseling (SAMHSA, 2008c). It is a systematic method of counseling with a demonstrated ability to help clients make positive changes in their lives. The efficacy of motivational interviewing has been proved in multiple studies (Rubak et al., 2005). At the heart of motivational interviewing is a style of counseling that helps clients to explore and overcome their own ambivalence (Rollnick & Miller, 1995).

Motivational interviewing diverges from client-centered therapy by being more directive. Whereas client-centered therapy traditionally uses reflection and active listening to let clients explore and find answers within themselves, motivational interviewing takes a more direct approach by actively encouraging clients to consider making changes (rather than passively allowing clients to find their own answers). It should be noted here that, on the surface, motivational interviewing would seem to be in direct conflict with client-centered therapy. In fact, the opposite is true. Motivational interviewing seeks to be nonjudgmental and nonconfrontational. The idea is not to engage in a power struggle with the client but to move alongside and serve as a co-facilitator or helper in the change process. In SAMHSA's treatment protocol on motivational interviewing, five principles of the counseling process are identified:

"The clinician practices motivational interviewing with five general principles in mind:
1. Express empathy through reflective listening.
2. Develop discrepancy between clients' goals or values and their current behavior.
3. Avoid argument and direct confrontation.

4. Adjust to client resistance rather than opposing it directly.
5. Support self-efficacy and optimism." (SAMHSA, 2008(c), p. 41)

Ego Psychology

This counseling technique has largely fallen from favor with most theorists, yet there are some basic tenets that still have application for counseling. *Ego psychology* (initially developed by Sigmund Freud and further developed by his daughter, Anna) is rooted in Freud's belief in an id, ego, and super-ego with the ego functioning as a buffer between the other two entities. Anna Freud carried on this body of work and developed the concept of the *ego defense mechanism*. Ego defense mechanisms are coping strategies that reduce the anxiety produced by negative or unwanted impulses (arising out of the id). Freud identified 10 specific mechanisms for defending the ego, and these were further defined and enumerated by his daughter (Freud, 1937). These 10 mechanisms are repression, regression, reaction formation, isolation, undoing, projection, introjection, turning against one's own person, reversal into the opposite, and sublimation or displacement. One of the main defense mechanisms still very much in use as part of the substance abuse counselor's lexicon is *repression* (often referred to as *denial*). Essentially, repression/denial is the pushing down or hiding of a feeling or behavior because it is thought to be unacceptable. It is common practice for a therapist to say "They are in denial." Essentially, the addict is reluctant to reveal to themselves and to others the extent of their drug usage. This often is one of the first obstacles a counselor has to overcome to be effective with a client. For our next, and final, discussion on clinical techniques, we will briefly examine some new and emerging models that have tremendous possibilities.

Internet-Based Counseling Tools

Technology is a fact of life, and it is no surprise that treatment programs are beginning to incorporate it into their services. Many programs now utilize computer-based programs and mobile phones to check in with clients and for scheduling. Insurance companies are more flexible in paying for telephone- and web-based counseling, especially in remote area where people are isolated and in crisis situations. However, technology is not the panacea that will solve all problems. One study points out that, even with the rapid advances in the use of communication devices, problems (such as confidentiality, security breaches) still exist (McClure et al., 2013). Despite the potential hazards, the use of social media (e.g., texts, blogs, online forms, electronic records, telehealth) will, in some part at least, become an integral part of the counselor's repertoire. Bartels and Naslund (2013) call for the use of social media (Facebook, Facetime, etc.) to serve as a treatment intervention for older adults who suffer from loneliness, depression, and other issues. It is a short leap from the utilization of social media to treat mental health issues to the use of social media in treating substance use disorders.

Choosing a Counseling Approach for Juanita

Steve uses this third session with Juanita to check out his initial assumptions that he formulated during their first meeting. He uses a combination of a client-centered therapy and motivational interviewing to draw her out about her feelings about her addiction, her desires to quit, and her fears about being a "treatment failure." Together they explore what it would mean for her to relapse and begin using again. She describes her fear of letting her children down once again and uses phrases like, "I don't know if I am up to this." As an experienced professional, Steve perceives Juanita's reluctance to fully engage in recovery as being a protective mechanism—designed to give herself an out if she does relapse. Steve's use of motivational interviewing helps him to avoid confronting her behavior, and instead he uses it as an opportunity to explore her underlying fear. He states, "What I hear you saying is that you feel afraid that recovery is scary for you and you fear that you will not be up to the challenges of living a clean and sober life. Is that accurate?" By not confronting or challenging Juanita, she begins to view Steve as an ally in the recovery process—someone who wants to help her—not someone who is waiting for her to make a mistake so he can send her back to court. Slowly, she is developing trust in Steve as her counselor and the helping process in general.

As the session comes to an end, but before Juanita leaves, Steve asks her to take a moment and complete the scale that will rate how she feels about today's session. The scale is short (only 10 questions), but it gives Steve a good understanding of how Juanita feels that the session went and whether she feels she is being helped—both very important towards her recovery.

CONCLUSION

Without a solid theoretical understanding of how and why addiction occurs, it is difficult to form a clear direction for how to treat that addiction. For years, counselors have relied on practice wisdom and their own intuition to guide their counseling. McLeod (2001) argues that we need a new paradigm wherein research guides what practitioners do with their clients. With the glut of information that we have today, clients are much more aware and apt to require that any techniques or practices be backed-up with empirical evidence that they are effective. And, ethically, we as helpers have a responsibility to those we work with to utilize the best practice standards possible. This chapter also reviewed some of the most prominent counseling approaches used in addiction counseling. As with all counseling approaches, there are strengths and limitations. Clients have varied needs, and counselors have varied strengths. Many counselors use several, or all, of these interventions based on how their client is presenting. Things to consider are the clients stage of change, strengths and limitations, developmental age, and cognitive ability.

Individual Counseling

INTRODUCTION

As usual, this chapter will begin with an overview of the Substance Abuse and Mental Health Services Administration (SAMSHA) competencies and the Council for Accreditation of Counseling and Related Educational Programs (CACREP) standards. Following that, we will continue to observe our client as she meets with her counselor in individual therapy near the end of her first 4 weeks in therapy and is becomes ready to move to the next phase—group counseling. In this chapter, we will demonstrate Steve and Juanita reviewing her treatment plan, discussing her progress in treatment, and discussing the next steps in Juanita's therapy process. We will also discuss how to deal with crisis situations when they arise and the techniques for using a treatment plan as a guide to counseling. Finally, we will discuss some documentation methods and the use of electronic medical records (EMRs) or electronic health records (EHRs). Listed here are the CACREP, Council on Social Work Education (CSWE), International Certification & Reciprocity Consortium (IC&RC), and SAMHSA standards associated with individual counseling.

CHAPTER COMPETENCIES AND STANDARDS

CACREP—Standards 19, 23–27
CSWE—Competencies 6–9
IC&RC—Domain II: Tasks 2 and 9; Domain III: Tasks 1–4 and 6; Domain IV: Task 7
SAMHSA–Competencies 17, 49–55, 67–87, 108–114, 120

MICRO COUNSELING SKILLS

The ways in which we communicate depend largely upon the situation. For instance, we communicate differently with clients than we do with colleagues, friends, or family members. In Chapter 2, we discussed two counseling skills—rapport building and engagement. This section introduces additional micro-counseling skills that are useful in helping clients work toward change. These skills are divided into *attending behaviors* and *interviewing skills*.

Attending Behaviors

Attending behaviors are indirect ways that we communicate with the client. This can be demonstrated through *body language*. Body language skills include:

- making *eye contact* to establish focus;
- *head movements,* like nodding, to demonstrate understanding;
- *mirroring* a client's behavior, such as leaning in or out to help clients relax (Geldard & Geldard, 2001);
- using your *tone of voice*, such as matching a client's excitement or lowering the tone when a client's voice starts to escalate;
- using *silence* to allow the client an opportunity collect thoughts;
- *positioning* your body to that there are no barriers between you and the client, such as a desk or folding your arms across your chest, and;
- using *facial expressions*, such as smiling or knitting your eyebrows to encourage further elaboration.

In addition, remember to be *genuine* with you client. This means that you are authentic, open, honest, and sincere with your client. Keep good boundaries without playing the role of "the professional" (I am here to fix you) or "the expert" (if you don't know something, admit it). Recognize the humanness of your client and join with them in the treatment process; do not tower above them. And, finally, demonstrate *warmth* by maintaining a positive, supportive, and nonjudgmental attitude.

Interviewing Skills

Interviewing skills are direct ways in which we communicate with our client. Listed here are 14 interviewing skills that are used in counseling. Some skills are used to solicit information (questions, simple encouragement) or assure an understanding of what the client is sharing (clarification, summarizing). Other skills are more advanced and used to increase knowledge (information giving) or to facilitate a deeper understanding with the client (confrontation, empowerment). Here, you will find an explanation and an example for each skill.

1. *Paraphrasing*: Translates into your own words the client's feelings, questions, ideas, and key words. For example; "So you're saying . . . " or "Tell me if I understand this correctly . . . ". This indicates careful listening and encourages further and deeper discussion.

2. *Restatement*: Takes the client's own thoughts and words about what the content of the event is and feeds them back to the client. Client: "I had a fight with her again last night." Counselor: "You and your wife had another fight last night." This is followed by a probe: "Tell me what happened" if the client does not voluntarily continue the discussion.

3. *Reflection of feeling (empathy)*: Most often phrased in the form of a guess or a hypothesis, reflections are worded so the client is free to accept or reject them. This is useful during conflict resolution and in discussing emotional issues: "It sounds like you are feeling frustrated."

4. *Open-ended questions*: Used to probe and elicit information: "Tell me about . . . "; "Can you please explain . . . "
   a. *How* questions enable discussion about feelings or processes: "How did you come to consider this?"
   b. *What* questions most often are used to gather information: "What brings you here today?"
   c. *When* questions help determine the timing of a problem: "When did you first notice experiencing blackouts?"
   d. *Where* questions can facilitate discussion about situation and environment: "Where did you go to shoot up?"
   e. *Could* questions invite an opportunity to discuss a difficult topic: "Could you tell me how you ended up in jail?"
   f. *Why* questions look for underlying causes or reasons: "Why do you think that?" These types of questions can lead a client to feel defensive, therefore, care should be taken when using them.

5. *Closed-ended questions*: Used to seek short, specific responses. Assessments and surveys are designed to have closed-ended questions to elicit limited response options like "yes/no" or "never/sometimes/frequently/always" to specific questions. Closed-ended questions are useful for confirming or refuting an observation: "Were you going to add something?"; "Was that your son in the lobby with you?" Or to quickly gather information to complete documentation: "How old are you?"; "When was your last doctor's visit?"

6. *Clarification*: Demonstrates an interest and a desire to understand the client and avoid misinterpretations: "I'm sorry, I don't understand what you mean." "Please explain that to me again."

7. *Summarization*: Condenses the content of the client's current state of events that surround the problem: "During the past 20 minutes you and I discussed your concerns about . . . " "Let's go over what we've discussed . . ." Emphasize important points.

8. *Simple encouragement*: Simple, short responses are effective for inviting further elaboration from a client. These are useful in limiting the participation of the counselor to make room for the client: "Tell me more."

9. *Information giving*: Education increases a client's knowledge related to the discussion. This can be done through sharing community resources that a client may need or through some educational material related to the client problem. "I have some information on signs and symptoms of depression. Let's go through these and see if any apply you."

10. *Problem-solving*: This encourages the individual to participate in identifying and assessing the problem. "Let's brainstorm some ideas together."

11. *Confrontation*: Used to challenge faulty thinking or false information. Client: "My probation officer told me that I don't have to be in counseling anymore." Counselor: "The letter I have here states that you are 'required to complete DUI classes.' What do you need to do to complete the classes?"

12. *Empowerment*: Emphasizing strengths and accomplishments empowers clients. "Regardless of all the obstacles you faced this week, you remained strong and stuck to your plan . . . "

13. *Self-disclosure*: Self-disclosure can be used in a limited capacity for positive role-modeling. Disclosures should always be at the benefit of the client and not the counselor. Appropriate self-disclosures: "When I feel overwhelmed at work, I talk with my supervisor to get direction and help. What have you tried that worked for you?" "As a parent myself, I understand the desire to be all things to your children. But even great parents cannot, and should not, meet their every demand."

14. *Interpretation*: Using empathy to explore deeper meaning and insight with the client. "It sounds like you were guarded when you went on the date. Being guarded is a defense mechanism where you limit what you share out of fear that there will be a negative consequence."

Individual Counseling with Juanita

Steve, as is his usual custom, opens the counseling session by "checking-in" with Juanita. He inquires about her week: "How things are going?" [open-ended question]. "Have you remained sober since our last visit?" [closed-ended question]. "What have been the challenges of staying sober?" [open-ended question]. He also is alert for any crises or other immediate problems that need to be dealt with before moving on.

This week, Juanita is in a state of minor crisis. She discovered some ma-rijuana in her son's room. She is afraid that he will become an addict, like she is, and once he starts to experiment with pot, he will continue wanting to get high—always seeking a more intense feeling from the drug. Steve senses that this is a real and immediate concern for Juanita, so, rather than note her concern and file it for future counseling, he decides to deal with her fears. Steve and Juanita spend some time exploring what finding out that her son is smoking marijuana means to her. What are her fears, her thoughts, and how does she feel about the situation? Juanita feels mixed emotions—on one hand, she knows that it is natural for kids to want to try new things—to experiment and find their own way and she is supportive of that. On the other hand, she is fearful that her son will like the high from pot so much that he will start to forsake his grades, let his schoolwork suffer, and pay more attention to getting high than to being a student. After taking about 20 minutes of the session to explore her feelings, Steve turns her attention to the treatment plan.

Juanita and Steve review the goals and objectives outlined in her treat-ment plan. Juanita has complied with the treatment plan by attending Alcoholic Anonymous (AA) meetings and Narcotics Anonymous (NA) meetings a minimum of once a day. On occasion, when she has felt tempted to use, she has attended two meetings in one day. She self-reports that she has identified a woman in one of the meetings who is serving as her tem-porary sponsor, and Juanita is considering asking her to be a permanent sponsor for her. Juanita reports that, "She is tough, and she doesn't cut me any slack, but I like her. She doesn't let me run any games down on her or myself." After reviewing the treatment plan, Steve turns the conversation to the next phase of treatment—participation in group therapy. Steve takes some time to explain what she can expect from group therapy, how many nights a week she will be expected to attend, and what the implications are for their own individual counseling sessions (Steve will be available to see Juanita for individual counseling if the group therapist thinks it would be beneficial.) Otherwise, Juanita will attend group 2 nights a week for the next 8 weeks and then, when she successfully completes group, she will again be meeting with Steve to plan the next phase of her treatment (family therapy). Juanita expresses some initial fear and trepidation about attending group, but after talking through her thoughts and the things she is concerned about with Steve, she agrees to begin attending group therapy. Steve agrees to help her get registered for the group with the receptionist as soon as their session ends. Before Juanita leaves, Steve asks her to complete a scale that rates her feelings about today's session (including questions about how she is progressing in treatment).

TREATMENT PLAN REVIEW

Addressing Treatment Goals and Objectives

The treatment plan should be regarded as a guide and, for that reason, frequently referred to by both the therapist and the client. Every counseling session should be reviewing progress toward achieving the clients' goals and objectives. This is documented in the clients record, and any changes that were identified during the session should be reflected in the treatment plan. This could be adding new a goal or objective or closing an existing goal or objective. However, there are instances where the therapist needs to set aside the treatment plan and focus on the immediate needs of the client. If you will notice in the case study just presented, Juanita was clearly in crisis. She was worried about a situation (finding drugs in her son's room), and it would be hard for her to focus on any other aspect of therapy until that was dealt with.

Dealing with Crisis

Whenever something happens to us, we have two components: our thoughts (about the event) and our emotions or feelings (about the event). One mistake that many helpers make is to focus on the thoughts ("Tell me what happened") and fail to explore the person's feelings. Often clients will be able to relate (sometimes in great detail) exactly what happened, but, unless the counselor spends time exploring what they were feeling (or how the event made them feel), clients will walk away with a vague sense that they weren't heard. So, Steve knew that he needed to spend time exploring with Juanita what she was feeling and what her underlying fears and concerns were. If he failed to do that, she would have left frustrated and still very anxious about the situation. By spending time with her and helping Juanita to sort out what her fears were, she left the session with a sense that Steve had listened and was going to help her deal with her son's behavior—*at the proper time* (later, when they were ready for family counseling). For now, she felt she could simply relax about the situation and not have to deal with it (because she has an ally in her counselor and together they will take on this larger issue of her son's use of marijuana). After Juanita leaves (and Steve helps her get registered for group with the receptionist), Steve spends some time documenting his session with Juanita.

DOCUMENTATION

We hope by now that it is becoming increasingly clear to you that one of the hallmarks of the counseling profession in general and substance abuse counseling specifically is that nothing is set in stone. Just as there are multiple forms for assessments and treatment plans, there are also a plethora of ways to document case records. We are going to review some of the most commonly used ones here. Chances are, the agency you are employed in will use one of the models that we show you. Before we delve into the various ways of recording case notes, we need to make a few general remarks. First and foremost, an old adage in the counseling field still applies today, "If you didn't document it, you didn't do it." This is where using the treatment plan's goals and objectives to guide treatment is beneficial. There are sometimes two types of case notes: *progress notes* and *counselor notes*. Progress notes are a written record regarding a counseling session with a client (regardless of whether it is an individual session or a group session). Counselor notes are simply ancillary notes that are directly related to a client's care. For example, you may have a release of information to discuss a client's treatment progress and treatment goals with her probation officer. If you make a phone call to the probation officer, you would record this under counselor notes.

Now, a few words about progress notes. Regardless of what format you use for recording your progress notes here are some simple guidelines:

1. Remember that the client file is a legal document and needs to be able to stand up to scrutiny if it is ever the subject of a court trial.
2. It is important to record case notes based on facts rather than your opinion (refer to item 1).

3. It is important to guard against recording other peoples' names in your file. For example, when discussing a client's spouse, you would record only their first initial (or their first and last initial but not their full name). Again, refer to item 1.

4. All documentation needs to be dated (when it was recorded) and signed (by the therapist).

Models for Record Keeping

Client records need to be succinct, yet accurate. Counselors learn to strike a delicate balance between writing too little and too much. Some counselors choose to have the client read and countersign their case notes so the client knows exactly what is being said about them. One advantage to this is that it truly makes a person think about what they are writing. In the next section, we will review some of the most common forms of writing case notes. Progress notes, when written well, can serve multiple functions. They assist the counselor in remembering what is going on with the client, what has been discussed, and what is the plan of action (this provides a historical record). This record is also important for others in the agency who may need to review the client's progress and see what treatment issues still need to be addressed.

SOAP ENTRY

The first example we will look at is the Subjective, Objective, Assessment, and Plan (SOAP) model. There are four components to the SOAP note. The first two (subjective and objective) consist entirely of what the client said and his or her behaviors. Beginning with the first one (Subjective), this is a short summation of what was discussed during the hour (from the client's point of view). The second entry (Objective) is the counselor's view of what was stated. Box 6.1 shows an example of a SOAP note. You may notice that the letters SOAP are clearly written out to the side of the case note. This helps anyone who is reading to know which category each entry falls under. The next section (Assessment) is the therapist's objective assessment of what is going on with the client, and the last section (Plan) is the specific plan for moving forward with the client. This may be as elaborate as stating the homework the client has agreed to complete during the week or simply stating that the plan is to meet with the client in 1 week.

Box 6.1

SOAP Entry for Juanita

Date; Time session began; Time session ended

S. Juanita reports using meth with a using friend last Tuesday. She relates that they met spontaneously outside of their children's school after dropping them off. The friend showed her a pipe and some meth and invited her to smoke. "It happened so quickly, like it was the most natural thing to do." "It wasn't until I got home that I realized that I really screwed up." Juanita reports feelings of guilt and shame and some anger at her friend who knew she had been arrested and ordered to take drug screens. "I could lose [custody] of my children!"

O. Juanita appeared to be extremely anxious and agitated as evidenced by wringing her hands, tears in her eyes, and constant movement in her chair. Juanita had a drawn look to her face when she spoke about the possibility of losing her children and being incarcerated.

A. Juanita was open and honest about her drug lapse in spite of her negative drug screen results. She appears to be in the *Preparation* stage of change as she recognizes that the benefits of staying drug-free outweighs any positive aspects of continuing to use.

P. Juanita has already contacted her sponsor and is attending 12-step meetings daily. She has arranged for her mother to drop off, and pick up, the children at school to avoid another encounter with her using friend. Juanita updated her Recovery Plan to reflect places, people and situations that she will avoid, and she will call her sponsor when she encounters another trigger before she acts.

                                         Signature of Counselor

DAP Entry

The second model we will review is Data, Assessment, and Plan (DAP) model. It essentially uses the same format as SOAP except that Subjective (S) is dropped. D (data) is simply a summarization of what was discussed during the session. The Assessment portion is the counselor's professional assessment of what is going on with the client, and the Plan (as in the SOAP model) is the direction that the counselor intends to go with the client. We will look at the same notes used in Box 6.1 but now written in DAP format (Box 6.2).

Box 6.2

DAP Entry for Meeting with Juanita

Date; Time session began; Time session ended

D. Juanita reports using meth with a using friend last Tuesday. She relates that they met spontaneously outside of their children's school after dropping them off. The friend showed her a pipe and some meth and invited her to smoke. "It happened so quickly, like it was the most natural thing to do." "It wasn't until I got home that I realized that I really screwed up." Juanita reports feelings of guilt and shame and some anger at her friend who knew she had been arrested and ordered to take drug screens. "I could lose [custody] of my children!" Juanita appeared to be extremely anxious and agitated as evidenced by wringing her hands, tears in her eyes, and constant movement in her chair. Juanita had a drawn look to her face when she spoke about the possibility of losing her children and being incarcerated.

A. Juanita was open and honest about her drug lapse in spite of her negative drug screen results. She appears to be in the *Preparation* stage of change as she recognizes that the benefits of staying drug-free outweighs any positive aspects of continuing to use.

P. Juanita has already contacted her sponsor and is attending 12-step meetings daily. She has arranged for her mother to drop off, and pick up, the children at school to avoid another encounter with her using friend. Juanita updated her Recovery Plan to reflect places, people and situations that she will avoid, and she will call her sponsor when she encounters another trigger before she acts.

Signature of Counselor

Problem-Oriented Record Keeping

Social work has borrowed ideas from other professions. One of these professions is the medical profession and the idea of Problem-Oriented Record Keeping (PORK). PORK has been utilized in the medical field for at least three decades. PORK (like its counterparts, SOAP and DAP) is a way to record in an organized fashion what is going on with the client and the counselor's therapeutic response to assist the client. In short, it asks What is the problem (with the client)? What is the response to the problem (diagnosis)? And what is the plan to treat this problem?

One of the criticisms of the medical model is that it is not "strengths-based" but "problem-based." When a counselor operates from the medical model (symptoms–diagnosis–prescription) or in counseling terms:

symptoms–diagnosis–treatment plan, it places the counselor in a dominant position and the client in a subservient role (tell me what is wrong and I will help to fix you). Social workers employ a "strengths-based" perspective—rather than looking at what is wrong (not working) with the client, social workers strive to find the client's strengths (what is working) and build from there. This places the client and counselor on an equal footing (the counselor assumes the role of co-helper with the client). The next section will review the Summary Model of record keeping.

Electronic Record Keeping

Keeping a manual (paper copy) of case notes is still in use in privately funded practice settings, however, increasingly more non–publicly funded agencies and counselors are turning to digital record keeping. Electronic record keeping has become an expectation for public agencies as the health industry has moved from a paper-based system to one integrating health information technology (health IT) with a large digital footprint, moving toward a national point-of-care health information system. The Medicare Access and CHIP Reauthorization Act of 2015 (MACRA) declared it a national objective to achieve the widespread exchange of health information using interoperable certified electronic health records and directed the Health and Human Services (HHS) agency to establish metrics to see if that objective has been met (US Department of HHS, 2015). Interoperability, which refers to the exchange of data between devices, programs, and even systems, "enables better workflows and reduced ambiguity, and allows data transfer among EHR systems and health care stakeholders . . . [and] improves the delivery of health care by making the right data available at the right time to the right people" (HealthIT.gov, n.d.).

There are a multitude of EMR and EHR programs available. For instance, one company that purports to be one of the largest providers of behavioral health EHRs offers addiction specific programs for medication-assisted treatment and abstinence-based treatment. For smaller agencies and private practices, there are also multiple options available for documentation, all with varied services that are standard or add-ons such as scheduling, electronic billing, patient portal, synching with devices, credit card processing, revenue tracking, storage, HIPAA compliance, online therapy portal, social media, coding, and notes. When considering purchasing an EHR program, keep in mind the size of your needs (agency vs. solo practice), the cost of the program and add-on services, the types of services offered, and the customer service available. Some programs offer a free trail that can be useful to determine the user friendliness and usability of the program itself. You can also search software venders through a web service that connects buyers and sellers of business software so that you can read reviews and ratings of mental health programs.

The National Council of Social Service (2007) recommends that, regardless of the format utilized to create and store records, documentation should adhere to the following guidelines: notes and records should be concise, accurate, up-to-date, meaningful, and internally consistent.

Documenting Ancillary Case Notes

Before we close this chapter on case notes and client recording, we need to say a few words about the documentation of other (ancillary) notes. Remember that the client file is a living document—a record of what has transpired with your client. As such, you need to make sure that everything is accurately recorded. Let us assume, for a moment, that our client, Juanita, can't make her appointment because her daughter is ill. Juanita calls the agency the morning of her appointment and leaves a message for Steve, her counselor, that she will not be in for her appointment because her daughter is ill. Juanita takes the opportunity to reschedule her appointment for later in the week. The receptionist passes the note to her counselor who records the following entry in her file:

> Counselor's Note: (Date), Telephone call from client. She needed to reschedule appointment due to child's illness. Appointment rescheduled for (date). Signed, (signature of counselor and date).

CONCLUSION

Counseling individuals goes beyond engagement and rapport and requires many micro-skills necessary to help our clients move through the stages of change. Using the treatment plan to guide this process helps provide both structure and focus. Treatment plans should be continually revised and updated with the client to reflect changes and progress toward goals and objectives. Documentation following an individual session should reflect the work that was done with the client. In addition, all other contacts regarding the client, such as a phone call, a collateral contact, or a letter written to a judge, should also be documented.

One of the most difficult challenges for counselors is balancing their time between documentation requirements and direct client contact. Documentation can be viewed as a painful necessity that is fit into the empty spots of a work day and written from a fading memory. Structuring your session around the treatment plan objectives can provide more clarity of what to document. Additionally, you can build in time for documentation directly after sessions and keep to this schedule by establishing good boundaries with your clients. A person-centered approach to documentation is to acknowledge that it is the client's record and therefore it is important to include the client in writing the note at the end of each session. For instance, always saving the last 10 minutes to discuss and record what transpired increases accuracy and can build collaboration and investment.

7

Group Counseling

INTRODUCTION

Within this chapter, we follow our client, Juanita, as she begins the next phase of her counseling process—attending group counseling. This chapter explores the most common types of groups: peer-led, educational, psycho-educational, and support. We will also review some of the settings for group counseling such as outpatient, intensive outpatient, and residential. This chapter will discuss the format for groups (open vs. closed) and how to establish group rules and will explore phases of groups. Finally, we will review some basic skills counselors use for conducting groups. Listed here are the Council for Accreditation of Counseling and Related Educational Programs (CACREP), Council on Social Work Education (CSWE), International Certification & Reciprocity Consortium (IC&RC), and Substance Abuse and Mental Health Services Administration (SAMHSA) standards associated with group counseling.

CHAPTER COMPETENCIES AND STANDARDS

CACREP—Standards 5, 13, 23–27
CSWE—Competencies 6–8
IC&RC—Domain III: Tasks 1–4, 8, Domain IV: Tasks 1 and 2
SAMHSA—Competencies 17, 88–93, 111, 117, 118, 120

Juanita's Group Counseling Session

When Juanita last met with her counselor, Steve, he had referred her to group counseling. After some discussion with Juanita about what to expect in group, the number of sessions she would be required to attend, and the overall purpose of group counseling, Juanita agreed to attend group and made a commitment to Steve to actively participate. Juanita was then scheduled to begin attending group the following week. The groups she would be attending would be held 2 nights per week for 8 weeks. The group leader, Marta, would work with the group on establishing group rules, behaviors and what the group members were expecting to get from the group.

Juanita attended her first group session the following week. The group was scheduled to run for 90 minutes. There were 12 other people who were scheduled to start the group. Most of the members sat in the lobby, nervously looking at each other or avoiding eye contact all together. Juanita had seen group counseling sessions portrayed on television and the movies, but she was unsure about what would go on within the group. Would she be asked to discuss why she was there? Would she be embarrassed by the group leader and humiliated by the group? This and other anxious thoughts ran through her mind as she looked around the room, waiting for the group session to begin.

Just as the clock on the wall reached the hour, a tall woman with graying hair walked out into the lobby and asked the group to follow her. When the group moved down the hall into a large room, they saw a group of chairs arranged in a circle. There was a total of 13 chairs—one for each person and Marta. After everyone found a seat, Marta took a moment to look around the room, making eye contact with those who would look at her. She then opened the session by introducing herself and talking for a few minutes about what could be expected (the focus of the group). Marta asked each of the group members to introduce themselves and to give as much (or as little) information about themselves as they felt comfortable sharing. The next half hour of the group was devoted to establishing some basic rules and guidelines. Marta talked about the importance of confidentiality (what's said in the group, stays in the group). Other group rules were discussed: only one person talks at a time, respect each other, no side-bar conversations (whatever is said needs to be said to the entire group), the need for being on time, and that once the group begins no one is to get up and leave until either break-time or the group ends. Marta spent some time discussing these rules and the rationale behind them. There were some questions about the different rules and some discussion among the group members. After each person had an opportunity to ask questions, all agreed that they could and would abide by the basic rules for group behavior. The last half hour of the group was spent discussing individual group members' expectations about the group. Marta asked members to talk about what they imagined the group would be like and what they would like to gain from attending the group. At the end of the session, Marta asked the group members to take about 5 minutes to complete a short questionnaire about their experience in the group that evening (the same scale Juanita and the other group members had been filling out in their individual counseling sessions).

TYPES OF GROUP COUNSELING

Before we begin an exploration of the various types of group counseling, we think it is important to establish a rationale for the use of group counseling. The most basic reason for referring a client to a group (rather than seeing them in individual counseling) is that groups are economical. It is much more effective to work with a group of 8 (minimum size) to 15 (maximum size for a group) than to see each person individually. By working with clients collectively (in a group), the group can be used to confront maladaptive behaviors, reinforce and encourage positive behaviors, and teach information. In short, it is easier to work with a group of clients than to try and provide treatment for them individually.

The SAMHSA (2005a) reports five types of groups commonly used in substance abuse treatment. These are:

1. *Psycho-educational groups*, which teach about substance abuse.
2. *Skills development groups*, which hone the skills necessary to break free of addictions.
3. *Cognitive-behavioral groups*, which rearrange patterns of thinking and action that lead to addiction.
4. *Support groups*, which comprise a forum where members can debunk each other's excuses and support constructive change.
5. *Interpersonal process group psychotherapy* (referred to hereafter as "interpersonal process groups" or "therapy groups"), which enable clients to recreate their pasts in the here-and-now of group and rethink the relational and other life problems that they have previously fled by means of addictive substances.

Educational Groups

As their name implies, educational groups are useful for teaching or imparting information. For that reason, they are often incorporated into treatment programs. An educational group may be used to impart specific information that a counselor may want to teach the group, such as the impact of addiction on the body, recovery dynamics, or symptoms of withdrawal. Or, a therapist may want to show a film that demonstrates the effect of tobacco usage. Educating and informing clients about the effects of their drug usage on themselves, their family, and others around them is an important part of the treatment process that can help to motivate clients to make positive changes. Often, though, educational groups alone are not enough. Next, we will review another type of group—the psycho-educational group.

Psycho-Educational Groups

Many counselors combine the use of education and intervention into what has become known as the "psycho-educational" group. Psycho-educational groups have two main goals: one goal is to educate the client about the behavioral, spiritual, physical, social, and psychological consequences of their drug usage. The second goal is to help motivate the client to change. The underlying theory is that behavior is a choice, and, given enough information and help to recover, clients will choose more pro-social and positive behaviors. Research has demonstrated that psycho-educational groups are an important and effective component of treatment (Hoagwood et al., 2010).

Skills Development Groups

Counselors utilize skills development groups to teach specific skills and to hone other skills that are a necessary part of living clean and sober lives. For example, skills groups may develop such skills as interpersonal communication, decision-making, anger management, and coping with anxiety and depression. These groups are often referred to as "life skills groups" because of their emphasis on the skills and behaviors necessary for coping with the stresses of daily living without using drugs.

Cognitive Behavioral Groups

Just as cognitive behavioral therapy is a useful therapeutic tool in individual counseling, this same technique can be successfully employed in group counseling. Groups entirely devoted to cognitive behavioral therapy assist clients in identifying thinking patterns and behaviors that lead to addiction and identifying new behaviors needed for their recovery. For example, when a person is active in her addiction, one pattern of her addiction may be to cash her paycheck and then drive to the dealer's house to buy drugs and get high. By identifying this pattern, the counselor can help the client to plan and practice new behaviors that will reinforce her sobriety. One way may be to help the client plan for what she will do when payday occurs. Exactly what will she do when she cashes her paycheck? Together they may plan for specific tasks to do rather than driving by the dealer's house (just to see if they are home). By helping one individual client work through this process in group, the entire group benefits (applying this situation to their own lives).

Support Groups

Peer-led groups (or support groups) are groups that do not have a therapist/counselor in charge, but are led by members of the treatment community themselves (Bottanari et al., 2012). One of the advantages of peer-led groups is that of equal status—everyone in the group is equal to the other group members (regardless of their profession, standing, or status in the larger community). One of the drawbacks of these type of groups is that without professional training in group leadership, it can be difficult to address clinical issues that drive individual behavior. It is important to draw distinctions between certain support groups that occur on a regular basis within any community and peer-led groups that are found in substance abuse treatment programs.

The idea of individuals helping other people with a similar problem is not a new phenomenon. One of the first internationally known support groups is Alcoholics Anonymous (AA), which began in 1935. Membership is free, and the only criteria to belong is a desire to quit using alcohol. The basic premise of AA is that people who are actively working to not drink (recover) are most qualified to help others who wish to become clean and sober. AA, then, uses a support system to share individuals' common strengths and hopes. AA meetings rely on individuals coming together to share their stories and rely on each other for strength and support. The model of support groups started by AA has now spread to a variety of addictions and problems and includes Narcotics Anonymous, Cocaine Anonymous, Overeaters Anonymous, Gambler's Anonymous, and Sex Addicts Anonymous. Outside of the addictions field, support groups can be found for cancer survivors, parents and family of those who committed suicide, and other issues.

Within the substance abuse treatment community are "peer-led" support groups in which members of a program (usually a residential program) can come together and both support (positive behaviors) and confront (negative behaviors) each other. One of the advantages of a peer-led support group is that they are economical—all that is needed is space for the group to meet and there exists no need for a clinician to lead the group. The downside to these type of groups is that they can only be as effective as the individual members who attend.

Interpersonal Process Group Psychotherapy (Therapy Groups)

Therapy groups usually require a leader with advanced education, licensing, and specialized training and skills. For instance, therapy groups can utilize trauma-focused therapy (helping clients to identify past traumatic events and then resolve them in present time) to assist addicts in identifying issues in their past that keep them stuck in their addiction and from living sober lives.

GROUP SETTINGS

Outpatient

Group counseling is found in a variety of treatment venues including outpatient, intensive outpatient, and residential treatment. Most states have specific guidelines and regulations about what constitutes various levels of treatment. Outpatient treatment is usually regarded as the patient receiving treatment no more than two times per week. If you will recall our discussion about the least restrictive forms of treatment in Chapter 4, you will remember that we want to utilize the treatment that causes the least amount of disruption to the client's life as possible. Usually this means outpatient treatment. Outpatient group counseling is no different—here the client would attend group no more than two times a week, usually for no more than 90 minutes per group.

Intensive Outpatient

Intensive outpatient (IOP) counseling services (either individual or group or a combination of both) are provided several times a week to clients. This usually means a minimum of three times per week, and, in some states, a certain number of hours are designated (e.g., not less than 6 hours per week and not more than 10 hours a week if a program is to be considered IOP). One study that conducted a meta-analysis of other studies found IOP services to be at least as effective as residential (inpatient) treatment for most clients (McCarty et al., 2014). Since IOP is more restrictive than outpatient counseling, the client also receives more frequent services.

Residential Treatment

Residential treatment (where a person lives at the treatment center) is some-times the best way to help someone become medically detoxified from drugs and then gain enough stability and sobriety to function in the community. Group counseling is a regular and integral part of residential treatment. Counselors use groups to help residents create support while addressing the crises and problems that resulted in them being placed in residential care. Groups can also be a way to help clients to gain insight into their own behavior by listening to those of their peers and to normalize the effects of their substance abuse by listening to others sharing similar effects. Table 7.1 is an example of various group descriptions for a residential facility.

Table 7.1 RESIDENTIAL GROUP DESCRIPTIONS

Group topic	Curriculum/Tools	Intervention	Group Description
Recovery dynamics through spiritual enrichment	Recovery Dynamics	Transpersonal psychotherapy	Counselor leads a discussion on accessing our higher power during times of struggle. May involve prayer or meditation.
Mind–body connection	Activity Therapy	Cognitive-behavioral	Each client selects and practices a physical activity that would relieve stress. Clients discuss differences between their thoughts and feelings before and after the activity.
Group cohesion	ROPES Course–Low Elements	Behavioral	Challenge course using physical activities that require members to work through problems together to complete the course.
Mindfulness	Mindfulness-based stress reduction (MBSR)	Cognitive	Mental state achieved by focusing one's awareness on the present moment while calmly acknowledging and accepting one's feelings, thoughts, and bodily sensations
Stress management techniques	Progressive muscle relaxation; guided imagery; thought stopping	Cognitive-behavioral	Various stress reduction techniques are taught and practiced. Discussions compare before and after stressful feelings and thoughts.

(continued)

Table 7.1 CONTINUED

Group topic	Curriculum/Tools	Intervention	Group Description
Coping skills group	Matrix model; recovery dynamics; criminal thinking, etc.	Psycho-educational	Education on various coping skills followed by discussions of personal application to improve daily functioning.
Process group	None	Motivational interviewing	
Peer support group	Wellness plan; crisis plan; recovery goals/ objectives	Support group	Group led by a trained or certified peer support specialist. Group focus is on modeling behaviors of recovery such as problem-solving activities, identifying and decreasing negative self-talk, identifying skills and supports, instilling hope for personal recovery.
Integrative therapy	Varies: art, music, reading, etc.	Integrative psychotherapy	Clients participate in an art expression activity such as creating a mask that portrays how they see themselves on one side of the mask and how others see them on the other. They discuss what they learned through their activity that assists in personal growth.
Relapse prevention	SAMHSA: *TAP 19 Counselors Manual for Relapse Prevention with Chemically Dependent Criminal Offenders*	Cognitive restructuring	Curriculum-based group that identifies and addresses relapse prevention techniques and reconstructs criminal thinking.
Twelve-step recovery group	Alcoholics Anonymous books and literature.	Support group	Peer-led group using a 12-step model of achieving sobriety. Groups can be "open" to the public or "closed" allowing only addicts to attend.
Anger management	SAMHSA: *Anger Management for Substance Abuse and Mental Health Clients: Participant Workbook*	Cognitive-behavioral	Curriculum-based groups designed to help identify triggers and reconstruct thoughts that lead to violent behavior.

ELEMENTS OF COUNSELING GROUPS

Open Versus Closed Group Formats

As you can see from the preceding discussion, there are several different types of groups. There are also different formats for group delivery, the most common being "open" versus "closed" groups. *Open groups* refer to groups that are ongoing—the beginning and ending point for each member is individualized. New members are admitted to the group on a regular basis, and, as group members meet the criteria for graduating from the group (either by demonstrating certain behaviors or by achieving a certain number of times attended), then they exit the group. One of the advantages of the open group format is that group members don't have to wait to join—new members are continuously incorporated into the group. One of the disadvantages of open groups is that the level of trust and honesty in the group is continually challenged by the admission of new members.

The second format is that of the "closed" group. *Closed groups* are groups that, once formed, are closed to new members. By nature, the group comprises the same individuals each time it meets. Closed groups, then, can develop a level of trust and honesty among group members much more quickly than open groups. We will now go on to examine some of the essentials of all types of groups.

Group Rules

One of the tasks of the counselor is to establish norms and rules for groups—especially when the group is just forming or when introducing new members to an existing open group. Group rules are those behavioral limits that help the group members to feel safe in the group and develop a level of trust necessary for deep, meaningful interactions. Rules vary from counselor to counselor and group to group, but they generally follow some basic guidelines such as:

- *Confidentiality*: Group members agree that whatever is said in group is not repeated outside of the group. Sanctions, such as admitting to and apologizing for a breach in confidentiality or being ejected from the group, may be imposed when violated.
- *Mutual respect*: Group members do not attack, discredit, or demean other members or use language that is hurtful or offensive to others. Sometimes this is called "shaming and blaming." These behaviors are

addressed immediately during the group, and repeat offenses can
result in dismissal from the group.

- *Attendance*: Group members agree to attend all sessions, be on time,
  and not leave early. There may be a penalty for missing a certain
  number of groups as well as for frequent tardiness.
- *Attentiveness*: Group members agree to be attentive during group and
  may be asked to turn off cell phones that can be distracting. However,
  group members are not sanctioned for not *participating*. Instead, they
  are gently encouraged by the other members and the counselor to
  share thoughts and experiences.

Group rules should be established before a group begins and then adapted
or added to as the group progresses. Box 7.1 shows an example of group rules
for an anger management group. You will notice that the counselor requires a
signature from each member's showing that he or she has been advised of these
rules. The counselor keeps the signed forms and gives each member a copy of
the rules to keep.

Box 7.1

ANGER MANAGEMENT GROUP RULES

1. *Confidentiality first*. What is said in the group, *stays* in the group.
   Anything said between any two or more group members at any time is
   part of the group and is confidential. I understand that everything said in
   group is confidential. I agree to keep secret the names of other members
   of the group and what is said in the group. I agree to keep secret anything
   which occurs between or among group members. I understand that
   there is an exception to this confidentiality which applies to the group
   leader. If the group leader believes that someone is in danger, the leader
   has a professional obligation to take direct action in order to keep
   everyone safe. I agree not to keep secret from the group anything which
   occurs within the group. Anything which occurs between or among any
   members is part of the group and is kept secret from anyone outside of
   the group but is not kept secret from the group. This also applies to any
   individual meetings you may have with a group leader. I understand that
   if I violate this confidentiality I could be removed from the group.
2. *Responsibilities of group leader and group members*. The group leader
   reserves the right to stop any side conversations, for the benefit of the
   group dynamic, to ensure the group remains on-task and in a timely

matter to cover necessary materials. I understand that it is the group
leader's responsibility to enforce these procedures and guidelines.
As a group member, it is my responsibility to attend group sessions,
engage and participate in group activities, and to complete and return
homework assignments.

3. *Accept each other without making judgments.* No group member is
   ever humiliated, hazed, or abused in any way. I agree to avoid this
   destructive behavior. Violence or intimidation toward other group
   members is never tolerated. I understand that I must never be violent
   or intimidating toward other group members and that if I threaten to
   harm persons or property I will be asked to leave the group.

4. *Avoid interrupting or having side conversations; listen to each other.*
   Give everyone an opportunity to share. Gossip and secret grudges can
   be very destructive in a group. I agree that if I have something to say
   to another group member, I will try to say it to the member directly
   rather than talk about him or her behind his or her back.

5. *Silence all cell phones, iPads, etc.*

6. *Always be honest and have a positive attitude.* This will make the group
   setting more beneficial and a better overall experience.

7. *Attendance and being on time.* I agree that I will attend every meeting
   unless an emergency arises. If an emergency should arise, I will notify
   the group leader prior to the meeting to tell him or her that I will be
   unable to attend. I understand that the group leader may tell the group
   what has happened. I understand that if I have two absences, my
   continued group membership will be discussed.

8. *Be respectful and sensitive to others; be supportive and encouraging to
   each other.* I agree that will never pressure other group members to
   participate in any discussion or activity after the member has passed
   or refused. I understand that the group leader is obliged to protect this
   right. I also understand that I will benefit more from group the more
   I am able to take risks in sharing and participating.

9. *Refrain from using offensive language.* Offensive language is more
   than "cuss" words. It also includes racist, sexists, and homophobic
   comments.

10. *Timeout.* The group leader reserves the right to call for a timeout. If
    a group member's anger begins to escalate out of control during a
    session, the leader will ask that member to take a timeout from the
    topic and the discussion. This means that the member, along with
    the rest of the members of the group, *will immediately stop talking
    about the issue* that is causing the member's anger to escalate. If the
    participant's anger has escalated to the point that he or she cannot

tolerate sitting in the group, the leader may ask the person to leave the group for 5 or 10 minutes or until he or she can cool down. The participant is then welcomed back to the group, provided he or she can tolerate continued discussion in the group.

11. *No drugs, alcohol, weapons.* Group members cannot participate in the group under the influence of alcohol or other mind-altering drugs. When under the influence of chemicals, persons do not have access to their emotions and have less control over their behavior. I understand that if the leader believes that I am under the influence of alcohol or other drugs, I will be asked to leave the group.

12. *Anger management group is ages 18+.* Children under 18 may not attend.

*Breaking these rules may result in dismissal for the day and count as an unexcused absence. If members are incapable of completing this group program, they will receive one "do-over," no more.

_____   _____

Group Member   Date

Stages and Phases of Groups

All groups have a beginning, middle, and end. Tuckman (1965) initially hypothesized that groups pass through four phases during the evolution of a group: forming, storming, norming, and performing. Later, Tuckman and Jensen (1977) added a fifth—adjourning. We will briefly look at each of these phases.

Forming: Group members are initially introduced to each other and reasons for being in the group (focus of the group) are discussed. This phase is characterized by formality and politeness among group members. Group rules are established for behavioral limits that help the group members to feel safe in the group and develop a level of trust necessary for healing to occur. Rules vary from therapist to therapist and group to group, but they generally follow some basic guidelines such as:

- *Confidentiality*: Whatever is said in group is not repeated outside of the group.

- *Mutual respect*: Group members do not attack or use language that is hurtful or offensive to other group members.
- *Attendance*: Group members agree to attend all group meetings, to be on time, and to stay in the group session until it concludes.
- *Participation*: Group members agree to participate in the group to the best of their ability.

As a counselor, it is often your task as group leader to teach members how to behave in the group. For example, when a group is in its infant stages, it is not uncommon for group members to direct remarks about other group members to the group leader. Part of the job of the group leader is to redirect those remarks by saying, "John, can you just repeat what you said to me, but this time, would you say it directly to Sophie?" In this way, group leaders are training group members to be direct in their communication.

Storming: As group members develop familiarity and comfort with others in the group, roles begin to emerge. Members may assume the role of group leader or mediators while others will may seek rescuing or remain an outsider due to minimal investment in the group process. This phase is characterized by confrontation among group members, usually with hostility and lack of direction. The group leader's role is to exert a great deal of influence and control over the group—directing and shaping group interaction.

Norming: As group members become more comfortable with each other, the initial hostility and chaos of the storming phase passes into the norming phase. Here, group members began to settle into their chosen roles and accept the differences within the group. This phase is characterized by a decrease in hostility and more focused confrontation—though group members who are trying to remain outsiders will still be quiet and reluctant to participate. The group leader has the task of drawing out those who seek to not participate and minimizing the influence of those who would dominate the group.

Performing: If the group has reached this phase, the group is then ready to tackle the issues/goals that were set in the beginning stage of the group. Group members in this phase have developed a comfort level in and trust with each other that allows work to deepen. This phase is characterized by group members cooperating, listening to each other, and providing feedback and advice. The group leader, at this point, does not have to exert a great deal of influence on the group other than to interject observations, keep the group focused, and facilitate the beginning and ending of the group.

Adjourning: Group members will often feel several different emotions when a closed group is preparing to terminate, or a member is leaving an open-ended group. Members could experience anger, indifference, anxiety, happiness, or sadness when exiting a group. For instance, group members may disclose their anxiety or fear at the loss of the support of the group, or become emotionally withdrawn from the group as a protective factor. It is the group leader's task to recognize these emotions and point them out to the group, thus helping to normalize feelings associated with separation and loss.

Group Cohesion

It should be noted here that one of the major factors that has been identified in all groups is the issue of *cohesion*. The more groups members feel bonded with each other and their therapist, the greater chance of a positive outcome (Budman et al., 1989; Burlingame et al., 2011). And while group cohesion is equivalent to a therapeutic alliance in individual counseling, achieving cohesion can often be a daunting process—especially for the new counselor. One study found that using group tasks (whereby the group had to work in a co-operative manner to complete the task) at the beginning of group helped to increase cohesion (Stockton et al., 1992).

GROUP FACILITATION SKILLS

Group counseling require skills for establishing and maintaining the focus of the group. Some basic skills for facilitating group members' interactions in the group are planning the agenda for each group, using body language to indirectly guide interactions, directly cutting off a member, redirecting interactions, linking content during the group process, drawing out group members, and facilitating activities that build understanding, cohesion, or insight.

Planning Group Agendas

Planning for each group helps ensure structure and focus for that specific group. Planning creates the agenda that counselors use to guide interactions that best meet the purpose and/or goals of the group. This agenda will vary based on the type of group that is established, but each group has a beginning, middle, and end with common elements. Box 7.2 shows sample outline for planning a group session with either a closed or open group format.

Box 7.2

GROUP AGENDA

Beginning
Counselor introduction of self and purpose of the group (first groups)
Introduction of members (first groups) or new members (open-ended groups)
Review of content from last group (if applicable)
Overview of this group's activities and/or goals/objectives (all groups)

Middle
Activity (e.g., educational component, warm-up exercise, reviewing homework assignment, check-ins, establishing/reviewing group goals/objectives, etc.)
Discussion of activity and application to members

End
Wrap-up activity (if applicable, such as an assignment related to educational content)
Closing discussion (final thoughts, questions, announcements, check-ins, etc.)
Summary (what was covered, explored, revealed)
Homework assignment (if applicable)

Another planning item is to establish an allotted time for items on the agenda. The length of time allotted, and the number of group members will have a determining factor on time allocations as well as on types and number of activities. For instance, larger groups (i.e., 12 or more members) and groups meeting for shorter periods (i.e., 45–50 minutes) may not allow enough time for a wrap-up activity. As another example, everyone checking in during the closing discussion would be more appropriate for a smaller group, while a large group would limit the discussion to any lingering questions from members.

Using Body Language

Body language is particularly helpful in directing interactions. Counselors can use eye contact with a member who is distracted to redirect attention back to the group or with a member not engaging in group to invite participation. Conversely, not making eye contact with members who are monopolizing the group helps decrease their interaction. Scanning throughout the group (making eye contact around the group) helps counselors identify body language from the group members that can be used collectively to check the mood of the group: "I can see that many of you disagree with that suggestion. What are the concern about moving the group time to 4:00?" It can also identify body language from individual group members to help draw them into the discussion: "Nathan, I see you nodding. Did you have a similar experience that you can share?"

Cutting Off Members

There are times when group members get off focus or when one group member monopolizes the group time. Cutting off a group member should be discussed by the counselor as a technique that will be used to help refocus the group when it goes "off topic," to change topics as part of the agenda, or to allow other members an opportunity to talk when someone is monopolizing the time: "There will be times when I say, 'I am going to cut you off here.' This is to bring the group back to the topic, or to allow other members a chance to add their thoughts."

Redirecting Interactions

When a group is in the beginning stage, it is not uncommon for group members to direct remarks about other group members to the group leader. Part of the job of the group leader is to redirect those remarks back to the intended member, "John, can you just repeat what you just said, but this time, would you say it directly to Sophie?" In this way, group leaders are training members to be direct in their communication. Redirection is also helpful when a question is asked and the counselor does not know the answer or wants to generate a discussion on the topic: "That is a great question to bring to the group. Can anyone answer Sara's question?"

Linking Content

As the group moves through the agenda, experiences and information will be shared that can be linked to the focus of the group. Linking reinforces learning by connecting educational content to discussions, and it also creates bonding opportunities among members by connecting shared experiences: "What you described fits the definition of a 'trigger' that we discussed earlier. Is this also a trigger for anyone else?"

Drawing Out Members

Group members should never be forced to participate even if they are court-ordered to attend the group. There are many reason for lack of participation, such as difficulty trusting, unsure or not confident of how they will be perceived, resistance to treatment by an involuntary member, depression or other mental health issue, or a physical limitation such as a speech or language disorder. In addition, a previously active group member may be going through a difficult time which may affect current participation. However, these members can be provided opportunities to participate. We mentioned previously that making eye contact is a way to engage group members and invite them to contribute. Activities, such as going around the room (round-robin) to do check-ins, provide an opportunity for participation. These are more indirect methods, whereas a direct method would be drawing the member in by using something they previously said or did: "It sounds like you are worried about how working outside the home will affect your ability to be a good parent. Christy, I remember you saying in your introduction that you are a working mother. What advice would you give Nancy based on your experiences?"

Facilitating Activities

Activities are an effective way to engage members, provide variety, and increase the energy of the group. They also provide opportunities to apply educational information that was presented. Preparation is important before conducting an activity. As we discussed earlier, the type of group, the number of members in a group, and the allotted time for a group will affect the number and type of activities you choose. Referring to the residential group described in Table 7.1, some groups are curriculum-based with activities already outlined (i.e., anger management groups). Education-based groups will have some learning content (counselor-led education) based on the topic being presented (i.e., stress management) and then an activity to practice a technique (i.e., progressive muscle relaxation). A discussion should always follow the activity with opportunities to link experiences to the educational content: "Jack mentioned that his headache disappeared by the end of the activity. Referring to the 'Signs of Stress' sheet that I handed out, what might have been the physical causes of Jack's headache?"

A common activity used in counseling groups is going around the room, person-by-person, to allow each member an opportunity to share. Sometimes referred to as a "round robin," this activity is good for both introductions and check-ins. It can also be used to start the discussion following an activity. One benefit of this activity is that everyone has an opportunity to talk. It is also useful when groups are new, and members are reluctant to volunteer to be the first to share. Providing directions for this exercise will provide clarity as to what is expected: "Starting on my left, let's go around the room and state your first name, the reason or events that led to you being in this group, and one expectation you have for this group." Or: "Let's check-in starting on my right. This time, share one situation you experienced since last group where you used a coping skill, even if it was not effective."

An Example of Juanita's Participation in Group

Let us return, for just a moment, to Juanita and the group she is attending. We will now examine the group counseling session from Juanita's point of view. Juanita arrived for her first group session a few minutes early. As she waited in the waiting room, she spent the time looking around, noticing the other group members as they arrived. Feeling somewhat anxious about the group session, she tried to hide her anxiety by pretending to be bored. As she leafed through a magazine that was left on the table, she saw at least three other people that she recognized from her AA and NA meetings she had been attending. She briefly looked at them and nodded a hello—they returned the greeting.

When the counselor, Marta, walked out to invite the group members into the group room, Juanita took a moment to look her over. Tall, around 50 years of age, long hair pulled back in a ponytail, Juanita thought to herself, "I wonder if she is in recovery? She has the look about her of someone who used to get high." Something about this thought seemed to calm Juanita's fear, and immediately she decided that she liked Marta.

The first 15 minutes of the group were spent with Marta talking. She welcomed everyone to the group and explained that it would be a "closed group" and what that meant. She then opened the session by introducing herself and talking for a few minutes about what could be expected. Marta asked each of the group members to introduce themselves and to give as much (or as little) information about themselves as they felt comfortable sharing. She also discussed some basic ground rules and expectations of the group. Juanita listened to what Marta was saying and decided that what she was asking of the group was not unreasonable—in fact, if she was honest about it—these were things designed to make the group a safe place. These activities reinforced Juanita's initial assessment that she liked Marta. After Marta explained the purpose of the group and group rules, the last half hour of the group was spent discussing individual group members' expectations about the group. Marta asked members to talk about what they imagined the group would be like and what they would like to gain from attending the group. When it was Juanita's turn to talk, she started out somewhat slow and spoke with hesitation in her voice. She had an underlying fear that others would laugh or make fun of her. After she spoke a few words, she noticed that at least some of the other group members were listening attentively to what she had to say. Feeling encouraged by the other's reaction, she began to open up and talk about her initial fears about attending the group. When she finished speaking, several of the group members were nodding and smiling at her. Marta thanked her for being honest and open about her feelings. Juanita felt proud of herself and enjoyed the group leader's compliments.

At the end of the session, Marta asked the group members to take about 5 minutes to complete a short questionnaire about their experience in the group that evening (the same scale Juanita and the other group members had been filling out in their individual counseling sessions). Juanita filled out her questionnaire. When she first arrived for the session, she was feeling anxious and a little afraid. After attending (and seeing some familiar faces), she felt some of her fear and trepidation begin to lessen. At the end of the session, she decided that group counseling may not be the scary process she initially imagined it to be. This change in her feelings was reflected in her evaluation of the evening's group.

CONCLUSION

Facilitating a group can be a difficult task, especially for new or inexperienced counselors. If a counselor does not keep the focus of the group, it can quickly devolve into a social group, or worse, into a platform for complaints about the program, the group, people outside of the group, and even the counselor. And an unskilled counselor may find the group monopolized by one or two members, miss opportunities to link content or common experiences, and ignore body language of the group members. If possible, it is beneficial to start out by co-facilitating a group with an experienced group counselor. Counselors can plan the group agenda together and then discuss the group dynamics and counseling skills used once the group is over (debriefing). This kind of supervision can provide insight on strengths and areas for improvement.

8

Family Counseling

INTRODUCTION

In this chapter, we begin by reviewing some of the theories of family therapy and best practices as delineated by the Substance Abuse and Mental Health Services Administration (SAMHSA). We will also review some important aspects for working with families: assessment, treatment planning, conducting counseling sessions, and referrals. As always, we will include practice questions and other resources. Listed here are the Council for Accreditation of Counseling and Related Educational Programs (CACREP), Council on Social Work Education (CSWE), International Certification & Reciprocity Consortium (IC&RC), and SAMHSA standards associated with family therapy.

CHAPTER COMPETENCIES AND STANDARDS

CACREP—Standards 2, 4, 7, 11, 13, 20–26
CSWE—Competencies 6–9
IC&RC—Domain III: Tasks 1–8
SAMHSA—Competencies 94–105

Juanita's Family Treatment

Juanita has now been in treatment for almost 3 months. During that time, she has managed to remain clean and sober, she has attended group therapy via intensive outpatient services, and she has been seen by her primary counselor, Steve, for individual counseling. Both Steve and Juanita have agreed that it is now time for her to begin counseling with her family (her son, her daughter, and her partner). Later, Steve may bring the children's father, Paco, into the counseling process, but for now, he focuses on Juanita's relationships with those living within the household. Steve begins his work with a family assessment. Later, he will develop a treatment plan to address the issues that are uncovered during the assessment. We will revisit Juanita, Steve, and the counseling process later in this chapter. But first, we need to examine some theories of family counseling and discuss the basic techniques for working with a family.

THEORIES OF FAMILY THERAPY: A BRIEF OVERVIEW

Founding (Seminal) Theories

Family therapy, at its heart, is imbedded in the belief that, regardless of where the problem started, whether an individual issue or a family issue, the solution lies in involving the entire family in the therapy process. Family therapy is a counterreaction to traditional counseling techniques that were rooted in psychodynamic theory. Psychodynamic theory postulated that human behavior is a result of impulses arising out of the subconscious mind. In psychoanalytic therapy, the subject forms bonds with the therapist and, through transference, unconsciously shifts feelings about others with whom the client has a conflict to the therapist. It was believed that involving other family members would impede the therapeutic process. By the 1950s, though, these ideas were being challenged. Challenges came from several directions, but, in part, they arose from a paradigm shift in science—the idea of *systems theory* (Minuchin, 1985). Systems theory, as it applies to families and family therapy, is the idea that families are interconnected and, therefore, changing an individual within a family would impact the entire family system (Bowen, 1974). Early pioneers in the field of communication and its role in the family and family therapy hypothesized that erroneous communication patterns could lead to schizophrenia (Bateson et al., 1956). Though this was later disproved, the authors went on to be influential in the developing field of family therapy. The group (later termed the Bateson Project) were faculty at Stanford University. Joined later by Virginia Satir, they became synonymous with family systems theory.

Other early fields of family therapy include structural family therapy and systemic family therapy, also referred to as the Milan systems model (Mackinnon & Miller, 1987). Later, Virginia Satir broke away and formed the experiential approach to family therapy (Cheung, 1997). Another type of family therapy that bears mentioning is what has become known as "intergenerational family therapy," usually associated with such therapists as Murray Bowen and James Framo. Intergenerational family therapy seeks to identify patterns of dysfunction within families, usually examining at least three generations, by using such techniques as the *genogram* (Framo, 1976). But perhaps the most prominently used therapeutic interventions in family therapy involving parent–child interactions rely on *cognitive-behavioral theory*. The use of shaping and modeling behavior is a prominent choice in many forms of parenting techniques taught and prescribed by child and family therapists. Now that we have a brief overview of the various genres of family therapy, we will examine some of these in broader detail, starting with theories centered around systems theories.

Systemic Theories

Systemic therapy or Milan family therapy focuses on the individual and collective development of members of the family rather than a proscribed set of techniques for working with a family. In essence, it is a way of conceptualizing or viewing the family that helps the therapist to understand how to approach the family in way that is helpful (McLeod et al., 1986). Systemic therapists are more interested in the systemic context of how the family operates rather than in individual behaviors. Therefore, they look for power struggles among family members, referred to as "family games" (Selvini-Palazzoli et al., 1978). Systemic-oriented therapists look for collective behaviors (usually in groups of three or more) and patterns of repeated maladaptive behavior (Sluzki, 1983). The therapist works to expose the maladaptive family games in multiple ways, such as using paradox and counter-paradox to challenge assumptions and gain new meanings, using circular questioning to expose new information, and assigning prescriptive homework, such as a new family ritual. Cottrell and Boston (2002) report that systemic therapy is a useful tool with families and has the ability to effect change with adolescents, but they also caution that more randomized trials (with a comparison group) need to be conducted.

Structural Theories

Salvador Minuchin was one of the founders of structural family therapy, along with his many colleagues (Edgar Auerswald, Braulio Montalvo, Harry Aponte, Jay Haley, Lynn Hoffman, Marianne Walters, Charles Fishman, and Jorge Colapinto). They believed that the structure of the family had a synergistic effect (the sum of the whole was greater than the individual parts) (Minuchin, 1974). Based on the idea that individuals are not isolated and that they react and interact based on their experiences with others within a family, they began to examine individuals in the light of their social context and through their interactions with others. "Structural family therapy is primarily a way of thinking about and operating in three related areas: the family, the presenting problem, and the process of change" (Colapinto, 1991, p. 422). Structural family therapists seek to enter into, and join, the family in a collaborative relationship so that they can understand the invisible rules that govern the functioning of the family. Structural theorists believed that pathology was a function of the family system, not of the individuals in that system. Major concepts of structural theory include examining boundaries, identifying power alignments within the family subsystems (especially triads and coalitions), exposing family rules, and addressing enmeshment and disengagement within the system.

Experiential Theories

Experiential family therapy was initially conceived and developed by Carl Whitaker. Later, one of its chief proponents was Virginia Satir. Whitaker and Keith (1981) emphasized that self-fulfillment was achieved through family cohesion. Experiential family therapists focus on the lived experience of group members and seek to uncover unexpressed and repressed emotions that hamper communication among family members.

As the name implies, experiential family therapy is less concerned with traditional talk therapy than it is with role-playing, guided imagery, and the use of props. *Family sculpting* is a technique developed by David Kantor, Fred Duhl, and Bunny Duhl whereby family members are physically placed in various spatial positions to one another to identify degrees of power and intimacy. Experiential therapists deal with the "here and now" (present-focused) as opposed to the "there and then" (past-focused). Current extensions of experiential therapy include such diverse forms as equine therapy, challenge courses and wilderness experience therapy, music therapy, art therapy, and psychodrama.

Cognitive Behavioral Theory

A primary premise of cognitive behavioral theory is that maladaptive behavior is reinforced by others as well as by one's own cognitive factors (thoughts, beliefs, attitudes, expectations, etc.). A cognitive-behavioral assessment might include a behavioral assessment, which is a detailed analysis of the problem in behavioral terms and a functional analysis (antecedents and consequences of the identified problem behaviors) (Falloon, 1991). Therefore, a child skipping school (problem behavior) because of being bullied (antecedent) resulted in mother leaving work (consequence) and the child getting detention (consequence). Cognitive behavioral interventions are centered around learning theory (John Dewey, Jean Piaget, Jerome Bruner, Lev Vygotsky, John B. Watson, Ivan Pavlov) and social learning theory (Albert Bandura, B. F. Skinner) and their use of conditioning, reinforcement, shaping, modeling, and schemas, with the therapist as teacher or trainer to introduce alternative behaviors.

Gerald Patterson and colleagues introduced behavioral parent training (BPT) using social learning theory by training parents to observe their child's problematic behaviors and then use specific social learning techniques to change the target behavior (Patterson et al., 1975). Examples are using "timeout" with a small child as a positive reinforcement, developing a behavioral contract with an adolescent who wants to drive the family car (i.e., curfew, miles limit, who is allowed in the car, no drinking, etc.), and creating a "token economy" through a reward checklist for a child surrounding specific home-related responsibilities (i.e., take dishes to sink, put clothes in hamper, make bed, brush teeth, complete homework, etc.) with desired rewards attached to levels of completion. The following section will examine the best practices in family therapy as identified by SAMHSA.

Best Practices

It should be noted here that family therapy with substance-abusing clients may be different than traditional family therapy. "Family therapy generally attends more to the process of family interaction, while substance abuse treatment is usually more concerned with the planned content of each session. The family therapist is trained to observe the interactions of family members and employ treatment methods in response to those observations" (SAMHSA, 2004, p. 35). SAMHSA recommends the following points for counselors (both those whose orientation is primarily as a substance abuse counselor and those whose training is as a family therapist):

If background and training are largely within the family therapy tradition, develop an ever-deepening understanding of the subtleties and pervasiveness of denial.

If background and training are largely within the substance abuse treatment field, develop an ever-deepening understanding of the subtleties and impact of family membership and family dynamics on the client and the members of the client's family.

When the going gets tough, get help. Both substance abuse counselors and family therapists are likely to need help from each other with different situations. Consultations and collaboration are key elements in ensuring clients' progress.

Develop thorough and effective assessment processes.

Consider specialized training on one or more specific family therapy techniques or approaches.

Match techniques to stage of change and phase of treatment. (SAMHSA, 2004, p. 71)

There is an emerging practice in family therapy known as the integrative problem centered metaframeworks (IPCM) therapy model. This model draws on the ideas of family system theory and also incorporates the latest empirical research from Bill Pinsof's *integrative problem-centered therapy*, and Doug Breunlin's, Dick Schwartz's, and Betty Karrer's *metaframeworks approach* (Breunlin et al., 2011; Pinsof et al., 2011). As the title implies, this model does not purport a specific "best practice for all," but instead advocates for the most direct approach to a problem, reserving more intensive approaches for when all else fails. This model is also feedback-driven, relying on the therapeutic alliance and the use of scales to help formulate treatment effectiveness. These are unique benefits, but a model this all-inclusive is not without its challenges. The family therapist using IPCM will need to be adept at multiple approaches and techniques or have a wide referral base. In addition, there does not seem to be a guiding practice as to when to change approaches, leaving choice up to the discretion of the therapist and/or client. However, with the development of empirical evidence, this model is promising.

Another emerging trend is *multidimensional family therapy* (MDFT). This empirically based model has evolved over the past two decades through research funded by the National Institute on Drug Abuse. This best-practice approach targets families with adolescents who have significant behavioral problems such as crime, delinquency, and substance abuse. MDFT is a multisystems model and involves five assessment and intervention modules: (1) interventions with the adolescent, (2) interventions with the parent(s), (3) interventions to change the parent–adolescent interaction, (4) interventions with other family members, and (5) interventions with systems external to the family (court, school, etc.) (Liddle, 2009). This model is further described in SAMHSA TIP 39 on Substance Abuse Treatment and Family Therapy (SAMHSA, 2004, pp. 90–91).

WORKING WITH THE FAMILY

Assessment

Assessment in family therapy is an important part of the entire process. It has been stated that there are four major steps in family therapy. These four steps are: assessment, contracting (treatment planning), therapy, and closure (Epstein & Bishop, 1981). Several measures exist that help the clinician to measure family functioning, including the Family Assessment Measure (Skinner et al., 1983), the McMaster Family Assessment Device (Epstein et al., 1983), and the Beaver's System Approach to Family Assessment (Beavers et al., 1985).

Regardless of how family assessment is conducted, the rudiments remain the same. It is important (as in individual therapy) to establish a therapeutic rapport with the client and then to assess the issues by listening carefully for both what is stated and what remains unspoken. Minuchin was the first family therapist to speak in terms of the *identified client* (the person in the family who is being designated as having the "problem"). Minuchin also warns that it is important to remember that the identified client may not be the central source of the family's problems (Minuchin, 1974). Box 8.1 lists the SAMHSA-recommended items to be collected during an assessment:

Box 8.1

SAMHSA ASSESSMENT ITEMS

Standard Medical History and Physical Exam, with Particular Attention to the Presence of Any of the Following:
- Physical signs or complaints (e.g., nicotine stains, dilated or constricted pupils, needle track marks, unsteady gait, tattoos that designate gang affiliation, "nodding off")
- Neurological signs or symptoms (e.g., blackouts or other periods of memory loss, insomnia or other sleep disturbances, tremors)
- Emotional or communicative difficulties (e.g., slurred, incoherent, or too rapid speech; agitation; difficulty following conversation or sticking to the point)

Skinner Trauma History
Since your eighteenth birthday, have you
- Had any fractures or dislocations to your bones or joints?
- Been injured in a road traffic accident?

- Injured your head?
- Been injured in an assault or fight (excluding injuries during sports)?
- Been injured after drinking? (Skinner et al., 1984)

Alcohol and Drug History
- Use of alcohol and drugs (begin with legal drugs first)
- Mode of use with drugs (e.g., smoking, snorting, inhaling, chewing, injecting)
- Quantity used
- Frequency of use
- Pattern of use: date of last drink or drug used, duration of sobriety, longest abstinence from substance of choice (when did it end?)
- Alcohol/drug combinations used
- Legal complications or consequences of drug use (selling, trafficking)
- Craving (as manifested in dreams, thoughts, desires)

Family/Social History
- Marital/cohabiting status
- Legal status (minor, in custody, immigration status)
- Alcohol or drug use by parents, siblings, relatives, children, spouse/partner (probe for type of alcohol or drug use by family members since this is frequently an important problem indicator: "Would you say they had a drinking problem? Can you tell me something about it?")
- Alienation from family
- Alcohol or drug use by friends
- Domestic violence history, child abuse, battering (many survivors and perpetrators of violence abuse drugs and alcohol)
- Other abuse history (physical, emotional, verbal, sexual)
- Educational level
- Occupation/work history (probe for sources of financial support that may be linked to addiction or drug-related activities such as participation in commercial sex industry)
- Interruptions in work or school history (ask for explanation)
- Arrest/citation history (e.g., DUI [driving under the influence], legal infractions, incarceration, probation)

Sexual History: Sample Questions and Considerations
- Sexual orientation/preference: "Are your sexual partners of the same sex? Opposite sex? Both?"
- Number of relationships: "How many sex partners have you had within the past 6 months? Year?"

- Types of sexual activity engaged in; problems with interest, performance, or satisfaction: "Do you have any problems feeling sexually excited? Achieving orgasm? Are you worried about your sexual functioning? Your ability to function as a spouse or partner? Do you think drugs or alcohol are affecting your sex life?" (A variety of drugs may be used or abused in efforts to improve sexual performance and increase sexual satisfaction; likewise, prescription and illicit drug use and alcohol use can diminish libido, sexual performance, and achievement of orgasm.)
- Whether the patient practices safe sex (research indicates that substance abuse is linked with unsafe sexual practices and exposure to HIV).
- Women's reproductive health history/pregnancy outcomes (in addition to obtaining information, this item offers an opportunity to provide some counseling about the effects of alcohol and drugs on fetal and maternal health).

Mental Health History: Sample Questions and Considerations
- Mood disorders: "Have you ever felt depressed or anxious or suffered from panic attacks? How long did these feelings last? Does anyone else in your family experience similar problems?" (If yes, do they receive medication for it?)
- Other mental disorders: "Have you ever been treated by a psychiatrist, psychologist, or other mental health professional? Has anyone in your family been treated? Can you tell me what they were treated for? Were they given medication?"
- Self-destructive or suicidal thoughts or actions: "Have you ever thought about committing suicide?" (If yes: "Have you ever made an attempt to kill yourself? Have you been thinking about suicide recently? Do you have a plan?" [If yes, "What means would you use?"] Depending on the patient's response and the clinician's judgment, a mental health assessment tool such as the Beck Depression Inventory or the Beck Hopelessness Scale may be used to obtain additional information, or the clinician may opt to implement his own predefined procedures for addressing potentially serious mental health issues.) (SAMHSA, 2004, pp. 39–41).

Establishing a Plan

Edwards and Steinglass (1995) found a relationship between gender, how much the drug-abusing spouse was invested in the relationship, and how the recovering addict perceived support from the other family members. Obviously, these factors would play a part in both family therapy and the treatment planning process. While family therapy is inherently more complex than individual therapy (simply because of the dynamics of multiple individuals involved) the basics for competent treatment planning still apply. A treatment plan needs to involve both the client (in this case the family) and the counselor, and it needs to have objectives that are measurable, observable, specific, and time-lined. Figure 8.1 is an example of a treatment plan that might be developed with Juanita and her family. You may notice that one of the goals is for Juanita to establish more effective communication with her children. The objective for this goal is to hold "Talking Circles" once a week. The idea behind the Talking Circle is simply to give each member of the household an opportunity to have a voice—to talk about anything they are feeling, thinking about, or wish to express—without fear of recriminations or being put down. This is a powerful tool in a family where everything in the family has been centered on the addict's using. The next section will examine a typical counseling session with Juanita and her family.

Counseling Sessions

One of the common pitfalls of the family of an addict is that all of the focus of the family is around the addict and his or her drug use. This becomes the central point that the family coalesces around. In recovery and, by extension, in treatment, the counselor needs to help to adjust the focus back to the entire family. One way of doing this is by asking for input from all family members. In counseling sessions, each family member has a chance to be heard, and what they have to say is validated by the therapist.

The therapist also understands that, with an addict, the same dynamics apply in family counseling as if the person has had an affair (except that the affair is with a drug and not another person). The addict is in love with the drug. The drug competes for their attention, for their time, and for their money—all being

SAMPLE FAMILY TREATMENT PLAN

Name of Client: _____

Date: _____

Date	Goal	Objectives	Steps/Methods	Date for Review
	1. Increased productive communication within the family	Family members will participate in one family meeting each week for a minimum of 30 minutes.	1. Family members will participate in a "Talking Circle" each week where each individual gets 5 minutes to speak about whatever is on their mind uninterrupted and without judgement 2. Family members use "I feel _____ because. . . ." statements to express and respond to each other (as learned in counseling) 3. Family meetings close with each family member identifying one or more positive outcome of the meeting.	Four weeks
	2. Increased safety of family members	Family member will be free of instances of neglect and abuse	1. Children will have safe and sustained supervision when parent is away. 2. Parent will take self and children to domestic violence shelter if abuse by partner is threatened or has occurred 3. Children will call 911 when threat or occurrence of violence is present	Weekly check-ins
	3. Increased support for children	Children will receive SUD-specific education and/or supportive counseling	1. Children ages five through twelve will participate in Children's SUD Education Group. 2. Teen-aged children will attend Al-Ateen group at least twice monthly	Monthly check-ins

Client Signature: _____ Date: _____

Counselor Signature: _____ Date: _____

Figure 8.1 Sample Family Treatment Plan

taken away from the primary relationship with the significant other. Other family members (especially children) are also impacted by this emotional withdrawal from the family. Part of the therapy, then, focuses on the feelings of betrayal and hurt that members have experienced. The counselor's job is to help family members find a voice to express these feelings in appropriate ways. For example, the therapist may want to teach members of the family how to confront others by expressing what behavior was exhibited and how it made them feel (when you came home drunk, I felt afraid and hurt).

Depending on the theoretical orientation of the counselor, the therapist may employ several different approaches. An experiential therapist like Satir or Whitaker may ask the family to engage in a role-play or a psychodrama where members act out an emotional scene that happened to the family and is still hurtful for family members. Others who subscribe to a multigenerational approach may ask the family to conduct a genogram and evaluate the recurring themes and patterns of substance abuse across several generations. Later in this chapter, we will view a sample session with Juanita and her children. But first, let's examine the issue of evaluating progress.

Evaluating Progress

We have stressed in other chapters the importance of establishing a therapeutic alliance with the client. This same principle holds true when engaging in family therapy. Research studies have demonstrated that a therapeutic alliance with the family and the families' perception of bonding with the therapist is an important predictor of how well the family will do in therapy (Friedlander et al., 2011; Norcross & Wampold, 2011).

Several scales are available for evaluating family cohesion and bonding, including the Family Adaptability and Cohesion Evaluation Scale IV (FACES IV; Olson, 2011). FACES IV has been widely used to measure family cohesion and the level at which families feel bonded to each other (Faulkner, 2001). Regardless of whether you choose a standardized scale such as FACES IV or choose to use a simple inventory that asks clients to rate how they feel their session went today, the importance is on gaining feedback. If clients feel engaged in the therapy session, they will make more progress.

Referrals

One important aspect of counseling is to know your own limitations. The National Association of Social Workers (NASW) has established a Code of

Ethics for social workers, and part of that code is referring a client when the social worker feels that they are not being effective or if they feel that the needs of the client exceed the capability of the therapist (NASW, 2008). Because Steve is a trained and competent family therapist, he will work with Juanita and her family. Later, after she has completed her treatment (and continues to exhibit growth in her sobriety), he will address the issue of her molestation by an uncle and refer her for sexual survivor counseling with a female therapist who specializes in working with abuse victims.

An Example of Juanita and Her Family in Counseling

Steve, Juanita's counselor, is now working with Juanita in family therapy. Today, Steve has invited Juanita's two children, Jorge (age 15) and Lucinda (Lucy, age 8) to begin a series of family counseling sessions with Juanita. Juanita has successfully completed group therapy, she has obtained a sponsor in Narcotics Anonymous, and she is doing well in her recovery. She and Steve both feel it is important to now involve her children in her counseling. The following is a synopsis of that session.

Steve invites Juanita and her two children into his office and asks them to find a seat, wherever they feel comfortable. Steve then explains a bit about what they will be doing today. He explains that, as part of their mother's treatment and recovery, it is important for them to be able to talk about how their mother's drug usage and drinking has impacted their lives. Steve also goes into some detail about the counseling office being a "safe place" for them to share their thoughts and feelings without having to worry about being in trouble for what they say.

Steve is aware that in a home where addiction is present, several rules govern the behavior of the members of that household. These rules are unwritten and unspoken, but all members of the home are aware of the rules and strictly abide by them. The rules are:

Don't talk. One never talks about the addiction, the bizarre behavior exhibited by the addict, or the impact that the drug abuse has on the family.

Don't trust. Family members (and children in particular) learn at an early age to not trust parents and caregivers because they break their promises often. Children also learn not to trust their own feelings.

Don't feel. Becoming emotionally numb by not allowing oneself to feel is a protective mechanism for children and others living with an addict.

Steve is aware that, to be successful in family therapy, he will have to confront these rules and also give the children permission to break these rules. He does this by quickly moving into a discussion of the rules. He tells the children that he is aware that these rules exist, and it is very common for families to have these rules. He goes on to state that part of their mother's job in recovery is to help them to break down these rules and learn to talk about what they are feeling, to learn to trust her, and to begin to allow themselves to feel all emotions. At this point, he asks them to tell him what he just said. Steve is asking for their input because it is very important that the children understand the paradigm shift that is occurring and that they be able to relate this back to him. When Steve is satisfied that both children fully understand what he has been saying, he moves on to the next portion of the session.

Steve begins to ask the children to talk about one time that they can remember when they felt either afraid, anxious or nervous, or uncomfortable about their mothers drug usage. Each child is invited to tell the story—as best they remember it and to voice how they felt when the incident occurred. Steve then turns to Juanita and asks her to tell the children how it feels to her when she hears them relate the story. By doing this, Steve is helping the children to break old taboos (that it is not right to talk) and it helps Juanita to take responsibility for what she has done (by telling the children how she feels). This also has the added benefit of modeling for the children a mother expressing her feelings. The remainder of the counseling session consists of Steve summarizing what they have discussed and negotiating some homework for the family to complete over the next week. The last thing Steve asks Juanita and her children to do is to complete a short survey that inquires about their feelings about the day's session. Steve then escorts them to the reception area to make an appointment for another counseling session in 1 weeks' time.

CONCLUSION

Family therapy has several seminal (foundational) theories that have helped to shape practice over the decades. Some of the most widely used theories in family therapy, such as systems theory, structural theory, experiential theories, and cognitive-behavioral theory, are being integrated into new best-practice approaches, such as MDFT and IFT. Family therapy can be challenging because there are more voices to pay attention to and additional dynamics at play as more individuals are added into the therapy session. In fact, it may seem overwhelming, even intimidating, compared to one-on-one counseling. Another challenge for family therapists is the commitment to participation from the family member. Sometimes therapist have to work against the family's expectation that the identified client just needs "fixed" (get clean and sober) and then everything will be right in the family. Unfortunately, there has been damage within the family system caused by the addiction that will not magically disappear at the end of treatment. This is why family and couples' treatment is so important and why attending training in this field and having great supervision is critical for the therapist.

Recovery and Relapse Dynamics

INTRODUCTION

In this chapter, we present several definitions of recovery, identify four essential dimensions of recovery, and discuss guiding principles that serve as a standard, unified working definition. We will then discuss six stages of recovery using a developmental model of recovery. In this chapter, we also define relapse and discuss relapse dynamics including 10 stages (or signs) and 37 symptoms that can be used to help identify or predict relapse. These signs and symptoms can help arrest or reverse the relapse process—even before the client returns to use. Finally, we have included the Advance WArning of RElapse (AWARE) Questionnaire 3.9 that is based on the symptoms of relapse and screening and monitoring during recovery. Listed here are the Council for Accreditation of Counseling and Related Educational Programs (CACREP), Council on Social Work Education (CSWE), International Certification & Reciprocity Consortium (IC&RC), and Substance Abuse and Mental Health Services Administration (SAMHSA) standards associated with recovery and relapse.

CHAPTER COMPETENCIES AND STANDARDS

CACREP—Standards 9, 13, 23, 26
CSWE—Competencies 7 and 8
IC&RC—Domain II: Tasks 2, 8, 9, 10; Domain III: 3, 4, 6, 8
SAMHSA—Competencies 5, 7, 10, 11, 62, 63

DEFINITIONS OF RECOVERY

It is important that we have a working definition and understanding of recovery, therefore, we present some examples here.

Many people agree that recovery is a journey of healing and transformation. In *SAMHSA's Working Definition of Recovery* (2010*a*), recovery is defined as "A process of change through which individuals improve their health and wellness, live a self-directed life, and strive to reach their full potential."

A summary of definitions of recovery by consumers can be found in the following quote by Anthony (1993) where recovery is described as:

" . . . ,a deeply personal, unique process of changing one's attitudes, values, feelings, goals, skills, and/or roles. It is a way of living a satisfying, hopeful, and contributing life even with limitations caused by illness. Recovery involves the development of new meaning and purpose in one's life as one grows beyond the catastrophic events of mental illness," (p. 15).

Finally, according to Deegan (1996), "Recovery does not mean cure. Rather recovery is an attitude, a stance, and a way of approaching the day's challenges. It is not a perfectly linear journey," (p. 96).

A common theme throughout these definitions is that recovery is not equated with cure but rather viewed as an ongoing process in which a person may be vulnerable to relapse and exacerbations of symptoms. Additionally, recovery involves a holistic transformation that includes systemic as well as individual changes. The out-of-control and harmful patterns of the addiction surrounding acquiring, using, and reacquiring the drug(s) of choice is replaced by controlled, healthy, and meaningful choices. The person in recovery is, perhaps, *reborn* mentally, physically, spiritually, and socially.

RECOVERY DIMENSIONS AND GUIDING PRINCIPALS

SAMHSA (2010*a*) identifies four major dimensions of recovery that are ecological in nature, relying on a person-in-environment framework within a holistic approach to recovery.

- *Health* (biological): overcoming or managing symptoms of addiction
- *Home* (environmental): having access to a stable and safe living environment
- *Purpose* (psychological): participating in meaningful activities and roles
- *Community* (social): engaged in relationships and social network that enhance recovery

With those dimensions of recovery as an umbrella, we will be drawing from two SAMHA renditions of guiding principles for recovery, one from 2007 and the other from 2010. First, the Center for Substance Abuse Treatment (CSAT), which falls under the umbrella of SAMHSA, identified 12 recovery principles during a 2005 National Summit on Recovery. "Participants at the summit represented a broad group of stakeholders, policymakers, advocates, consumers, clinicians, and administrators from diverse ethnic and professional backgrounds" (Sheedy & Whitter, 2009). Second, SAMHSA led another collaborative meeting in August 2010 as part of its Recovery Support Initiative that included behavioral health specialist, people in recovery, SAMHSA representatives, and consultation with other stakeholders, with the goal of establishing "A standard, unified working definition [that] will help advance recovery opportunities" (SAMHSA, 2010a). The result of that meeting led to the publication of *SAMHSA's Working Definition of Recovery* (SAMHSA, 2010a), which identifies "10 Guiding Principles." Here, we present both collaborations as a combined framework with 14 guiding principles for recovery and effective addiction treatment.

Fourteen Guiding Principles

1. The first guiding principle is based on the belief that *hope* (SAMHSA, 2010a) and *gratitude* (Sheedy & Whitter, 2009) are needed to overcome recovery challenges. Identifying strengths, acknowledging movement toward change, and removing barriers to recovery are ways that counselors can increase hope for a client. Hope cultivates a sense of gratitude for each opportunity that helps the addict remain in recovery.
2. Recovery requires clients to be active in deciding their own life goals, therefore, treatment should be *person-driven* (SAMHSA, 2010a) and *self-directed* (Sheedy & Whitter, 2009).
3. And, because recovery comes in many unique ways for individuals, treatment options should *occur via many pathways* (SAMHSA, 2010a; Sheedy & Whitter, 2009) such as peer support, group counseling, medication, and incorporation of spirituality/faith.
4. Recovery is *holistic* (SAMHSA, 2010a; Sheedy & Whitter, 2009) for the individual, and offering a supportive and community will attend to each client's unique care and can include transportation, family counseling, and mental health services.
5. When recovery is *supported by peers and allies* (SAMHSA, 2010a; Sheedy & Whitter, 2009) through mutual support networks and groups, individuals find that helping others' is also a form of self-care through building a recovery community.

6. In addition, recovery is *relational*, and identifying support through relationships and social networks (SAMHSA, 2010*a*) such as friends, family, church, work, and volunteer activities can increase a sense of inclusion and belonging outside the recovery community.

7. Treatment should always take into consideration how recovery is *culturally based and influenced* (SAMHSA, 2010*a*; Sheedy & Whitter, 2009). Cultural awareness and social diversity include understanding the impact and influence of a client's economic status, cultural background, physical and mental ability, language, environmental situation, and lifestyle preferences on his or her recovery. Counselors should always practice only within the scope of their knowledge and skills, therefore, participating in trainings and seeking supervision related to culture and diversity is part of being a competent counselor and a lifelong learner.

8. Additionally, treatment should be *supported by addressing trauma* (SAMHSA, 2010*a*). Trauma is often uncovered during recovery, and trauma experiences can greatly impede the recovery process. Trauma-informed care can help create a safe and supportive venue for sharing. Trauma experiences include domestic violence, environmental disasters (tornado, hurricane, fire, etc.), child physical abuse, sexual abuse including rape, emotional abuse, child neglect, police- and military-related violence such as riots or war, and others traumas, such as a motor vehicle accident or secondary trauma that involves witnessing (watching or hearing) traumatic events.

9. Recovery also *involves individual, family, and community strengths and responsibility* (SAMHSA, 2010*a*) including *rejoining or rebuilding a life in the community* (Sheedy & Whitter, 2009). Obtaining employment, seeking education, rebuilding relationships, and active involvement in the community are examples of ways to gain what is lost and/or desired.

10. *Respect* (SAMHSA, 2010*a*) is a guiding principle that is both internal and external. It takes great courage to seeks treatment and make the changes and choices necessary to work a recovery. Not only does an individual have responsibilities to speak out for himself and others, but families and communities also have a responsibility to foster the inclusion of recovering individuals and their families. Respect also involves *addressing discrimination and transcending shame and stigma* (Sheedy & Whitter, 2009). For instance, some communities invite shelters, half-way houses, and treatment facilities into their county while others take a stand referred to as "not in my back yard." These communities tend to

ignore that substance abuse already exists, although many times hidden from public view, and community members feel that a treatment facility or shelter will bring the problem to them. Education presented by counselors and personal testimonies by addicts at town/city meetings is powerful advocacy and support for the recovering population and can help counter systemic prejudices. Acknowledging the accomplishments resulting from recovery in meaningful ways facilitates both acceptance and support.

11. Recovery exists on a *continuum of improved health and wellness* (Sheedy & Whitter, 2009). Healing from addiction can sometimes be slow and feel painful. Many times, relapse can be part of this journey. Even non–drug-related setbacks, such as a family or financial crisis, can interfere with one's emotional or physical health and wellness. However, improvements are gradual and seeking balance is a goal of recovery.

12. Recovery involves *recognition of the need for change* (Sheedy & Whitter, 2009). In a previous chapter, we discussed the stages of change that occur; precontemplation, contemplation, preparation, action, maintenance, and relapse. Recovery is a commitment that requires a high degree of motivation, the recognition that change is necessary, and an understanding that change can involve all areas of one's life (emotional, physical, relational, spiritual, social, etc.). Change does not stop at the end of treatment, but is ongoing for a lifetime.

13. Recovery *involves a process of healing and self-redefinition* (Sheedy & Whitter, 2009). Addicts spend an incredible amount of time and energy both denying and hiding their addiction. They are defined by their need to acquire and use drugs and have a wasteland of damage and regrets that will need healing over time. Recovery poses a challenge and an opportunity for a new self-definition.

14. *Recovery is a reality* (Sheedy & Whitter, 2009). Regardless of how long or severe the addiction, or how old or young the addict, recovery can and does occur and is available to everyone.

DEVELOPMENTAL MODEL OF RECOVERY

SAMHSA has delineated a *developmental model of recovery* (DMR) with six stages or periods of recovery. "The DMR has been devised to help recovering people and treatment professionals identify appropriate recovery plans, set treatment goals, and measure progress" (SAMHSA, 2006b). Here, we examine the process of recovery using this DMR as a framework.

Transition Stage: Denial

During the transition stage, the addict can be temporarily successful at safely controlling their alcohol or drug consumption or stopping their use in an effort to convince themselves or others that they are not addicted. However, they discover time and again that these attempts never work very long. There is a pattern of preoccupation associated with the addiction that includes obsessive thoughts (cognitive), compulsive behaviors (behavioral), and physical cravings (biological) caused or aggravated by the addiction. These patterns become programmed due to the rituals and lifestyles of addiction, creating a sense of normality formed with other using peers. This normality reinforces the addict to return to use, and the associated behaviors surrounding use that can include criminal activity.

> The major cause of inability to abstain during the transition stage is the belief that there is a way to control use. (SAMHSA, 2008*b*)

Stabilization Period: Symptom Management

Once an addict seeks help, there is great need to manage the physical withdrawals and psychological conditioning that are a result of long-term use. Acute withdrawal symptoms can be intense and include physical symptoms that can be painful as well as dangerous, depending on the drug. Additionally, individuals can continue to experience withdrawal symptoms for up to 2 years. These symptoms are called *postacute withdrawal syndrome* (PAWS) and include milder physical symptoms, but more emotional and psychological withdrawal symptoms. Bob Carty (2016), the director of clinical services at Hazelden in Chicago, lists some common symptoms including an inability to think clearly, memory problems, emotional overreactions or numbness, sleep disturbances, physical coordination problems, and stress sensitivity. Additionally, SAMHSA's TAP 19 (2006*b*) reports that the most common PAWS symptoms are mood swings, anxiety, irritability, tiredness, variable energy, low enthusiasm, variable concentration, and disturbed sleep. As you can see, there are multiple PAWS symptoms that can be experienced as individuals work through strengthening their recovery. Identifying these symptoms and helping individuals understand that some of these symptoms are a normal part of recovery is critical. Research demonstrates that helping clients to manage relapse by recognizing early warning signs leads to positive outcomes in recovery (Bennett et al., 2005; Clarke & Myers, 2012; Dodge et al., 2013; Gorski, 1990). One way to do this is to incorporate education about the nature of relapse and create a daily checklist for the client to review as part of the treatment plan.

The major cause of inability to abstain during the stabilization period is the lack of stabilization management skills. (SAMHSA, 2008a)

Early Recovery Period: Learning Recovery

This early recovery period requires much education, support, and resources. The recovering individual must learn about the aspects of addiction and recovery and develop new ways of thinking (cognitive), feeling (affective), acting (behavioral), relating (social), and believing/valuing (spiritual) to establish a chemical-free lifestyle. This involves separating from using friends and building relationships that support long-term recovery. The thoughts, feelings, and behaviors developed over time require major interventions that teach new skills and insights to replace the conditioned patterns of the addict's past. Because of the multiple changes this period requires, many professionals and individuals in the recovering community warn against any unnecessary major commitments (i.e., starting new relationships) or changes (i.e., moving home or work) for the first year of recovery.

The primary cause of relapse during the early recovery period is the lack of effective social and recovery skills necessary to build a sobriety-based lifestyle. (SAMHSA, 2008a)

Middle Recovery Period: Working Recovery

This period of recovery marks a shift in focus from understanding, accepting, and managing one's disease to working on repairing and constructing a new sober lifestyle. Many times, this period is signified by a change in treatment from a protected environment, such as residential care, to one less restrictive, where the recovering person is mainstreamed into the larger society. The harm caused to others in the past is addressed during this period and amends are made in an attempt to repair the damage. During this time, new goals are established in the recovery plan such as occupation, social outlets, and sober support networks, and the skills and attitudes learned in treatment are applied to real-life problems. Developing a balanced and meaningful lifestyle is critical during this period.

> The major cause of relapse during the middle recovery period is the stress of real-life problems. (SAMHSA, 2008a)

Late Recovery Period: Self-Actualizing Recovery

Late recovery is marked by a period of deeper discovery. As the recovering person becomes more accustomed to a sober lifestyle, they are more aware of triggers that can lead to a relapse. There may be underlying issues, such as personality traits, dysfunctional relationship patterns, mental health concerns, and physical limitations or illness that interfere with feeling balanced and affect a sense of well-being. Past trauma experiences, such as child maltreatment, can create self-defeating thoughts and behaviors that make the recovering person vulnerable to relapse. Sometimes this requires additional treatment interventions, but many times the recovering person makes conscious decisions regarding changes needed to remove triggers and maintain sobriety. Some of these decisions can be major changes, such as divorce, change in employment, retirement, gaining more education or training, or practicing a faith. Other decisions can seem more minor but are still very significant, such as setting a boundary, forgiving someone, starting a hobby, taking medication, and losing weight.

> The major cause of relapse during the late recovery period is either the inability to cope with the stress of unresolved childhood issues or an evasion of the need to develop a functional personality style. (SAMHSA, 2008a)

Maintenance Stage: Maintaining Recovery

Recovery is a life-long process of managing one's life problems and guarding against relapse. Any use of alcohol or drugs will reactivate the disease and cause any continued growth and development to be arrested. Being diligent in maintaining a recovery program is critical—even with years of sobriety. A recovery plan requires structure, like being on a meal plan for diabetes, and it is not difficult to start making excuses for not following the plan. In fact, maybe one *deserves* a break. After all, what harm will it cause just this once? In reality, these lapses of thinking are triggers. Doing something dangerous, like a diabetic eating a piece of birthday cake at a party or an addict holding a glass of champagne on New Year's Eve, is never a reward for good behavior. It is a denial of a disease.

> The major causes of relapse during the maintenance stage are the failure to maintain a recovery program and encountering major life transitions. (SAMHSA, 2008*a*)

DEFINING RELAPSE

In medical terms, *relapse* is the return of signs and symptoms of a disease after a recovery or remission. In addictions, the signs and symptoms of the disease is the return to drug-seeking behaviors that usually result in resumption of use after a period of abstinence or sobriety. Like recovery, relapse is many times not a spontaneous event, but instead a process where the signs and symptoms can be identified, arrested, and treated. There was a time in the not too distant past when substance abuse counselors believed that relapse was simply a return to the use of the psychoactive substance of the addict's choice. However, as counselors learned more about early warning signs of relapse, this belief system began to change. Gorski and Miller (1982) were some of the first authors to identify relapse as a process—not an event. In fact, drug usage is the end result of the relapse process—not the beginning.

RELAPSE WARNING SIGNS

Gorski and Miller (1982) argued that relapse begins before the addict returns to using and identified 37 warning signs that signal a possible relapse. Therefore, by understanding the warning signs, an addict can monitor his or her own daily recovery and identify when he or she is slipping toward a return to using (Miller & Harris, 2000). The following list is an overview of Gorski and Miller's 10 phases (or signs) of the relapse episode. Within these 10 phases are 37 symptoms that can indicate that a relapse is occurring.

> *Phase 1: Return of Denial:* During this phase the dependent person becomes unable to recognize and honestly tell others what he or she is thinking or feeling. The most common symptoms are:
>   1. Concern about well-being.
>   2. Denial of the concern.

Phase 2: Avoidance and Defensive Behavior: During this phase the dependent person doesn't want to think about anything that will cause painful and uncomfortable feelings to come back. As a result, he or she begins to avoid anything or anybody that will force an honest look at self. When asked direct questions about well-being, he or she becomes defensive. The most common symptoms are:

    3. Believing "I'll never drink again."
    4. Worrying about others instead of self.
    5. Defensiveness.
    6. Compulsive behavior.
    7. Impulsive behavior.
    8. Tendencies toward loneliness

Phase 3: Crisis Building: During this phase the dependent person begins experiencing a sequence of life problems that are caused by denying personal feelings, isolating self, and neglecting the recovery program. Even though he or she wants to solve these problems and work hard at it, two new problems pop up to replace every problem that is solved. The most common symptoms are:

    9. Tunnel vision.
    10. Minor depression.
    11. Loss of constructive planning.
    12. Plans begin to fail.

Phase 4: Immobilization: During this phase the dependent person is totally unable to initiate action. He or she goes through the motions of living but is controlled by life rather than controlling life. The most common symptoms are:

    13. Daydreaming and wishful thinking.
    14. Feeling that nothing can be solved.
    15. Immature wish to be happy.

Phase 5: Confusion and Overreaction: During this phase the dependent person can't think clearly. He or she becomes upset with self and those around her or him, is irritable, and overreacts to small things. Common symptoms are:

    16. Periods of confusion.
    17. Irritation with friends.
    18. Easily angered.

Phase 6: Depression: During this phase the dependent person becomes so depressed that he or she has difficulty keeping to normal routines. At times there may be thoughts of suicide, drinking, or drug use as a way to end the depression. The depression is severe and persistent and cannot be easily ignored or hidden from others. The most common symptoms are:

19. Irregular eating habits.
20. Lack of desire to take action.
21. Irregular sleeping habits.
22. Loss of daily structure.
23. Periods of deep depression.

Phase 7: Behavioral Loss of Control: During this phase the dependent person becomes unable to control or regulate personal behavior and daily schedule. There is still heavy denial and no full awareness of being out of control. His or her life becomes chaotic, and many problems are created in all areas of life and recovery. The most common symptoms are:

24. Irregular attendance at AA and treatment meetings.
25. Development of an "I don't care" attitude.
26. Open rejection of help.
27. Dissatisfaction with life.
28. Feeling of powerlessness and helplessness.

Phase 8: Recognition of Loss Control: The dependent person's denial breaks and suddenly he or she recognizes how severe the problems are, how unmanageable life has become, and how little power and control he or she has to solve any of the problems. This awareness is extremely painful and frightening. By this time, he or she has become so isolated that it seems that there is no one to turn to for help. The most common symptoms are:

29. Self-pity.
30. Thoughts of social drinking.
31. Conscious lying.
32. Complete loss of self-confidence.

Phase 9: Option Reduction: During this phase the dependent person feels trapped by the pain and inability to manage his or her life. There seem to be only three ways out: insanity, suicide, or drug use. This person no longer believes that anyone or anything can help him. The most common symptoms are:

33. Unreasonable resentment.
34. Discontinues all treatment and AA.
35. Overwhelming loneliness, frustration, anger and tension.

Phase 10: The Relapse Episode: During this phase the dependent person begins to use alcohol or drugs again, typically struggling to control or regain abstinence. Some people, especially those who have developed a recovery or crisis plan, are able to quickly reach out and get help before catastrophic consequences occur. The struggle to control use, however, often leads to shame and guilt when the attempt ultimately fails. Eventually, all control is gone, and serious biopsychosocial problems develop and continue to progress. The most common symptoms are:

36. Loss of behavioral control.
37. Acute relapse.

This model is compatible with other treatments modalities such as 12-step programs and family therapy, as well as with less rigid varieties of cognitive, affective, and behavioral therapy models, but it is not as compatible with nondirective or client-centered approaches (Gorski, 2007). The primary strategies used in this model are to teach the client to (1) understand the relapse process, (2) identify and cope with high-risk situations, (3) manage cravings and urges, (4) develop and use a relapse plan during a lapse to minimize consequences, (5) continue in treatment during recovery from a relapse, and (6) create a balanced lifestyle.

In Figure 9.1 we present the AWARE Questionnaire, which is based on the warning signs identified Gorski and Miller. This tool can be used in a variety of ways: it can be given to a client while they are waiting for their session, it can be used as part of a counseling interview, or it can be sent home as homework (for the client to complete on their own and then bring it back on their next visit). This instrument was originally developed through research funded by the National Institute on Alcohol Abuse and Alcoholism (NIAAA) and is in the public domain. Therefore, it may be used without specific permission provided that proper acknowledgment is given to its source (Miller & Harris, 2000).

	Never	Rarely	Some-times	Fairly Often	Often	Almost Always	Always
1. I feel nervous or unsure of my ability to stay sober.	1	2	3	4	5	6	7
2. I have many problems in my life.	1	2	3	4	5	6	7
3. I tend to overreact or act impulsively.	1	2	3	4	5	6	7
4. I keep to myself and feel lonely.	1	2	3	4	5	6	7
5. I get too focused on one area of my life.	1	2	3	4	5	6	7
6. I feel blue, down, listless, or depressed.	1	2	3	4	5	6	7
7. I engage in wishful thinking.	1	2	3	4	5	6	7
8. The plans that I make succeed.	1	2	3	4	5	6	7
9. I have trouble concentrating and prefer to dream about how things could be.	1	2	3	4	5	6	7
10. Things usually don't work out well for me.	1	2	3	4	5	6	7
11. I feel confused.	1	2	3	4	5	6	7
12. I get irritated or annoyed with my friends.	1	2	3	4	5	6	7
13. I feel angry or frustrated.	1	2	3	4	5	6	7
14. I have good eating habits.	1	2	3	4	5	6	7
15. I feel trapped and stuck, like there is no way out.	1	2	3	4	5	6	7
16. I have trouble sleeping.	1	2	3	4	5	6	7
17. I have periods of serious depression.	1	2	3	4	5	6	7
18. I don't really care what happens.	1	2	3	4	5	6	7
19. I feel like things are so bad that I might as well drink.	1	2	3	4	5	6	7

Figure 9.1 AWARE Questionnaire (Revised Form)

Gorski, Terence T. and Miller, Merlene, Staying Sober – A Guide for Relapse Prevention, Herald House - Independence Press, Independence, MO, 1986 for the warning signs.

20. I am able to think clearly.	1	2	3	4	5	6	7
21. I feel sorry for myself.	1	2	3	4	5	6	7
22. I think about drinking.	1	2	3	4	5	6	7
23. I lie to other people.	1	2	3	4	5	6	7
24. I feel hopeful and confident.	1	2	3	4	5	6	7
25. I feel angry at the world in general.	1	2	3	4	5	6	7
26. I am doing things to stay sober.	1	2	3	4	5	6	7
27. I am afraid that I am losing my mind.	1	2	3	4	5	6	7
28. I am drinking out of control.	1	2	3	4	5	6	7

Total Score

Scoring: Total the numbers circled for all items but reverse the scoring for the following five items: 8, 14, 20, 24, 26.

For these five items only:

If the client circles this number: 1 2 3 4 5 6 7

Add this number to the total score: 7 6 5 4 3 2 1

Interpretation: The higher the score for each column, the more warning signs of relapse are being reported by the client. The range of scores is from 28 (lowest possible score) to 196 (highest possible score).

AWARE Score	Relapse Risk Indicator
Very Low Risk	0–27
Low Risk	28–69
Medium Risk	70–97
High Risk	98–125
Very High Risk	126–196

Relapse probability: Based on a client's AWARE score, the following table indicates the risk of relapse during the next 2 months, within in the first year after treatment (Miller & Harris, 2000).

Probability of Heavy Drinking During the Next Two Months		
AWARE Score	If already drinking in prior 2 months	If abstinent during the prior 2 months
28-55	37%	11%
56-69	62%	21%
70-83	72%	24%
84-97	82%	25%
98-111	86%	28%
112-125	77%	37%
126-168	90%	43%
169-196	>95%	53%

Figure 9.1 Continued

The Case of Juanita

Juanita and Steve begin the counseling session by reviewing her progress in treatment to date. Juanita has progressed through individual counseling with Steve, group counseling led by Marta, family counseling with her children, and is now learning about relapse dynamics with Steve. Juanita completes the AWARE Questionnaire and she scores a 60, which signifies a low risk for relapse. Juanita is encouraged by this result. She identified in the questionnaire that she experiences symptom #3 (I tend to overreact or act impulsively) *often* (score of 5) and symptom #17 (I have periods of serious depression) *almost always* (score of 6). Juanita and Steve develop a plan to address her impulsivity through cognitive-behavioral techniques and also agree that a medical referral to evaluate her depression is indicated.

Juanita agreed to take home copies of the AWARE Questionnaire and complete it daily to help monitor relapse symptoms. Juanita will bring the completed Questionnaires when she sees Steve for weekly individual counseling. Depending on her progress over the next 4 weeks, Juanita will then transition into an aftercare group. Once Juanita reaches the aftercare group, her involvement with Steve will be reduced to one counseling session per month (for approximately 3 months), at which time they will both evaluate her progress and readiness for discharge. Juanita has mixed feelings about her progress in treatment. On one hand, she is proud of the work she has done and her "clean time" (the amount of time she has gone without using any drugs or alcohol). On the other hand, she is feeling a bit of trepidation and anxiety about losing her support system in Steve. She has come to view Steve as an honest and supportive friend whom she can depend will be honest with her—even when she doesn't like what he says. Not having weekly access to his counsel is a bit daunting for her, and she shares these fears with Steve. Together, they discuss her feelings of dependency on Steve and how, while this is not unusual in treatment, it can impede her steps to take responsibility for her own recovery. At the end of the session, Steve again asks Juanita to complete a session rating scale that measures how she feels about the day's counseling session.

CONCLUSION

This chapter examined the dynamics between recovery and relapse as it pertains to substance abuse and substance abuse counseling. Prior to the 1970s, recovery with abstinence and relapse was regarded as a return to the use of alcohol and other drugs. During the following decades (the 1970s and '80s) the counseling profession underwent a paradigm shift based on multiple new research findings to viewing recovery as a holistic change (biological, psychological, social, and spiritual) *with* abstinence and relapse as a process that can be detected *before* the return to use.

To help the client manage relapse symptoms, counselors need to understand how recovery works. Clients do not spring, fully formed, into recovery. Recovery is a process. Each day, as the client struggles with new challenges, there are also new opportunities for growth. The recovering addict must learn to negotiate new territory without the help of mind-altering substances. Development that is normally experienced with age-related stages of life is many times arrested during active use. The recovering person struggles to catch up emotionally and socially with peers and may present as immature.

Ordinary events and things that most of us take for granted can be overwhelming for someone who has not performed these tasks clean and sober. Addicts are hampered by *state-dependent learning*—the idea that whatever task, skill, or behavior learned while under the influence of a drug must now be relearned while sober. For example, if an addict learned to drive a car while under the influence, driving while sober will be a challenge. The same holds true for any activity (playing pool, dancing, talking with someone of the opposite sex): all are activities that must be relearned. Fortunately, the relearning process is not as difficult as the process for initially learning these tasks, skills, and behaviors.

10

Aftercare and Discharge Planning

INTRODUCTION

In this chapter, we define and discuss aftercare and how it is utilized as part of a continuum of care for treatment and recovery. This involves helping the client to identify and utilize a support system, develop aftercare plans to stay healthy in recovery, and access information on 12-step programs as a part of recovery. This chapter will also discuss discharge planning, provides an example of a discharge summary form, and address unresolved treatment issues. Listed here are the Council for Accreditation of Counseling and Related Educational Programs (CACREP), Council on Social Work Education (CSWE), International Certification & Reciprocity Consortium (IC&RC), and Substance Abuse and Mental Health Services Administration (SAMHSA) standards associated with aftercare and discharge planning.

CHAPTER COMPETENCIES AND STANDARDS

CACREP—Standards 3, 11, 12, 25, 26
CSWE—Competencies 4, 8, 9
IC&RC—Domain II: Tasks 3, 5, 8, 10; Domain III: Task 3
SAMHSA—Competencies 24–26, 28, 33, 75–76, 111

DEFINING AFTERCARE

Aftercare has two distinct connotations. Aftercare is a formalized treatment protocol that occurs after residential, intensive outpatient, or outpatient treatment. Additionally, aftercare is a lifelong process that continues throughout an addict's lifetime. It is during that process that clients reflect on their lives, recognizing issues (i.e., character defects, faults) and problems that need to be addressed, and then take steps to correct those issues and problems. Less formal than aftercare treatment, participating in aftercare is when a recovering addict can make the transition from the structured environment of treatment to the unstructured world of daily living.

In the New Beginnings Agency where our client Juanita has been receiving treatment, aftercare is a treatment protocol that occurs before discharge. Generally, aftercare is regarded as a place where clients learn to manage their own sobriety and recovery with the management of relapse being a primary goal (Hawkins & Catalano, 1985). Aftercare has been demonstrated to be effective in reducing recidivism rates (returning to the use of drugs) among substance abusers (Matheson et al., 2011; Ouimette et al., 1998).

Aftercare for Juanita

In the last chapter, Juanita and Steve met to review her progress in treatment. Steve and Juanita also reviewed her treatment plan and discussed ways that Juanita will manage her relapse warning signs. The plan was for Juanita to see Steve for individual counseling one time per week for the next 4 weeks and then to transition into an aftercare group. Once Juanita reached the aftercare group, her involvement with Steve would be reduced to one counseling session per month (for approximately 3 months), at which time they will both evaluate her progress and readiness for discharge.

Today, Juanita is to begin her aftercare group. Aftercare will consist of Juanita attending one group per week (for about an hour). In the group, she will be expected to discuss her sobriety, recovery, and any challenges she is having. The difference with this group is that Juanita will be expected to take a proactive approach to her recovery (moving away from treatment dependency). In this group, members are expected to be honest and open about their struggles and openly disclose any struggles they may be having. In addition to the weekly group meetings, group members are expected to attend a 12-step meeting a minimum of one time per week. Juanita arrives for her first aftercare session a few minutes early.

The group begins promptly on the hour, with 12 members attending. This is an open-ended group, and Juanita recognizes and greets some of the members from her intensive outpatient group. The group is opened by the group leader, Alison, who introduces herself and her co-leader, Tony. Tony is a recovering addict who has been in recovery for about 3 years, and he briefly tells his story about being a client at the center and then eventually becoming a Peer Support Specialist. He states to the group, "Being a Peer Support Specialist is one way that I can give back to the recovery community, and it also helps me to stay clean and sober because it reminds me of how much I have to be grateful for." Alison then opens the group discussion by discussing aftercare as a place where people can find continuing support, discuss their struggles in sobriety, and begin to transition away from treatment and into a life-time of recovery. Since Juanita is a new member to the group, Alison welcomes her by having everyone introduce themselves in round-robin style by stating their name and length of recovery. The remainder of the hour is spent with clients providing a "check-in," a process where clients discuss their triumphs and trials in recovery since the last group meeting. At the end of the group, Alison assigns members homework to write out an analysis of where they are in the 12-step process and what they need to work on toward the next step. This homework will be a major part of the group discussion for next week's group. To close the group, Alison and Tony take a few minutes to wrap up by summarizing what was discussed and answering any questions group members may have.

AFTERCARE PLANNING

Recovery from addiction is not something that simply happens to a client—it takes work and planning. Plans for aftercare usually include some type of *recovery or sobriety plan,* which may include a *crisis plan* (or there may be a separate crisis plan). Steve spends time with Juanita helping her to identify those areas that are potentially problematic for her in recovery. Using Juanita's initial biopsychosocial assessment as a guide, Steve and Juanita review the issues that were originally identified when she first presented for treatment. Together, Steve and Juanita identify four areas that she needs to address and work on as part of her continued Recovery Plan. The first three areas are things that she will begin to address over the next 6 months, the fourth issue, concerning her sexual abuse as a child, will be placed "on hold" until she is better equipped to deal with it. The following Recovery Plan lists the three identified issues and the corresponding action plan for Juanita.

Recovery Plan

Identified Issue 1: *Education*

Juanita wants to return to school to begin working on a degree as a Registered Nurse. The nursing degree will fulfill a life-long dream, and it will provide financial stability for her and her children.

Action Plan: Juanita is going to enroll at the local university in courses to obtain her Registered Nurse license. The university has a "bridge program" that will allow her to apply credits she has earned as a nurse's aide toward her degree as a registered nurse. She plans to take two courses starting in the next semester, and, depending on how those go, she may eventually go full time.

Identified Issue 2: *Recreation*

Juanita realizes that her socialization has centered around the use of drugs with her friends. Now that she has several months of uninterrupted sobriety, she has found that her old friends have dropped the friendship (in large part because they now have little in common). Her new goal is to develop new friendships with people who do not use drugs (preferably those who are active in a 12-step program).

Action Plan: Juanita will begin participating in some of the social activities that are regularly sponsored by her Alcoholics Anonymous (AA) Group. The group holds monthly dances, sponsors outings to the theater, and organizes other social events for its members. Juanita plans to become active in these social outings.

Identified Issue 3: *Spirituality*

Juanita was raised as a Roman Catholic but she still harbors resentments toward God because of the abuse she suffered as a child. She finds it hard to reconcile the image of a loving God allowing a child to be abused.

Action Plan: Juanita has an appointment to talk with a priest about her feelings about God and her ambivalence toward religion. The priest is a friend of her sponsor in AA, and he is highly recommended as someone who will listen, not judge or criticize her, and allow Juanita the freedom to explore her feelings. She reports to Steve that she has mixed feelings about doing this, but since God and spirituality are such a big part of AA, she wants to give it a try. "If nothing else, to at least resolve this whole spirituality issue" she tells him.

Planning for Crises

Most recovering addicts deal with some major issue during their initial recovery. These can range from being diagnosed with a catastrophic illness, the death of a family member or friend, divorce, or loss of a job. Having a plan for coping with and managing crisis situations will help the recovering addict in times of conflict and need. Problems are a part of life; how the addict chooses to deal with those problems is the hallmark of recovery. In Chapter 6, we thoroughly discussed crisis planning as part of developing a treatment plan. It is equally essential for aftercare planning to update an existing crisis plan or create a new one prior to discharge.

SAMHSA (2002) has developed an excellent resource guide titled, "Action Planning for Prevention and Recovery: A Self-Help Guide" available at http:// store.samhsa.gov/product/Action-Planning-for-Prevention-and-Recovery-A-Self-help-Guide/SMA-3720. And, as always, this is a free publication. We highly recommend you download and read this pamphlet.

Identifying a Support System

Part of the counselor's task is to help the client with the identification of a support system. In the case of Juanita, her primary support system will be her sponsor and the 12-step group that she attends. For others, primary support systems may include friends, family member, co-religionists/church members, work colleagues, or, participants involved in common hobbies, organizations, or activities. There are four main "talking points" when discussing a support system with a client:

1. Help clients understand the importance of a support system.
2. Help clients identify specific people who will be the key individuals in providing help/support.
3. Help clients identify any impediments or barriers to developing a support system (i.e., accessibility, availability, environmental barriers).
4. Help clients articulate how they will approach potential support persons (i.e., role play, visualization, steps, scenarios).

One support system available for anyone, either face-to-face or by Internet, is through AA and is discussed in the next section. Many recovery plans include attendance at 12-step support group meetings, working a 12-step program, and securing a sponsor as a means of support from a sober community.

TWELVE-STEP PROGRAMS IN RECOVERY

There is no doubt that 12-step programs like AA and Narcotics Anonymous (NA) are beneficial. These groups are free of charge and have helped literally thousands of addicts become clean and sober and go on to live productive lives. Research has also demonstrated that they are an important addition to traditional treatment services (Bahr et al., 2012; Donovan et al., 2013). Twelve-step programs are based on the belief that addicts can best help other addicts to recover by sharing their common struggles, hopes, strengths, and stories. Together they form a support group. There are no professional group leaders, and no member has any status higher than another regardless of their occupation or standing in the community. In the 12-step community, all share the same status as members who are struggling to lead clean and sober lives. That is the one criteria for admission—a desire to be clean and sober. AA, NA, Cocaine Anonymous, Gambler's Anonymous, and other 12-step programs are all based on 12 simple yet profound steps to sobriety. The following is a quote from SAMHSA regarding 12-step programs:

> Twelve-Step groups emphasize abstinence and have 12 core developmental "steps" to recovering from dependence. Other elements of 12-Step groups include taking responsibility for recovery, sharing personal narratives, helping others, and recognizing and incorporating into daily life the existence of a higher power. Participants often maintain a close relationship with a sponsor, an experienced member with long-term abstinence, and lifetime participation is expected. (SAMHSA, 2008*a*)

Surprisingly, alcohol is only mentioned in the first step, which states, "We admitted we were powerless over alcohol (or insert the particular addiction) and our lives had become unmanageable" (Alcoholics Anonymous, 2001, p. 59). The entire 12 steps are reproduced in Box 10.1.

One of the strengths of the 12-step programs is the use of a "sponsor." A sponsor is someone who agrees to function as a mentor to a new member. Sponsors often take on the responsibility of assigning homework to their wards, such as asking them to list the ways in which life has become unmanageable. Sponsors hold recovering addicts accountable for their thoughts, feelings, and behaviors and are generally available to talk 24 hours a day, especially in a crisis. As new members gain sobriety and work their plan of recovery, many will eventually go on to serve as sponsors themselves for new members as they enter the program—thus giving back what they have received. The next section will focus on discharge planning and what that entails.

Box 10.1

THE TWELVE STEPS OF ALCOHOLICS ANONYMOUS

1. "We admitted we were powerless over alcohol—that our lives had become unmanageable.
2. Came to believe that a Power greater than ourselves could restore us to sanity.
3. Made a decision to turn our will and our lives over to the care of God as we understood Him.
4. Made a searching and fearless moral inventory of ourselves.
5. Admitted to God, to ourselves, and to another human being the exact nature of our wrongs.
6. Were entirely ready to have God remove all these defects of character.
7. Humbly asked Him to remove our shortcomings.
8. Made a list of all persons we had harmed, and became willing to make amends to them all.
9. Made direct amends to such people wherever possible, except when to do so would injure them or others.
10. Continued to take personal inventory and when we were wrong promptly admitted it.
11. Sought through prayer and meditation to improve our conscious contact with God, as we understood Him, praying only for knowledge of His will for us and the power to carry that out.
12. Having had a spiritual awakening as the result of these Steps, we tried to carry this message to alcoholics, and to practice these principles in all our affairs" (Alcoholics Anonymous, 2012)

DISCHARGE PLANNING

Discharge planning (like treatment plans) will have many different looks, depending on where you work. Some agencies will have a specific form that you will be expected to complete upon the client's discharge, and this form may be recorded as a hard copy, electronically, or both. Figure 10.1 shows a sample form. However, we would like to emphasize that this is only an example—each agency tends to have its own criteria for information to record upon a client discharge.

When a client is court-mandated to treatment, you may be asked to write a formal report or letter to the court system upon the client's discharge or

NEW BEGINNINGS, INC.
DISCHARGE SUMMARY

Counselor Name and Credentials: _____

Client Name: _____ DOB: _____/ _____/ _____

Admission Date: _____/ _____/ _____ Discharge Date: ____/ ____/ ____

Presenting Problem at Admission/Intake:

_____

_____

_____

Treatment Issues Identified by Client at Admission:

_____

_____

_____

STRENGTH, NEEDS, ABILITIES AND PREFERENCES OF CLIENT AT DISCHARGE:

_____

_____

_____

TREATMENT PROVIDED
☐ Inpatient/Residential Treatment   ☐ Outpatient Treatment

☐ Intensive Outpatient Treatment   ☐ Aftercare

SERVICES PROVIDED (Check all that apply)
☐ Individual Therapy   ☐ Group Therapy   ☐ Family Therapy

☐ Drug/Alcohol Education   ☐ Individual Drug/Alcohol Counseling

☐ Group Drug/Alcohol Counseling   ☐ Family Drug/Alcohol Counseling

☐ Parenting Education   ☐ Individual Rehabilitation   ☐ Group Rehabilitation

☐ Medication Management Referral (provide physician name):

_____

Figure 10.1 Discharge summary

☐ Support Group Referral (specify type and/or name of support group):

_____

☐ Other:

_____

REASON FOR DISCHARGE
☐ Overall Achievement of Treatment Plan Goal(s)/Objective(s):

☐Minimal   ☐ Moderate   ☐ Substantial

☐ Treatment Plan Objectives <u>Not</u> Completed, if Not completed please complete the following:

☐ Client Referred to Another Level of Care (explain): _____

☐ Client Transferred to Another Agency (explain reason for transfer):

_____

☐ Client Terminated Against Recommendation of Agency

☐ Client Deceased: Provide explanation of circumstances:

_____

☐ Client Moved and Left No Forwarding Address or Contact Information

☐ Client Unable to Participate Due to Loss of Abilities, explain loss:

_____

☐ Other:_____

SUMMARY OF TREATMENT OUTCOMES AND RESULTS
(From Treatment Plan)
Problem /Goal 1:

  Objective 1a:

  Objective 2b:

  Objective 3c:

  Objective 4d:

Figure 10.1 Continued

Current Progress on Objectives:

_____

_____

_____

Problem /Goal 2:

   Objective 1a:

   Objective 2b:

   Objective 3c:

   Objective 4d:

Current Progress on Objectives:

_____

_____

_____

Problem /Goal 3:

   Objective 1a:

   Objective 2b:

   Objective 3c:

   Objective 4d:

Current Progress on Objectives:

_____

_____

_____

Problem /Goal 4:

   Objective 1a:

   Objective 2b:

   Objective 3c:

   Objective 4d:

Figure 10.1 Continued

Current Progress on Objectives:

_____

_____

_____

OTHER GAINS BY CLIENT WHILE IN TREATMENT:

_____

_____

_____

STATUS OF CLIENT AT DISCHARGE

Acute   *Yes   No*   If yes, explain why <u>and</u> any/all transition/referral/support services activated:

_____

_____

_____

Chronic   *Yes   No*   If chronic, is client currently stable? *Yes No* If No, explain why and any/all transition/referral/support services activated:

_____

_____

_____

MEDICATION SUMMARY

Prescribing Physician	Name of Medication	Type of Medication	Dosage, Strength, Frequency of Medication	Efficacy of Medication	Length of time on Medication

Figure 10.1 Continued

CONTINUING CARE PLAN:

_____

_____

_____

Client Consents to Follow-Up: *YES*   *NO*

If No, why did client choose to refuse consent for follow-up?

_____

_____

_____

If Yes, when and how does client agree to be contacted for Follow-Up?

☐ 30 days   ☐ 60 days   ☐ 90 days

☐ mailed questionnaire   ☐ telephone interview   ☐ in-person interview

Written Recommendations for Services and Supports:

_____

_____

_____

Special Circumstances of Client (if any):

_____

_____

_____

Services Needed by Client (if any):

_____

_____

_____

Figure 10.1 Continued

REFERRAL(S) (check all that apply)

☐ Inpatient Alcohol and Other Drug Services   ☐ Case Management (Adult)

☐ Case Management (Child)   ☐ Medical Services

☐ Community Housing Program   ☐ Domestic Violence Services

☐ Crisis Intervention Services   ☐ Inpatient Mental Health Services

☐ Medication Management Services, specify physician name:_____

☐ Psychiatric Services, specify physician name: _____

☐ Legal Services (Juvenile Bureau, Legal Aid, etc.)

  Specify _____

☐ Physical/Occupational Therapy   ☐ Dietary Services

☐ Educational Services

☐ Return back to referral source   ☐ Refer to primary physician

☐ Placement/Living Program or Service (i.e. shelter, group home, home health, long-term care):

Please specify _____

☐ Support/Self-help Groups (i.e. Twelve Steps, Parent Support Group, Faith-Based Group):

Please specify:_____

☐ Social/Protective Services: (i.e. TANF, Protective Services, Salvation Army, Red Cross):

Please specify: _____

☐ Vocational Rehabilitative Services (i.e. Physical/Occupational, Audio/Visual/Speech, Other):

Please specify: _____

☐ Other, please specify: _____

Contact Information for Referral Sources Selected:

_____

_____

_____

Figure 10.1 Continued

Summary Statement:

_____

_____

_____

Person designated to track follow-up schedule after discharge:

_____   _____

Counselor Signature and Credentials _____ Date _____

Figure 10.1 Continued

completion of treatment (as in the case of Juanita). If that is the case, you could use information that is included in the discharge summary for this report. In addition, a discharge from one level of care with an admission to a different level of care may be required.

UNRESOLVED TREATMENT ISSUES

Since the primary function of aftercare is to help the client maintain sobriety and learn to manage his or her recovery, one of the most important aspects for the client is learning to recognize and manage unresolved issues. For Juanita, one major unresolved issue that has not been addressed during her treatment is the issue of her childhood sexual molestation. Because she is new to recovery, it is not wise to take on an issue of such magnitude. Conventional treatment wisdom would say it is better for her to develop some solid sobriety and, at some later point, to seek counseling for her childhood abuse. If she tries to deal with this issue too soon in recovery, it could jeopardize her sobriety.

We know that a sense of powerlessness and loss of control are common reactions to all types of abuse and maltreatment, and it is not uncommon for victims to deal with this sense of powerlessness by turning to psychoactive substances (Dass-Brailsford & Myrick, 2010; Shorey et al., 2013). When a person has suffered abuse and then uses mood-altering drugs to cope with the pain of that abuse, the abuse itself becomes a "core" issue—an underlying problem that must be dealt with after a person has achieved stability in his or her recovery. There is no specified amount of time for how much sobriety a person needs before confronting these underlying issues. This is highly individualized and depends on the client. For some, it may be appropriate to confront the pain of abuse within the first 2 years of initiating recovery; for others, a longer period may be indicated. The key issues are stability in recovery, willingness to confront the pain and anxiety inherent in the treatment process, and the client's own ability to deal with turmoil.

In the case of Juanita, Steve and Juanita have discussed the need for her to seek professional help to deal with the unresolved trauma of her childhood abuse "when she is ready." Steve emphasized to Juanita the importance of establishing a solid support group, having stability in recovery, and feeling psychologically ready to confront those issues. In the interim, Steve and Juanita identified other, more immediate issues for her to work on. We will examine those in the next chapter.

CONCLUSION

Counselors work with clients as they near the end of their treatment to help them identify possible problematic situations that may cause them trouble during their recovery. Substance abuse treatment professionals, then, work with the client to not only identify possible "sticking points" in their recovery, but also to find ways to manage and deal with these issues as they arise. Also, counselors help clients to identify treatment issues that still need to be dealt with at some point in the future. These tasks occur before discharge from treatment and are part of the aftercare planning. When clients are discharged from treatment, the discharge summary represents the overview of what occurred during treatment and the treatment outcomes, and it can also include a treatment prognosis (a prediction of how well the client will do in recovery based on treatment outcomes). Prognoses are generally identified as excellent, good, fair, and poor and are generally based on multiple factors such as the client's propensity for insight regarding his or addiction; acceptance of responsibility for thoughts, feelings, and behaviors; readiness/motivation to remain clean and sober; and ability to form supportive alliances, to name a few. But regardless of the prognosis, aftercare should include a meaningful, useful, comprehensive/ holistic and achievable recovery plan to help create the best possible outcomes in recovery.

11

Co-Occurring Disorders

INTRODUCTION

This chapter examines the complexities of people who are dealing with both addiction and mental illness. We will review how prevalent these issues are and some of the barriers experienced by people who suffer from co-occurring disorders. This chapter will provide an overview of treatment issues that may arise, as well as some approaches to therapy. Listed here are the Council for Accreditation of Counseling and Related Educational Programs (CACREP), Council on Social Work Education (CSWE), International Certification & Reciprocity Consortium (IC&RC), and Substance Abuse and Mental Health Services Administration (SAMHSA) standards associated with co-occurring disorders.

CHAPTER COMPETENCIES AND STANDARDS

CACREP—Standards 5, 8, 26
CSWE—Competencies 7 and 8
IC&RC—Domain I: Task 6; Domain II: Tasks 1–8; Domain IV: Task 4
SAMHSA—Competencies 4, 31, 52

PREVALENCE OF CO-OCCURRING DISORDERS

Estimating the number of individuals who have co-occurring substance abuse issues and mental health problems is a moving target—at best. SAMHSA estimates that 5.2 million people in the United States were dealing with co-occurring disorders (SAMHSA, 2007). In another publication, SAMHSA estimates that between 20% and 50% of people in mental health settings have a co-occurring substance use and mental health disorder (SAMHSA, 2010c). The National Alliance on Mental Illness (2014) estimates that more than half of adolescents with a substance abuse disorder also suffer from a mental illness. Other research has corroborated the findings that a large percentage of the substance abusing population suffer from other, co-occurring mental disorders. For example Hasin et al. (2005) published results from the National Epidemiological Survey on Alcoholism and Related Conditions. They report that more than 5% of the population surveyed reported a major depressive disorder within the past 12 months, and more than 13% had a major depressive episode over the course of a lifetime. Cranford et al. (2011) found similar results using the same data set. In another study, Mericle et al. (2012) reported a correlation between ethnicity and psychiatric disorders, with Caucasians reporting the highest incidence of co-occurring disorders over the course of a lifetime. The authors conclude that 8.2% of whites, 5.4% of blacks, and 5.2% of Latinos self-reported a co-occurring disorder over the course of their lifetime.

The issue of co-occurring mental disorders becomes even more problematic when we examine the issue of co-occurring disorders and prisoners. One study (Baillargeon et al., 2010) found that at least 50% of the prison population had a substance abuse problem, but among those with co-occurring disorders there was a much higher risk for reincarceration. In another study (Lynch et al., 2014), the researchers reported that 38% of the females who were included in the study reported a co-occurrence of mental health issues and substance abuse. But while it may be difficult to ascertain exactly how many individuals are dealing with co-occurring disorders, we do know how to deal with these issues. We will turn to that next.

PRIORITIZING TREATMENT OPTIONS

For many years, substance abuse counselors have grappled with the question, "If we have a client with a dual diagnosis, which problem should we treat first?" Some would argue that you deal with the substance abuse issue—then a clinician can know exactly what mental health issues are impacting the client (once they are detoxed from the drug of abuse). Others would argue that it is important to deal with the mental illness first. Today, the current thinking is to deal with both problems simultaneously (Drake et al., 2001). Drake and his co-authors recommend that a clinician (or team of clinicians) develop "integrated" services—seamless services provided by one provider that would treat both the substance abuse and the mental health issue. Others have argued for a simultaneous delivery of services that treat both the substance abuse and mental health issues (Smelson et al., 2012; Suarez et al., 2012).

It should be noted here that, ethically a counselor should not attempt to treat above his or her training or capability. Obviously, if a client has a mental illness that is beyond a person's ability to deal with, then a referral to another therapist is in order. Knowing when to refer is an important skill and doesn't mean that a person is incompetent. It actually means just the opposite—that a person knows his or her own limitations and is putting the client's best interest first. By referring to another therapist for help, you create a situation where the client can get the help he or she needs (while still working on addiction issues).

RECOGNIZING AND ASSESSING MENTAL HEALTH DISORDERS

We are going to open this discussion about the recognition and assessment of mental health disorders with an assumption. This assumption is that you are working with a client who has already been detoxified (withdrawn) from whatever psychoactive substances he or she have been using. If a client is still under the influence or in early stages of withdrawal, the mental state can often reflect that of someone who is experiencing mental illness (depression, anxiety, hallucinations, etc.). For a thorough discussion and clinical guide to detoxification of a client, we refer you to the *Detoxification and Substance Abuse Guide* (SAMHSA, 2006*a*). However, if your client is not actively using any drugs, then the following are markers to look for when there are signs of a change in mental functioning:

Symptoms and signs of conditions that require immediate medical attention:

- Change in mental status
- Increasing anxiety
- Hallucinations

Immediate mental health needs (mental health issues that require immediate attention):
- Suicidality (assess for suicidal ideation, plan, and past attempts)
- Homicidal thoughts (impulses to hurt themselves or someone else)
- Anger and aggression
- Lack of orientation (is the person oriented to person, time, and place? Do they know who they are, where they are, and what time/ day it is?)
- Inability to carry on a conversation and exhibit logical, sequential thoughts

Any of these conditions suggest the need for further psychological screening. It is possible that the client is experiencing a serious psychological break with reality and may require medical intervention. There are some general questions that counselors can use to ascertain clients' level of functioning and their ability to track information. You may want to employ some of these questions if you have doubts about your client's orientation and alertness:

- Ask them to tell you what date and time it is.
- Ask them to tell you where they are.
- Ask them to tell you their first name and last name.
- Ask them why they are here.

These four simple questions should give you an indication of the client's mental orientation (or lack thereof). This is referred to as oriented times four (time, place, person and situation) and written Ox4. Inability to answer these questions suggests a need for further (more in-depth) screening. Let us return, for just a moment, to our discussion in earlier chapters regarding postacute withdrawal syndrome (PAWS). Recall that symptoms fall into three categories: physical, emotional, and mental. Physical symptoms can be as varied as headaches, nausea, inability to sleep, and physical discomfort including aches and muscle pain. Emotional symptoms include depression, anxiety, thoughts of suicide, and mood swings. Mental symptoms include confusion, difficulty in forming coherent thoughts, interference with short-term memory, and gaps in long-term memory.

One of the tasks of the therapist, then, is to determine if the symptoms and issues being displayed by the client are caused by PAWS or by an underlying mental condition. This can sometimes be difficult to determine, but here are some guidelines:

- When was the last time the client used any psychoactive substance (PAWS symptoms usually pass by the sixth month of abstinence)?
- Does the client have a history of mental illness?
  - If yes, what has been the nature of the problem (depression, anxiety, etc.)?
  - When did the problem first occur (age at onset)?
  - When was the last episode?
  - Has the client received treatment for the mental illness?
  - Has the client taken medication?
    - If yes, what medication?
    - Are they still taking it? Dosage last taken?

These questions should help you to form a better picture of what is going on with your client. Depending on the answers to these questions, it may be necessary to make a referral for psychiatric help while helping the client with his or her substance abuse issues.

ADDRESSING MEDICATION IN RECOVERY

In the substance abuse treatment community, you will find a great deal of debate regarding the use of medications and recovery. First, a debate exists about the use of "harm reduction therapy" such as buprenorphine, methadone, and other drugs used to help opioid addicts to manage their addiction and lead responsible lives. Second, a debate exists as to whether dually diagnosed recovering substance abusers should use medications to help them manage their mental illness. The question is, "If an addict is taking a drug for mental illness, are they truly in recovery?" (Ginter, 2012; White, 2009; Woods & Joseph, 2012).

Today, this debate almost sounds ludicrous. If a person was a diabetic and needed insulin to live, we would not question their recovery because they were dependent on insulin, but as laughable as it sounds, the debate still continues. People who are dependent on medications (for depression, anxiety, bipolar disorders, schizophrenia, and a host of other mental illnesses) are still having their recovery called into question by other recovering addicts (and even some treatment professionals) (Redden et al., 2013; Zweben & Ashbrook, 2012).

This leaves the recovering addict with the question, "Can I be in recovery and be taking medication?" The answer needs to be a resounding, "Yes." Yes, a person can be recovering from alcohol and other mood-altering substances and still be taking prescription medications to help them manage their mental health issues. The operative word here is "mood-altering substances." If an individual is using a compound or behavior (food, drugs, sex, gambling, etc.) to alter his or her mood (and escape reality) then recovery must be called into question. They are simply exchanging one addiction for another—much like the alcoholic who quits drinking but begins smoking marijuana on a regular basis. But when an addict is using a prescription medication (prescribed by their physician or psychiatrist) to manage a mental health issue, then they are acting responsibly and should be considered actively in recovery. Recovery means that the individual is working to meet the challenges of daily living without the coping mechanism of mood-altering drugs or behaviors, and they are actively seeking to improve themselves and their relationships with others. The fact that they are dependent on medication to help them manage does not change the fact that they are seeking to recover from the addiction.

CONCLUSION

This chapter takes up the sometimes hotly contested debate of co-occurring disorders (substance abuse and mental health issues) and recovery. Several different debates arise over this subject. The first question is what issue to treat first (the substance abuse or the mental illness). The second question asks if a person who is "in recovery" from alcohol, other drugs, or other behaviors (such as gambling addiction) be in recovery if he or she is actively taking medication for a mental illness. Another question that arises is, if a person is on a harm reduction therapy regime (such as taking buprenorphine for opiate addiction), can they still be considered in recovery? Though these questions have been debated for decades, most treatment professionals today are beginning to modify their stance (on at least some of these questions). Most professionals would accept a client taking medication for a mental illness while simultaneously participating in a recovery program for alcohol and other substances. And many professionals are beginning to accept harm reduction models as a legitimate means of treatment (because of the potential for allowing the client to lead a normal, healthy, and productive life while in treatment), though this is still a matter of some debate.

12

Diversity Issues

INTRODUCTION

In this chapter, we address working with specific populations that have their own unique sets of challenges. We will be discussing some of the unique counseling challenges of LGBTQ, adolescents, women, people of color, older persons, people with infectious diseases, and the military. Listed here are the Council for Accreditation of Counseling and Related Educational Programs (CACREP), Council on Social Work Education (CSWE), International Certification & Reciprocity Consortium (IC&RC), and Substance Abuse and Mental Health Services Administration (SAMHSA) standards associated with diversity issues.

CHAPTER COMPETENCIES AND STANDARDS

CACREP—Standards 13, 16
CSWE—Competencies 2 and 3
IC&RC—Domain III: Tasks 4, 7; Domain IV: Task 2
SAMHSA—Competencies 12, 18–23, 99–107

RECOVERY CONSIDERATIONS

It can be assumed that treatment programs and their counselors that use best practice models and approaches specific to substance abuse, would expect better recovery outcomes than those programs that do not. Additionally, programs and counselors that prepare for and address the diversity of their population by developing a framework for cultural competence, would expect to see even greater outcomes. As you will see in the next sections, there is growing need for substance abuse treatment programs that understand and provide services to under-served populations. We will be addressing; women, people of color, the LGBTQ community, adolescents, the aged, and military personnel and their families. However, it is also important to mention that there is a lack of services for substance abuse treatment in rural communities, especially those where high rates of prescription drug and other opioid abuse is found, (Faulkner et al, 2015).

Working with LGBTQ

Because this population remains predominately hidden, it is difficult to determine how many people in the U.S. identify as lesbian, gay, bisexual, transgendered, and questioning or LGBTQ. And even more difficult is determining how many LGBTQ are in treatment. However, one study (Gates, 2011) reports that approximately 9 million Americans self-report as being lesbian, gay, bisexual, or transgendered. Others have reported that this population contains s a disproportionate number of people who self-report mental illness and other psychological problems (Haas et al., 2010; Hester et al., 2012; Mustanski et al., 2010). Part of this increased rate of psychological problems can be directly attributed to the increased rate of prejudice and stigma associated with being queer. The Centers for Disease Control (2011) reports that adolescents and young men who reported rejection from their families were:

- 8.4 times more likely to have tried to commit suicide
- 5.9 times more likely to report high levels of depression
- 3.4 times more likely to use illegal drugs
- 3.4 times more likely to have risky sex

While precise incidence and prevalence rates of substance use and abuse by LGBTQ individuals are difficult to determine for several reasons: reliable information on the size of the LGBTQ population is not available, epidemiologic studies on alcohol and drug abuse rarely ask about sexual orientation, and research studies cannot be compared because of inconsistent methodologies.

SAMHSA (2001) states that, when compared with the general population, LGBTQ people are more likely to use alcohol and drugs, have higher rates of substance abuse, are less likely to abstain from use, and are more likely to continue heavy drinking into later life. This is compounded when the client is also a person of color. SAMHSA states:

In addition to understanding a client's ethnic background, counselors should keep in mind how the client's culture views LGBT individuals and the effect this viewpoint has on the client. Each ethnic minority group has norms and values about LGBT members and behavior. Providers may be helpful to a client if they remember these multilayered, and sometimes opposing, influences on the client. For the LGBT person from an ethnic or racial minority, coping with one's sexual orientation takes place amid a tangle of cultural traditions, values, and norms. LGBT persons of color cope with trying to fit into the gay and lesbian communities in the face of racism and discrimination. For some, the added burden of these issues makes finding a comfortable place in society even more complex and difficult. Major ethnic minorities in the United States react differently to issues of sexual orientation. It is important for the provider to assess how an LGBT client from a minority group feels about his or her culture. Some may be alienated by their culture, whereas others may be supported by it. (SAMHSA, 2001, p. xv)

Working with Adolescents

Adolescents present their own unique set of challenges in treatment. While they may not have experienced some of the negative consequences from their drinking and drug abuse that long-term users experience. Consequences associated with teenage drinking and substance use include; injuries or death from motor vehicle accidents, suicides, homicides, violence, delinquency, psychiatric disorders, and risky sexual practices, (SAMHSA, 1999).

One study concluded that adolescents are highly underserved as a treatment population (Brannigan et al., 2004). Others have concluded that adolescents have different treatment needs than adults, and programs designed for adults are not effective with teenagers (Winters et al., 2011). Furthermore, it is recommended that adolescents respond best to treatment when the following factors are considered: the developmental stage of the individual adolescent, the family, ethnicity, gender, co-existing disorders (including any medications the person may be taking), and environment (including any negative school, peer and community influences). Researchers found that family therapy was the most effective treatment tool for adolescents (Baldwin et al., 2012; Tanner-Smith et al., 2013; Williams & Chang, 2000).

Several researchers have found that adolescents can present with co-occurring disorders (Chan et al., 2008; Wilens & Morrison, 2011; Wise et al., 2001). The issue, then, is how best to treat adolescents who present with co-occurring disorders. As stated earlier, the first issue is to involve the family. Other research has shown that adolescents, like adults, respond well to both therapeutic alliance and cognitive behavioral approaches (Burke, 2010; Duppong Hurley et al., 2013).

Working with Women

Women who use drugs often suffer from other serious health problems, sexually transmitted diseases, and mental health problems, such as depression. Research has demonstrated a positive outcome between gender-responsive therapy (counseling targeted specifically for women) and sustained sobriety after release from treatment (Messina et al., 2010; Prendergast, 2011; Tuchman, 2010).

The National Institute on Drug Abuse (NIDA, 2012*b*) states the following about women and drug abuse in treatment,

> Gender-related drug abuse treatment should attend not only to biological differences but also to social and environmental factors, all of which can influence the motivations for drug use, the reasons for seeking treatment, the types of environments where treatment is obtained, the treatments that are most effective, and the consequences of not receiving treatment. Many life circumstances predominate in women as a group, which may require a specialized treatment approach. For example, research has shown that physical and sexual trauma followed by post-traumatic stress disorder (PTSD) is more common in drug-abusing women than in men seeking treatment. Other factors unique to women that can influence the treatment process include issues around how they come into treatment (as women are more likely than men to seek the assistance of a general or mental health practitioner), financial independence, and pregnancy and child care, (pp. 19–20).

Women who use drugs are at greater risk for unwanted pregnancy. When a pregnant woman uses drugs, she and her unborn child face serious health problems. During pregnancy, the drugs used by the mother can enter the baby's bloodstream. The most serious effects on the baby can be HIV infection, AIDS, prematurity, low birth weight, sudden infant death syndrome, small head size, stunted growth, poor motor skills, and behavior problems. Figure 12.1 shows some of the health risks faced by children whose mothers used drugs while pregnant (US Department of Health and Human Services, 1994).

Mother	Baby
Poor Nutrition	Prematurity
High Blood Pressure	Low Birth Weight
Rapid Heart Beat	Infections
Low Weight Gain	Small Head Size
Low Self Esteem	Sudden Infant Death Syndrome
Preterm Labor	Birth Defects
Sexually Transmitted Disease	Stunted Growth
Early Delivery	Poor Motor Skills
HIV/AIDS	HIV/AIDS
Depression	Learning Disabilities
Physical Abuse	Neurological Problems

Figure 12.1 Health issues in children associated with maternal drug abuse

NIDA research shows that women drug abusers have improved treatment outcomes when treatment is culturally relevant and includes accommodating specific needs. Some women need basic services of food, shelter, and clothing. Others also need transportation, child care, and parenting training. Women may need medical care, mental health therapy, and legal assistance. A comprehensive treatment plan may also include external referrals, such as classes to learn new skills on how to search and interview for a job. Treatment programs, dominated by male clients, often do not address women's issues or services.

(SAMHSA, 2009b) chap. 1) advises developing the following treatment protocols for women:

- *Acknowledge the importance and role of socioeconomic issues and differences among women.* Biological, cognitive-behavioral, and psychological dimensions of women's substance use and abuse should be framed in their socioeconomic contexts including, but not limited to, employment, educational status, transportation, housing, literacy levels, and income.
- *Promote cultural competence specific to women.* Treatment professionals and staff must understand the worldviews and experiences of women from different ethnic and cultural backgrounds, as well as the interaction among gender, culture, and substance use to provide effective substance abuse treatment. In addition, effective treatment will depend equally on attention and sensitivity to the vast diversity among the female population, including overlapping

identities of race, class, sexual orientation, age, national origin, marital status, disability, and religion.

- *Recognize the role and significance of relationships in women's lives.* The relational model recognizes the centrality of relationships or connections in women's lives and the importance of those relationships with respect to alcohol, tobacco, and drug use. While substance use may initially play an integral role in making or maintaining connections in relationships, the relational approach views the development of substance use disorders as a "disconnection" and stresses the development and repair of connections to others, oneself, one's beliefs, and one's culture as critical for recovery. The relational model takes a family-focused perspective, using a broad definition of family as those individuals a woman views as her significant support system. In this model, a woman's children are included in her treatment, and prevention and treatment services must be provided directly to her children and family.

- *Address women's unique health concerns.* Women possess distinctive risk factors associated with onset of use, have greater propensity for health-related consequences from drug and alcohol consumption, exhibit higher risks for infectious diseases associated with drug use, and display greater frequency of various co-occurring disorders. Moreover, women who abuse substances are more likely to encounter problems associated with reproduction, including fetal effects from substance use during pregnancy, spontaneous abortion, infertility, and early onset of menopause. Substance abuse treatment needs to address women's unique health concerns throughout the course of treatment.

- *Endorse a developmental perspective.* In general, women experience unique life course issues. Specific to women who abuse substances, these life course issues, along with developmental milestones, impact their patterns of use, engagement in treatment, and recovery. Substance use and abuse affect women differently at different times in their lives. It is important to consider age-specific and other developmental concerns starting with the assessment process and continuing through continuing care and long-term recovery.

- *Attend to the relevance and influence of various caregiver roles that women often assume throughout the course of their lives.* Regardless of substance abuse, women are more likely to assume primary caregiving responsibilities for their children, grandchildren, parents, and other dependents. These roles may heavily influence a woman's willingness to seek help for substance abuse, and also may interfere with her ability to fully engage in the treatment process or to adhere to treatment recommendations.

- *Recognize that ascribed roles and gender expectations across cultures affect societal attitudes toward women who abuse substances.* Whether or not a woman neglects her roles as a caregiver, engages in alcohol or drug-induced sexual activity, continues to use despite pregnancy, or uses sex to secure her next supply of drugs or alcohol, women with substance use disorders are significantly stigmatized by societal attitudes and stereotypes of women who drink and use drugs. As a result, women may experience feelings of shame associated with their use and the consequences of their use.

- *Adopt a trauma-informed perspective.* Current and past violence, victimization, and abuse greatly affect many women who abuse alcohol and drugs. Substance abuse treatment approaches need to help women find safety, develop effective coping strategies, and recover from the effects of trauma and violence.

- *Utilize a strengths-based model for women's treatment.* A strengths-based approach builds on the woman's strengths and uses available resources to develop and enhance resiliency and recovery skills, deepen a sense of competency, and improve the quality of her life. These strengths may include personality traits, abilities, knowledge, cultural values, spirituality, and other assets; while resources may involve supportive relationships, environments, and professional support.

- *Incorporate an integrated and multidisciplinary approach to women's treatment.* Treatment needs to integrate current knowledge, research, theory, experience, and treatment models from diverse disciplines critical to understanding women and substance abuse treatment. In addition to incorporating and blending information from the mental health, women's health, and social and behavioral sciences fields, treatment providers must network and collaborate with other agencies to provide comprehensive case management and treatment planning to address the complexity of biopsychosocial and cultural issues that women may exhibit throughout treatment.

- *Maintain a gender-responsive treatment environment across settings.* Effective treatment for women begins with a collaborative environment that is nurturing, supportive, and empowering. Women with substance use disorders are more likely to remain in a treatment setting that feels familiar and safe, includes their children, utilizes proactive case management, and fosters the development of supportive relationships across the continuum of care.

- *Support the development of gender-competency specific to women's issues.* Administrative commitment and vigilance is needed to ensure that staff members are provided gender-specific training and supervision to promote the development of gender competency for women."

Working with People of Color

SAMHSA (2014) defines cultural competence as "the ability to recognize the importance of race, ethnicity, and culture in the provision of behavioral health services," (p. 9). To do this, counselors need to acknowledge cultural biases and make changes to address those biases. Similarly, treatment program can increase cultural competence by demonstrating empathy and understanding of cultural differences in treatment design, implementation, and evaluation. SAMHSA (2006, chap. 4) states that a culturally competent treatment program is characterized by:

- Staff knowledge of or sensitivity to the first language of clients
- Staff understanding of the cultural nuances of the client population
- Staff backgrounds similar to those of the client population
- Treatment methods that reflect the culture-specific values and treatment needs of clients
- Inclusion of the client population in program policymaking and decision making.

Cultural competence involves more than understanding minority populations, it requires an investment by administrators and program staff in the people served by the program. Researchers (Burrow-Sanchez et al., 2011; Guerro et al., 2012) have found that cultural competence has an impact on treatment outcomes (at least with Hispanic populations). This research corroborates earlier findings by Mat (1994). But while minorities represent one of the fastest growing segments of our population, let us turn briefly to another quickly expanding group—older persons.

Working with Older Persons

It is no secret that the largest and fastest growing segment of the US population (comprising nearly 30% of the nation's total) are the "baby boomers"—those born between 1946 and 1964. Researchers are discovering that this population is also at increased risk for substance abuse (Arndt et al., 2011). Schonfeld et al.

(2010) reports that prescription medication was the most widely abused drug among this population (followed by alcohol). One study found that "More than one in five older adults ever had a substance use disorder, and more than 1 in 20 had a disorder in the past 12 months, primarily involving alcohol or tobacco" (Lin et al., 2011, p. 297). SAMHSA states that "People 65 and older consume more prescribed and over-the-counter medications than any other age group in the United States. Prescription drug misuse and abuse is prevalent among older adults not only because more drugs are prescribed to them but also because, as with alcohol, aging makes the body more vulnerable to drugs' effects" (SAMHSA, 1998, p. xvi).

Part of what complicates the problems of drug abuse among the elderly is the fact that baby boomers have a history of illicit drug abuse, combined with tolerant attitudes toward the use of psychoactive substances (such as marijuana, cocaine, and other drugs). Volkow (2011) writes,

The social and physical changes that accompany aging may well increase vulnerability to drug-related problems. The loss of loved ones, juggling of multiple roles, and retirement or other alterations in employment and income may cause some older people to use illicit drugs as self-medication for anxiety or depression, especially if they have a history of taking drugs to cope. Slowing metabolism can increase sensitivity to the effects of drugs. Furthermore, the effects of drugs of abuse in older adults may be influenced by age-related health conditions and medications—contingencies that are more problematic when patients hide their drug abuse.

We know that certain factors increase a person's likelihood of illicit drug use. These factors include being male, being unmarried, initiating use at an early age, and having experienced depression, alcohol use, and tobacco use in the past year (Blank, 2009). Research shows that alcohol is the most commonly abused drug among the aging (with prescription drug abuse a close second). Older adults are less likely than younger adults to recognize or seek treatment for substance use disorders. However, when older persons engage in treatment, they are as likely to benefit from treatment as younger people (Wang & Andrade, 2013). Substance abuse counselors, doctors, nurses, and other healthcare professionals need to be cognizant of the potential for substance abuse among the elderly and routinely screen for any signs of abuse or dependence.

Working with Clients with Infectious Diseases

People who abuse drugs are more likely to contract infectious diseases. Bloodborne diseases such as hepatitis, HIV/AIDS, and sexually transmitted diseases are transmitted through body fluids like urine and semen. Other diseases include tuberculosis; endocarditis, an infection of the heart valves by certain bacterial and fungal organisms; bacteremia/septicemia, bacterial invasion of the bloodstream that may result from use or sharing of contaminated needles and other drug paraphernalia; body lice/scabies; and venereal warts (SAMHSA, 1993). When substance abuse programs were surveyed to determine their level of care for patients with infectious diseases a substantial proportion of programs were found to not offer services (particularly medical services) for these infections. The most commonly cited barriers were funding, health insurance benefits, patient acceptance, and staff training (Bini et al., 2011). Furthermore, Chadwick et al. (2014) found that a significant number of people who were entering substance abuse treatment for the first time had never been tested for HIV/AIDS. One study reported that substance use dependence or abuse is associated with higher mortality among HIV-infected patients (DeLorenze et al., 2011). Chan et al. (2011) reported that risky sexual practices and the sharing of needles increase the exposure to HIV/AIDS, although the initial symptoms may not manifest themselves for several years.

The issue, then, is how to decrease these risky behaviors. Researchers report that HIV/AIDS can be significantly reduced by a strict regimen of testing and treating patients (Bernstein et al., 2012; Gardner et al., 2011). This would imply a regular procedure for testing all clients who enter treatment and then helping those who test positive for infectious diseases to find help—something that is not being done on a regular basis. The analyses suggest that private nonprofit facilities, which are the largest providers of outpatient substance abuse treatment (OSAT) are less likely than public facilities to offer sexually transmitted infectious disease testing or to report adequate client utilization rates. Higher utilization was instead associated with professionally accredited facilities and with facilities whose majority of clients were Latino/a, reported a history of treatment, stayed in treatment longer, or received case management (Guerrero & Cederbaum, 2011). SAMHSA (2011) recommends that all counselors provide screening measures for hepatitis and provides the following tips:

- Consider screening to be more than just a blood test. It is an opportunity to educate the client about hepatitis its effects on health, and prevention strategies. It is an opportunity for clients to identify their risk factors and learn how they can reduce the risk of contracting or transmitting viruses.
- Be aware that many clients may not know whether they have been screened for hepatitis in the past or they might not know the results. They might confuse HIV screening or any blood test with hepatitis

screening, and they might erroneously believe that they are—or are not—infected.

- Clearly explain that the hepatitis test is optional. Clients may not understand what disease the test will detect or that they have the option not to give consent;
- Follow up with clients regardless of the results. Failure to follow up is a missed opportunity to deliver or reinforce prevention messages, (pp. 16–17).

Friedland (2010) states that reducing the spread of infectious diseases is possible with integrated programs and services. However, prejudices need to be addressed before widespread change will be seen.

Working with Veterans, Active Duty Military, and Their Dependents

Military personnel and their families have their own unique set of problems. Veterans returning from wars such as the ongoing operations in Iraq (Operation Iraqi Freedom; OIF) and Afghanistan (Operation Enduring Freedom; OEF) continue to strain military resources. NIDA reports that substance abuse is a key concern. While the 2008 Department of Defense Health Behavior Survey reveals general reductions over time in tobacco use and illicit drug use, it reported increases in other areas, such as prescription drug abuse and heavy alcohol use. In fact, prescription drug abuse doubled among US military personnel from 2002 to 2005 and almost tripled between 2005 and 2008. Alcohol abuse is the most prevalent problem and one which poses a significant health risk. A study of Army soldiers screened 3–4 months after returning from deployment to Iraq showed that 27% met criteria for alcohol abuse and were at increased risk for related harmful behaviors (e.g., drinking and driving, using illicit drugs). And although soldiers frequently report alcohol concerns, few are referred to alcohol treatment. Research findings highlight the need to improve screening and access to care for alcohol-related problems among service members returning from combat deployments (NIDA, 2011b).

Studies show that alcohol misuse and abuse, hazardous drinking, and binge drinking are common among OEF and OIF veterans. Veterans sometimes drink alcohol as a way to numb difficult feelings and erase memories related to their war experiences. For example, increased combat exposure involving violence or human trauma among OIF veterans was linked to more frequent and greater quantities of alcohol use than was less exposure to such combat (SAMHSA, 2012).

Families of service personnel also have their issues to deal with. Cohoon (2011) reports that children with a parent deployed in the military suffer from greater anxiety and more emotional difficulties and psychological distress than other children. Research shows that children with preexisting psychological conditions, such as anxiety and depression, may be particularly vulnerable, as well as children with specific risk factors, such as child abuse, family violence, or parental substance abuse (Lincoln et al., 2008). Other research suggests that children of parents who are deployed may be at greater risk for domestic violence, drinking and other substance abuse problems (Acion et al., 2013; Sayers et al., 2009).

However, specific strategies designed to work with families who are undergoing stress due to deployment are showing some promise. These techniques include education, communication skills, helping families to recognize stress triggers, teaching emotional regulation skills, and parenting classes (Beardslee et al., 2011; Gewirtz et al., 2011; Lester et al., 2011; Murphy & Fairbank, 2013; Saltzman et al., 2011). Ahmadi and Green (2011) advocate using the screening, brief intervention, and referral to treatment model that SAMHSA recommends.

The military has shown progress in decreasing cigarette smoking and illicit drug use. Additional emphasis should be placed on understanding increases in prescription drug misuse, heavy alcohol use, PTSD, and suicide attempts, and on planning additional effective interventions and prevention programs. Challenges also remain in understanding and addressing military mental health needs (Bray et al., 2010). Coll et al. (2011) advocate for counselors, therapists, and other front-line workers to be trained in a variety of skills including anger management, substance abuse therapy, parenting skills, and stress management in order to properly assist returning soldiers and their families. As we learn more about this vulnerable population, and as technology continues to expand, we will become better equipped to serve those who have served our country.

CONCLUSION

This chapter takes a brief look at some of the most vulnerable populations served by substance abuse counselors and mental health professionals. These populations are often misunderstood, misrepresented, and improperly served by those who most want to be helpful. It is important for counselors to acquire knowledge of the best practices for helping these specialized populations. It is also important to become culturally competent in order to best help those we serve.

13

Drug Classifications

INTRODUCTION

In this chapter, we review four classifications of psychoactive drugs: central nervous system depressants, hallucinogens, central nervous system stimulants, and narcotics. In addition, we will review alcohol and some of its propensity to affect the body and the brain. The last section of this chapter will deal with treatment implications for clients who are abusing one or more of these drugs. Listed here are the Council for Accreditation of Counseling and Related Educational Programs (CACREP), Council on Social Work Education (CSWE), International Certification & Reciprocity Consortium (IC&RC), and Substance Abuse and Mental Health Services Administration (SAMHSA) standards associated with drug classification.

CHAPTER COMPETENCIES AND STANDARDS

CACREP—Standards 5, 8, 14, 22–25
CSWE—Competencies 4, 6, and 7
IC&RC—Domain II: Task 3, 6; Domain III: Task 8
SAMHSA—Competencies 3, 4, 14, 117

PRESCRIPTION DRUG MONITORING PROGRAMS

Most states have instituted prescription monitoring programs (PMP) or prescription drug monitoring programs (PDMP). According to the National Alliance for Model State Drug Laws (NAMSDL, 2008), these programs may serve several purposes such as:

1. support access to legitimate medical use of controlled substances,
2. identify and deter or prevent drug abuse and diversion,

3. facilitate and encourage the identification of, intervention with, and treatment of persons addicted to prescription drugs,
4. inform public health initiatives through outlining of use and abuse trends, and
5. educate individuals about PDMPs and the use, abuse, and diversion of and addiction to prescription drugs, (p. 1).

MAJOR DRUG CLASSIFICATIONS

Like many other aspects of the field of chemical dependency counseling, there is much disagreement about how drugs should be classified. A quick search of the Internet or any scholarly work will reveal a plethora of different opinions—all of them logical and plausible. By no means are we attempting to solve this argument. This chapter will simply utilize what we feel is a basic approach that places the most commonly abused drugs into a logical order for classification and consideration.

Non-Alcohol Central Nervous System Depressants

Certain drugs are used to slow down the action of the central nervous system (CNS), and these are sometimes referred to as either sedatives or tranquilizers. These drugs, when used medically, can have beneficial effect to treat seizure disorders, reduce anxiety and panic attacks, relieve muscle tension, and relieve pain (analgesics). These drugs include both synthetic compounds and compounds naturally occurring in nature. Natural compounds might include such drugs as valerian root, kava, and, technically, alcohol and opioids (though we will take up those in a separate section).

EFFECTS ON THE BRAIN AND BODY

Synthetically, there are a variety of CNS depressants and most work in the brain to decrease brain activity by interacting with the chemicals that deliver messages between cells. Most CNS depressants act on the brain by affecting the neurotransmitter gamma-aminobutyric acid (GABA). The two most widely used categories of CNS depressants are the barbiturates and benzodiazepines. Barbiturates include mephobarbital and pentobarbital sodium (Nembutal); these are used to treat anxiety, tension, and sleep disorders. Benzodiazepines include diazepam (Valium), chlordiazepoxide HCl (Librium), and alprazolam (Xanax), which can be prescribed to treat anxiety, acute stress reactions, and panic attacks. One possible side effect of sudden withdrawal from these drugs is seizures. Dassanayake et al. (2012) report that patients who overdose on CNS depressants are left with significant mental impairment.

POTENTIAL FOR ADDICTION

Barbiturates are extremely habit-forming (both psychologically and physically) and are potentially dangerous if a person withdraws from them without medical supervision. The CNS develops a dependence on these compounds and quickly adapts to functioning with the drugs in a person's system. Long-term usage of either barbiturates or benzodiazepines can result in increased tolerance and the need for increased dosage to achieve a therapeutic effect. Continued use can also lead to physical dependence and withdrawal when use is abruptly reduced or stopped.

DETOXIFICATION AND WITHDRAWAL

Barbiturates have the ability to be habit-forming both physically and mentally, and any client who has a long-term addiction to one of these drugs should be medically supervised before beginning withdrawal. Sudden withdrawal from a barbiturate can be life-threatening and dangerous—medical supervision is advised. The barbiturate addict shows many of the symptoms associated with chronic alcoholism, including blackouts, irrationality, slurred speech, poor motor coordination, emotional deterioration, mood swings, and psychosis. Benzodiazepines, while carrying a potential for psychological addiction, are not as physically dangerous to withdraw from, although common sense and good practice would always dictate seeking a physician's opinion.

There is another not so apparent danger in withdrawal from benzodiazepines, however. SAMHSA warns that benzodiazepines carry with them the possibility of "protracted withdrawal." Protracted withdrawal, according to SAMHSA, encompasses the signs and symptoms of acute withdrawal that persist beyond the normal time frame (SAMHSA, 2010b). For example, if normal withdrawal symptoms last between 3 days and a week, but are still present several weeks after cessation of a drug, this is protracted withdrawal. Research demonstrates that one effect of protracted withdrawal is the experiencing of anhedonia (the inability to experience pleasure from normal activities such as listening to music). Anhedonia can last for up to a year after withdrawal from the drug (Pozzi et al., 2008). And, although anhedonia occurs with benzodiazepine withdrawal, it is not confined to this particular drug but also can be a result of other drug usage (including alcohol and opioids), as we will see later.

Hallucinogens

Hallucinogenic drugs are not new. Native Americans and other cultures have utilized the psychoactive properties of various plants for thousands of years, including peyote, psilocybin mushrooms, datura, and morning glory seeds to name a few. Today, there are many synthetic drugs classified as hallucinogens. These include LSD, ketamine, PCP, STP, DET, DMT, and DPT.[1]

EFFECTS ON THE BRAIN AND BODY

Hallucinogens are generally divided into two categories: *hallucinogenics* (those that cause a person to see and hear things that are not real) and *dissociative drugs* (those drugs that cause a person to feel detached). LSD, peyote, psilocybin, and PCP are drugs that cause hallucinations, which are profound distortions in a person's perception of reality. Under the influence of hallucinogens, people see images, hear sounds, and feel sensations that seem real but are not. Some hallucinogens also produce rapid, intense emotional swings. LSD, peyote, and psilocybin cause their effects by initially disrupting the interaction of nerve cells and the neurotransmitter serotonin. The National Institute on Drug Abuse (NIDA, 2009, p. 3) reports the following effects of hallucinogens on the brain:

> *LSD:* Sensations and feelings change much more dramatically than the physical signs in people under the influence of LSD. The user may feel several different emotions at once or swing rapidly from one emotion to another. If taken in large enough doses, the drug produces delusions and visual hallucinations. The user's sense of time and self is altered. Experiences may seem to "cross over" different senses, giving the user the feeling of hearing colors and seeing sounds. These changes can be frightening and can cause panic. Some LSD users experience severe, terrifying thoughts and feelings of despair, fear of losing control, or fear of insanity and death while using LSD. Most users of LSD voluntarily decrease or stop its use over time. LSD is not considered an addictive drug since it does not produce compulsive drug-seeking behavior. However, LSD does produce tolerance, so some users who take the drug repeatedly must take progressively higher doses to achieve the state of intoxication that they had previously achieved.
>
> *Psilocybin:* The active compounds in psilocybin-containing "magic" mushrooms have LSD-like properties and produce alterations of

---

1 LSD, lysergic acid diethylamide; PCP, phencyclidine; STP, 2,5 dimethoxy-4-methylamphetamine (DOM); DET, diethyltryptamine; DMT, N, N-dimethyltryptamine; DPT, N, N-dipropyltryptamine.

autonomic function, motor reflexes, behavior, and perception. The psychological consequences of psilocybin use include hallucinations, an altered perception of time, and an inability to discern fantasy from reality. Panic reactions and psychosis also may occur, particularly if a user ingests a large dose.

PCP: The use of PCP as an approved anesthetic in humans was discontinued in 1965 because patients often became agitated, delusional, and irrational while recovering from its anesthetic effects. PCP is a "dissociative drug," meaning that it distorts perceptions of sight and sound and produces feelings of detachment (dissociation) from the environment and self. Among the adverse psychological effects reported are—

- Symptoms that mimic schizophrenia, such as delusions, hallucinations, paranoia, disordered thinking, and a sensation of distance from one's environment.
- Mood disturbances: Approximately 50 percent of individuals brought to emergency rooms because of PCP-induced problems—related to use within the past 48 hours—report significant elevations in anxiety symptoms.
- People who have abused PCP for long periods of time have reported memory loss, difficulties with speech and thinking, depression, and weight loss. These symptoms can persist up to one year after stopping PCP abuse.
- Addiction: PCP is addictive—its repeated abuse can lead to craving and compulsive PCP-seeking behavior, despite severe adverse consequences.

POTENTIAL FOR ADDICTION

Most of the time, when hallucinogens are described, the user is referring to the use of psychedelic drugs such as LSD or psilocybin (magic mushrooms). Dissociative drugs, such as ketamine, actually do have a high potential for causing addiction but these drugs are not always considered hallucinogenic. The dissociative qualities of ketamine can cause some to classify it as a hallucinogen but most people don't think of a prescription medication such as ketamine as an actual hallucinogen.

LSD is actually not considered an addictive hallucinogen as it does not cause any distinct desire or craving to use it after it has been abused. Addiction is the presence of physical or psychological dependence that develops as a result of having used a drug in repeated doses. While a user may take LSD in multiple instances, the ability of this drug to cause physical dependence or a psychological craving to continue using is typically not present. Other hallucinogens, such as PCP, however, do have the potential to be both psychologically and physically addicting.

Detoxification and Withdrawal

Because most hallucinogens do not carry with them the potential for dependency (in the traditional sense of the word), detoxification is contraindicated. There is no need to admit someone to a medical detoxification unit to withdraw from the effects of a hallucinogen (as opposed to someone who is withdrawing from long-term barbiturate use/addiction, which would necessitate medically supervised withdrawal).

Opioids (Narcotics)

We generally think of narcotics as being those drugs that have analgesic (pain-relieving) properties. These drugs have existed for millennia as opium, morphine, and, more recently, codeine and heroin. Originally, all narcotics/opioids were derived from the Asian poppy plant. Extracts of the plant were ingested, smoked, or injected intravenously to relieve pain or for their euphoric effects. Today, synthetic opioids such as fentanyl, Demerol (meperidine) Dilaudid (hydromorphone), Percocet (oxycodone), Vicodin (hydromorphone), and other drugs are available (through both prescription and the illegal market).

Effects on the Brain and Body

According to NIDA (2011a), opiates act by attaching to specific proteins called *opioid receptors*, which are found in the brain, spinal cord, gastrointestinal tract, and other organs in the body. When these drugs attach to their receptors, they reduce the perception of pain. Opioids can also produce drowsiness, mental confusion, nausea, constipation, and, depending upon the amount of drug taken, can depress respiration. Some people experience a euphoric response to opioid medications since these drugs also affect the brain regions involved in feeling pleasure.

Narcotics can have both short- and long-term effects on the body. The short-term effects include euphoria, hallucinations, mood swings, dizziness and nausea, confusion, constipation, and possible coma. Long-term effects are more serious and can include collapsed or scarred veins, infectious diseases like HIV/AIDS or hepatitis B contracted from needle sharing, infections, liver and kidney disease, and brain damage. In high doses, opioids can lead to death due to respiratory failure.

POTENTIAL FOR ADDICTION
Opioids should be considered highly addicting (both physically and psychologically). Because of their ability to block pain, produce euphoria and a general sense of well-being, and react with the brain's reward or pleasure centers, they have the potential to be addictive with only minimal use (creating a psychological dependence or feeling of "need" for the drug). In addition, these drugs' reactions with the body make them highly addictive on a physical level. Nutt et al. (2007) developed a scale to measure a drug's potential for addiction (based on a scale of 0–3, with three being the highest/most addictive). The scale was based on three potential aspects of each drug: its potential for dependence based on physical addiction, psychological addiction, and pleasure. The opioids rated the highest, with an average composite rating of 3.0.

DETOXIFICATION AND WITHDRAWAL
Withdrawal from narcotics can take from 3 to 7 days and can be extremely painful (though not life-threatening, as with barbiturates or alcohol). Acute withdrawal symptoms include headache, diarrhea, extreme body aches (mimicking having the flu), nausea, insomnia, and vomiting. Other symptoms may include a runny nose, anxiety, depression, and abdominal cramps.

In the past decade, new drugs have come on the market that help with withdrawal and are part of a treatment approach known as "harm reduction." By taking these drugs on a regular basis (under the care of a physician) an addict can have either milder withdrawal symptoms or no symptoms at all. These drugs (e.g., buprenorphine) have several trade names such as Suboxone. Suboxone's use in the management of opioid addiction and therapy is still a matter of debate among treatment professionals.

Alcohol

Technically, because of alcohol's depressant effect on the CNS, it would be classified as a CNS depressant. Because alcohol is such a widely used and abused drug, we have decided to give it a separate category. We will then discuss alcohol in terms of its characteristics, its impact on the body, its potential for both addiction, and its implications for withdrawal.

EFFECTS ON THE BRAIN AND BODY
In extremely small doses, alcohol can have a stimulating effect on the body. However, it is generally a depressant. Alcohol works progressively in the body, starting first with the emotions, then impacting (progressively) the voluntary

motor skills (speech, gait, cognitions), the semi-voluntary motor skills (e.g., blinking of the eyes), and eventually the involuntary systems (circulation, breathing, and brain function).

The human body can metabolize about 1 ounce of alcohol every hour. This is the equivalent of one drink (there is about 1 ounce of alcohol in one beer, one glass of wine, or one shot of distilled liquor). Thus, if a person has five drinks in 1 hour, it will take them (on average) about 5 hours to process (metabolize) the alcohol. The liver, the organ responsible for breaking down the alcohol in the body, can only handle 1 ounce at a time: the rest of the alcohol must be circulated throughout the body until the liver can break down another ounce of alcohol.

Research has demonstrated that low to moderate intake of alcohol can have a beneficial effect (Ronksley et al., 2011). However, the opposite is true when alcohol is consumed at higher rates, resulting in liver disease, cardiopulmonary disease, increased risk of gout, and possible links to prostate cancer (Dennis & Hayes, 2013).

POTENTIAL FOR ADDICTION

Alcohol carries with it the potential to be extremely addictive. One of the major predictors of alcoholism is a history of alcoholism in the family. A familial history of addiction is an indication that the possibility of addiction exists and means that a closer examination should be made. Earlier in the text we discussed the different theories of addiction. One of the leading theories today is the genetic theory of addiction. Current thinking is that there exist two types of alcoholics: type I and type II. Type I alcoholics tend to develop drinking patterns of binge drinking followed by periods of abstinence. Signs of addiction in type I alcoholics tend to manifest later in their drinking careers than in type II alcoholics. Type II alcoholics, conversely, tend to show signs of addiction much earlier in their drinking (usually beginning drinking during adolescence and developing signs of addiction much more quickly) (Cloninger et al., 1996).

DETOXIFICATION AND WITHDRAWAL

Like barbiturates, alcohol carries with it a potential for physical dependence and thus a risk when a person decides to discontinue use. Depending on the age of the drinker, their drinking history, use and abuse of alcohol, and past experiences with withdrawal, it is always advisable to seek medical advice before someone stops using alcohol. This becomes even more problematic for someone who has a long history of uninterrupted drinking (binge drinking) and a history of delirium tremens (DTs) when withdrawing. As a general rule of thumb, if a person has been drinking daily for more than a month, it is recommended that he or she seeks medical help before withdrawing from alcohol. Complications during detoxification can include dehydration; hallucinations; restlessness; irritability; anxiety; agitation; anorexia; nausea; vomiting; hallucinations (auditory, visual, or tactile); insomnia; intense dreaming; nightmares; grand mal seizures; increased sensitivity to sound, light, and tactile sensations; delusions, usually of paranoid or persecutory varieties; tremor; elevated heart rate; increased blood pressure; poor concentration; impaired memory and judgment; delirium/disorientation with regard to time, place, person, and situation; and fluctuation in level of consciousness (SAMHSA, 2006a).

SMOKING ALCOHOL

Smoking alcohol (the process of pouring alcohol over dry ice and inhaling it, either directly or through a straw) is beginning to gain some popularity in the United States. One of the attractions of ingesting alcohol in this way rather than drinking it is that it eliminates all of the calories, but maintains the high. One major downside is that it is difficult to keep track of how much you are consuming.

Other Drugs

The following section is a brief discussion of a host of other drugs, including those who have a long history of abuse (such as marijuana and cocaine) and those that are relatively new on the list of abused drugs (such as Krokodil). This list is not meant to be exhaustive, but more of an overview of the types of drugs currently in vogue.

MARIJUANA

Marijuana (*Cannabis sativa*) is a plant that has a long and varied history in the world. Its psychoactive properties have been known for a long time, but in the past hundred years, it has become increasingly popular in the United States. Cannabis is often consumed for its psychoactive properties of heightened mood or euphoria and relaxation. Some immediate undesired side effects include a decrease in short-term memory, dry mouth, impaired motor skills, and reddening of the eyes. Cannabis is usually consumed by smoking, though it is possible to also ingest it by mixing it with food and eating it.

About 15% of people who acknowledge moderate to heavy use reported a withdrawal syndrome with symptoms of nervousness, sleep disturbance, and appetite change. Many adults who are marijuana-dependent report affective (i.e., mood) symptoms and craving during periods of abstinence when they present for treatment. The contribution of physical dependence to chronic marijuana use is not yet clear, but the existence of a dependence syndrome is fairly certain (SAMHSA, 2005*a*). Research does suggest, however, that early-onset usage (in adolescence) is a strong predictor of continued use later in life (Patrick et al., 2011). *Hashish* (also known as hash) is a derivative of the cannabis plant. It is also smoked (and sometimes eaten) like marijuana. Hash contains the same psychoactive ingredients (tetrahydrocannabinol) as marijuana, but in a more concentrated form.

COCAINE

Cocaine is a derivative of the coca plant, native to South America. For centuries, natives where cocaine grows have chewed the leaves to give them energy and suppress the appetite, thus allowing them to withstand rigorous physical work. Powdered cocaine can be ingested either by inhaling (snorting) or by dissolving in water and injecting into the bloodstream. *Crack* (a relatively new invention that emerged during the mid-1980s) is a smokeable form of cocaine (also known as "free-basing). Prior to the invention of crack, a person would have to mix cocaine with ether in order to smoke it.

Cocaine is a strong CNS stimulant that increases levels of the neurotransmitter dopamine in brain circuits regulating pleasure and movement. Normally, dopamine is released by neurons in these circuits in response to potential rewards (like the smell of good food) and then recycled back into the cell that released it, thus shutting off the signal between neurons. Cocaine prevents the dopamine from being recycled, causing excessive amounts to build up in the synapse, or junction between neurons. This amplifies the dopamine signal and ultimately disrupts normal brain communication. It is this flood of dopamine that causes cocaine's characteristic high.

Cocaine affects the body in a variety of ways. It constricts blood vessels, dilates pupils, and increases body temperature, heart rate, and blood pressure. It can also cause headaches and gastrointestinal complications such as abdominal pain and nausea. Because cocaine tends to decrease appetite, chronic users can become malnourished as well. Most seriously, people who use cocaine can suffer heart attacks or strokes, which may cause sudden death. Cocaine-related deaths are often a result of the heart stopping (cardiac arrest) followed by an arrest of breathing (NIDA, 2013).

KROKODIL

Krokodil (desomorphine) is a derivative of morphine but anywhere from seven to ten times more powerful. Desomorphine, like methamphetamine, is relatively easy to produce and in cases where other opioids are not available, many addicts have turned to Krokodil as a substitute. In the United States, at this writing, Krokodil is still a relatively unknown drug, but it is gaining popularity in Russia and other European countries (Sikharulidze,

2014). One of the most insidious properties of this drug is the fact that it has the potential to kill flesh at an alarming rate (leaving bone exposed). This property is thought to be a by-product of the iodine and other products required to produce it.

Bath Salts

Bath salts is a term used to describe several different designer drugs sold under such trade names as Cloud Nine, Purple Wave, and Zoom. They are sold as "bath salts" to circumvent federal drug regulations that prohibit the sale of unregulated psychoactive substances. Bath salts can be snorted, swallowed, smoked, or injected. Little is known about their interaction or long-term effects on the brain. Users report a high similar to that from amphetamines with their stimulant effects. The potential for overdosing and accidental poisoning from these drugs is considered very high.

Spice

Spice refers to a wide variety of drugs that are considered to be alternative, "legal" forms of marijuana. Sold under many names, including K2, fake weed, Yucatan Fire, Skunk, Moon Rocks, and others—and labeled "not for human consumption"—these products contain dried, shredded plant material and chemical additives that are responsible for their psychoactive (mind-altering) effects. Spice users report experiences similar to those produced by marijuana—elevated mood, relaxation, and altered perception—and in some cases the effects are even stronger than those of marijuana. Some users report psychotic effects like extreme anxiety, paranoia, and hallucinations (NIDA, 2012; Rosenbaum et al., 2012).

CONCLUSION

This chapter reviews some of the most popular drugs that are currently abused. This chapter examines the drug itself, its effects on the body, and the potential for addiction (including the implications for detoxification and withdrawal). The chapter surveyed categories of drugs such as the CNS depressants, stimulants, and hallucinogens. Also included are popular drugs of abuse such as alcohol, marijuana, cocaine, and some of the new and emerging drugs (like Krokodil). The next chapter will review other forms of addiction such as eating disorders and gambling.

14

Emerging Fields of Addiction

INTRODUCTION

In this chapter, we examine the three most common, non-substance, co-occurring disorders that substance abuse counselors will encounter; gambling, sex addiction, and eating disorders. We will examine each of these independently, including their signs and symptoms, scales for assessment, and approaches to treatment. Listed here are the Council for Accreditation of Counseling and Related Educational Programs (CACREP), Council on Social Work Education (CSWE), International Certification & Reciprocity Consortium (IC&RC), and Substance Abuse and Mental Health Services Administration (SAMHSA) standards associated with individual counseling.

CHAPTER COMPETENCIES AND STANDARDS

CACREP—Standards 3, 15, 20, 23, 25
CSWE—Competencies 2, 4, 7–9
IC&RC—Domain I: Tasks 3–7
SAMHSA—Competencies 1, 118

GAMBLING ADDICTION

Gambling is a controversial topic and not all professionals agree that compulsive gambling is an "addiction," especially as it relates to the disease model of drug abuse (Peele, 2001). However, compulsive gambling has the ability to alter mood by creating a high that leads to the desire to gamble more, much like drug seeking. Gambling addiction (also known as *ludomania*) is a compulsion to gamble in spite of negative consequences or one's desire to stop. The DSM 5 reclassified Gambling Disorder from a disorder of impulse control to a behavioral addiction. While gambling does not require the ingestion of a substance in order to alter mood and behavior, it presents with many of the same symptoms as drugs of abuse (Bowden-Jones & George, 2011).

Signs and Symptoms of Compulsive Gambling

Gambling can be a serious problem if a person is exhibiting the following symptoms:

- *Preoccupation*: The person spends much of his or her time thinking about gambling (either past gambling experiences, present activities around gambling, or future/fantasy thoughts about gambling).
- *Tolerance*: The gambler requires larger wagers or more frequent wagers to satisfy his or her desire to gamble or to receive the initial high or rush from the gambling experience.
- *Withdrawal*: The individual experiences feelings of irritability, anxiety, or nervousness after a period of not being able to gamble.
- *Escape*: The person uses gambling as a means of altering mood or to escape unwanted feelings.
- *Chasing*: The individual continues to gamble to make up for losses.
- *Lying*: The person uses deception and lies to hide the frequency and amount of his or her gambling.
- *Loss of control*: The person tries (unsuccessfully) to curtail his or her gambling activity, or the person attempts to limit gambling activity to only certain days or times of the week.
- *Illegal activities*: The person has either engaged in illegal activities to gain money to cover gambling losses or to acquire money to gamble.
- *Trouble with family and friends*: The person continues to gamble despite objections of family and friends.
- *Trouble with employers*: The person's gambling activities interfere with employment (missing work, calling in sick, etc.).

It is important for substance abuse counselors to recognize that gambling often present as a co-occurring disorder (coinciding with another addiction like substance abuse) but it can also be an addiction without any substance abuse or other disorders.

Standardized Scales for Assessing Compulsive Gambling

There are many diagnostic and screening instruments available (for a fee) on the Internet and market today. However, none is as simple and easy to administer as the Lie/Bet screening tool (Johnson et al., 1988). This two-item scale simply asks the individual whether or not he or she has ever felt the need to bet increasing amounts of money, and, a second question, if he or she has ever lied to family or people important to them about their gambling. A positive answer to one or both questions suggests a need for further screening/diagnosis. Other brief screening tools include the National Council on Problem Gambling's (NCOG) Brief Biosocial Gambling Screen (BBGS) and Gambler's Anonymous—Twenty Questions.

Of course, screening tools are useful for initial indication and identification of a problem, but for more definitive results, more sophisticated measures are required. Lesieur and Blume (1992) modified the Addictions Severity Index for use with gamblers and have developed the Gambler's Severity Index (GSI). The *Diagnostic and Statistical Manual of Mental Disorders* fifth edition (DSM-5) categorizes gambling disorder as a behavioral addiction (much like substance abuse) because of the similarities in brain function, physiology, behavioral patterns, and comorbidity (American Psychiatric Association, 2013).

Support Groups for Compulsive Gamblers

Like other addictions such as alcoholism or addiction to cocaine or narcotics, there exists a 12-step support group for compulsive gamblers: Gambler's Anonymous (GA). GA is based on the same principles of Alcoholics Anonymous (AA) and other support groups: that addicts can help each other gain sobriety and overcome their addiction through adherence to the 12 steps. Whereas the first step of AA is "Admitted we were powerless over alcohol and that our lives had become unmanageable" (Alcoholics Anonymous, 2001, p. 59), GA substitutes the words "powerless over alcohol" for "powerless over gambling." All the other steps are almost identical. Box 14.1 lists the 12 steps of GA.

Box 14.1

12 STEPS OF GAMBLER'S ANONYMOUS

1. We admitted we were powerless over gambling—that our lives had become unmanageable.
2. Came to believe that a Power greater than ourselves could restore us to a normal way of thinking and living.
3. Made a decision to turn our will and our lives over to the care of this Power of our own understanding.
4. Made a searching and fearless moral and financial inventory of ourselves.
5. Admitted to ourselves and to another human being the exact nature of our wrongs.
6. Were entirely ready to have these defects of character removed.
7. Humbly asked God (of our understanding) to remove our shortcomings.
8. Made a list of all persons we had harmed and became willing to make amends to them all.
9. Make direct amends to such people wherever possible, except when to do so would injure them or others.
10. Continued to take personal inventory and when we were wrong, promptly admitted it.
11. Sought through prayer and meditation to improve our conscious contact with God as we understood Him, praying only for knowledge of His will for us and the power to carry that out.
12. Having made an effort to practice these principles in all our affairs, we tried to carry this message to other compulsive gamblers.

Other support groups also exist for gamblers. For example, DailyStrength.org is a free, online group that helps with a number of behavioral addictions (including gambling). Recovery World (recovery-world.com) is another online support group that has chat rooms for a variety of addictions (including gambling).

COMPULSIVE SEXUAL BEHAVIOR

Compulsive sexual behavior or sex addiction is a term used to describe people who report being unable to control their sexual urges, behaviors, or thoughts.

Other terms and other models for sexual addiction or aspects of it include hypersexuality, erotomania, nymphomania, and satyriasis. Whether sexual addiction should be included in the DSM is a subject of debate and controversy among therapists, psychologists, sociologists, and other professionals. Proponents of a sexual addiction model draw parallels between it and substance abuse addiction and gambling. One of the chief proponents of the idea that sex addiction exists is Dr. Patrick Carnes. Carnes is an early pioneer in this field, and, as a leading authority, he has written extensively on the subject. Dr. Carnes has many achievements, including designing the United States' first in-patient treatment facility for sexual addiction—the Golden Valley Treatment Facility in Golden Valley, Minnesota (Carnes, 2014).

Signs and Symptoms of Compulsive Sexual Behavior

Compulsive sexual behavior may consist of generally acceptable sexual acts taken to an extreme (e.g., compulsive masturbation). These behaviors become problems when they become an obsession that is disruptive or harmful to the individual. Other compulsive sexual behaviors are outside the bounds of commonly accepted conduct. Known as *paraphilia's*, these behaviors range from compulsive cross-dressing to having sexual desires toward children (pedophilia). Some of the symptoms that sexual behavior may have reached a point of being problematic include:

- Sexual impulses are intense and feel as if they're beyond the person's control.
- A person may feel compelled to engage in certain sexual behaviors, regardless of whether they find the activity enjoyable.
- The sexual behavior becomes an escape from other problems, such as loneliness, depression, anxiety, or stress.
- The individual continues to engage in sexual behavior despite serious consequences, such as the potential for getting or giving someone else a sexually transmitted disease, the loss of important relationships, trouble at work, or legal problems.
- A person has difficulty establishing and maintaining emotional closeness, even if married or in a committed relationship. (Fong, 2006)

Again, we draw your attention to the degree that these symptoms and range of behaviors mimic those of substance abuse addiction (e.g., the feeling of loss of control, the willingness to engage in behaviors that the person knows will have negative consequences, the inability to maintain personal relationships).

Standardized Scales for Assessing Compulsive Sexual Behavior

Before we delve into the issue of various scales available for assessment of hypersexuality, we need to make clear that there is a lack of consensus among treatment professionals as to what, exactly, is meant by terms such as *sexual addiction, hypersexuality*, and other compulsive sexual behaviors. Because of this lack of agreement, research on these behaviors is difficult. With that said, there are several scales available to screen for and measure sexual addiction. Below is a sample of screening scales identified by (Hook et al., 2010):

- Sexual Addiction Scale of the Disorders Screening Inventory
- Compulsive Sexual Behavior Inventory
- Sexual Dependency Inventory-Revised
- Perceived Sexual Control Scale
- Garos Sexual Behavior Index
- Sexual Compulsivity Scale
- Sex Addicts Anonymous Questionnaire
- Sexual Symptom Assessment Scale
- Sexual Addiction Screening Test
- Sexual Addiction Screening Test–Gay Men
- Internet Sex Screening Test
- Sexual Outlet Inventory
- Diagnostic Interview for Sexual Compulsivity
- Yale-Brown Obsessive Compulsive Scale–Compulsive Sexual Behavior
- Cognitive and Behavioral Outcomes of Sexual Behavior Scale
- Compulsive Sexual Behavior Consequences Scale

These scales are divided into three categories: objective sexual addiction symptoms, subjective sexual addiction symptoms, and consequences of sexual addiction. The Sexual Outlet Inventory, the Diagnostic Interview for Sexual Compulsivity, and the Yale-Brown Obsessive Compulsive Scale–Compulsive Sexual Behavior Scale should be considered tools for clinicians. Thus, they are appropriate for a diagnosis, but may require more extensive training for their use and interpretation.

Twelve-Step Groups for Sexual Addiction

As with substance abuse and gambling, there are several support groups available for those who self-identify as being a "sexual compulsive" and want to seek help. One of the best known of these groups is Sex Addicts Anonymous (SAA).

SAA, like other 12-step programs, utilizes the 12 steps and 12 traditions. The first step is "We admitted we were powerless over addictive sexual behavior—that our lives had become unmanageable" (Sex Addicts Anonymous, 2004, p. 20). Box 14.2 includes the entire 12 steps of SA.

Other 12-step programs include Sexaholics Anonymous (SA). SA was the first of the 12-step groups for sex addicts. It grew out of the AA tradition and was founded by a member of AA who was in recovery from alcohol and other drugs but was cheating on his wife. SA places strong emphasis on refraining from any sexual activity outside of marriage (including masturbation). Sexual Compulsives Anonymous (SCA) was begun by gay men who wanted a safe place

---

Box 14.2

SEX ADDICTS ANONYMOUS: 12 STEPS
(Sex Addicts Anonymous, 2004, pp. 20–21).

1. We admitted were powerless over addictive sexual behavior—that our lives had become unmanageable.
2. Came to believe that a power greater than ourselves could restore us to sanity.
3. Made a decision to turn our will and our lives over to the care of God as we understood God.
4. Made a searching and fearless moral inventory of ourselves.
5. Admitted to God, to ourselves and to another human being the exact nature of our wrongs.
6. Were entirely ready to have God remove all of these defect from our character.
7. Humbly asked God to remove our shortcomings.
8. Made a list of all persons we had harmed and became willing to make amends to them all.
9. Make direct amends to such people wherever possible, except when to do so would injure them or others.
10. Continued to take personal inventory and when we were wrong, promptly admitted it.
11. Sought through prayer and meditation to improve our conscious contact with God as we understood Him, praying only for knowledge of His will for us and the power to carry that out.
12. Having made an effort to practice these principles in all our affairs, we tried to carry this message to other sex addicts and to practice these principles in our lives. (Sex Addicts Anonymous, 2004, pp. 20–21)

---

to recover from their compulsive sexual behavior. Sexual Recovery Anonymous (SRA) is an off-shoot of SA—the founding members of SRA reacted to SA's strong stance that sex should only occur in marriage. Members of SRA believe that sex should be confined to a "committed relationship" (Gilkerson, 2009).

EATING DISORDERS

Eating disorders are difficult to recognize in the early stages and are complex to treat once diagnosed. For instance, if a person is abusing alcohol or other drugs, they can stop using the drug. However, with compulsive eating disorders not eating is not an option. While a popular misconception is that eating disorders are problems that plague women, the truth is both males and females can have eating disorders. For our discussion, we will simply define an eating disorder as any abnormal eating that is detrimental to one's body or health. We begin by examining some of the signs and symptoms of eating disorders.

Types and Symptoms of Eating Disorders

One of the most dangerous of the eating disorders is known as anorexia nervosa (commonly called *anorexia*). Anorexia is the skipping of meals or voluntarily refusing food. Anorexia is commonly characterized by weight loss due to refusal to eat, excessive exercise, or the compulsive use of laxatives. Anorexia is essentially a perception problem: people who are anorexic view themselves as overweight, regardless of how thin they become.

A second common disorder is bulimia nervosa (binging and then purging afterward). One indicator of people who purge (make themselves throw up) is a quick trip to the bathroom after a meal. You may also hear the sound of vomiting if a person is forcing themselves to throw up. Other means of purging include the use of laxatives. People who suffer from bulimia tend to have feelings of remorse about loss of control over how much they have eaten.

A third common disorder is compulsive (binge) eating. Here, the person consumes large amounts of calories (to the point of being sick). They, too, feel a loss of control over their eating. The difference between bulimia nervosa and bulimia is the lack of purging after eating.

It can be difficult to recognize eating disorders, but some common symptoms are the wearing of baggy clothes (to hide extreme changes in either weight gain, or weight loss); preoccupation with food (counting bites of food, or refusing to eat), extreme exercise, and denial that excessive exercise and eating behaviors or loss of weight/thinness is a problem.

Standardized Scales for Assessing Eating Disorders

Assessing eating disorders can be difficult, especially if the client is trying to hide the disorder. Anderson et al. (2004) recommend that practitioners pay attention to: body weight, binge eating and compensatory behavior, over-concern with body weight and shape, dietary restraint, body image disturbance, and affective disturbance. There are several assessment scales available, including the Eating Assessment Test (EAT, Garner et al., 1983), the Dutch Eating Behavior Questionnaire (DEBQ, Van Strien et al., 1986), the SCOFF Questionnaire (Morgan et al., 1999), the Emotional Eating Scale (Arnow et al., 1995), and a self-rating scale for bulimia, the BITE (Henderson & Freeman, 1987). The named scales here are simply a sampling of the various scales on the market.

Support Groups for Eating Disorders

As with other addiction, people who are dealing with an eating disorder may have available to them 12-step groups that they can turn to for support. These include Eating Disorders Anonymous and Overeaters' Anonymous (OA). Box 14.3 presents the 12 steps of Overeaters Anonymous in their entirety. Notice the similarity to other 12-step programs. One other group that we include here is the National Association of Anorexia Nervosa and Associated Eating Disorders (ANAD).

Box 14.3

THE TWELVE STEPS OF OVEREATERS ANONYMOUS

1. We admitted we were powerless over food—that our lives had become unmanageable.
2. Came to believe that a Power greater than ourselves could restore us to sanity.
3. Made a decision to turn our will and our lives over to the care of God *as we understood Him.*
4. Made a searching and fearless moral inventory of ourselves.
5. Admitted to God, to ourselves and to another human being the exact nature of our wrongs.
6. Were entirely ready to have God remove all these defects of character.
7. Humbly asked Him to remove our shortcomings.

8. Made a list of all persons we had harmed and became willing to make amends to them all.
9. Made direct amends to such people wherever possible, except when to do so would injure them or others.
10. Continued to take personal inventory and when we were wrong, promptly admitted it.
11. Sought through prayer and meditation to improve our conscious contact with God *as we understood Him*, praying only for knowledge of His will for us and the power to carry that out.
12. Having had a spiritual awakening as the result of these Steps, we tried to carry this message to compulsive overeaters and to practice these principles in all our affairs.

CONCLUSION

This chapter examined three non-substance-related addictions; gambling, sex and eating. These may co-occur with other addictions (e.g., a person may have a primary addiction of substance abuse and a secondary addiction to gambling), or they may be a stand-alone addiction. As clients begin to recover and make changes in their lives, it is not uncommon for the symptoms of secondary addictions to begin to manifest themselves.

15

Certification as a Substance Abuse Counselor

INTRODUCTION

In this last chapter of the text, we discuss seeking certification as a substance abuse counselor. The chapter also covers why it is important to be certified, the benefits of joining the International Certification & Reciprocity Consortium, transferring certification from state to state, and certification versus licensure. Listed here are the Council for Accreditation of Counseling and Related Educational Programs (CACREP), Council on Social Work Education (CSWE), International Certification & Reciprocity Consortium (IC&RC), and Substance Abuse and Mental Health Services Administration (SAMHSA) standards associated with certification.

CHAPTER COMPETENCIES AND STANDARDS

CACREP—Standards 4, 6, 9, 12, 20–23
CSWE—Competencies 6 and 7
IC&RC—Domain I: Tasks 1–6
SAMHSA—Competencies 24–26, 28, 33, 75–76, 111

BENEFITS OF CERTIFICATION

You may be wondering to yourself, "Why should I spend the time and energy that it takes to become certified (or licensed)?" This is an excellent question and well worth asking yourself—especially considering the time and energy that is required to reach this level of education and/or training.

The short answer to this is, "It depends on your career goals." If you want to work with people who are affected by addictions (addicts or their families), then it is important that you can certify to the public that you are a trained professional. In days past, someone with a desire to work in addictions only needed to open an office and they could conduct business as an addiction specialist. Today, consumers hold treatment professionals to a high standard. They expect someone in the field of addictions counseling to have the knowledge, skills, values, and training suitable to their needs. Being certified is one way to demonstrate at least a minimum level of skill and proficiency in the field. By being credentialed you are able to make a statement to the public that you have met a minimum set of standards required for practice as verified by an independent evaluator. Also, certification is now required by all 50 states in order to practice as a substance abuse counselor. This requirement helps ensures public safety (do no harm) and professional integrity (accreditation/credentialing).

You should know that there are a variety of levels to be a certified alcohol and drug counselor. The levels range from allowing you to practice with less than a bachelor's degree all the way up to requiring a master's degree. Various states have different requirements (and levels of certification): we encourage you to check with your state credentialing board to determine the levels open to you. In addition to being certified at your state level, you may wish to seek national certification. There are several national certifications available, and we will discuss some of the most widely recognized ones.

INTERNATIONAL CERTIFICATION AND RECIPROCITY CONSORTIUM

The IC&RC is a worldwide network that was originally organized in 1981. The consortium began as an idea in the late 1970s. Several Midwestern states discussed the possibility of an interstate agreement that would allow certified substance abuse counselors to transfer their certifications between states. Over time, the idea grew and eventually became known as the National Certification and Reciprocity Consortium (NCRC) in 1989. As foreign countries began to express interest and to join the growing consortium, the name changed again in 1992, to become the International Certification & Reciprocity Consortium (IC&RC).

The profession of alcohol and drug abuse counseling has grown, changed, and become more specialized over the decades since the inception of the IC&RC. To meet the changing needs of the profession, the board has developed several specializations. These include Alcohol and Drug Counselor (1981), Clinical Supervisor (1992), Prevention Specialist (1994), Advanced Alcohol and Drug Counselor (1999), Criminal Justice Addictions Professional (2002), Co-Occurring Disorders Professional/Diplomate (2007), and Peer Recovery (2012).

One of the benefits of being certified by the IC&RC is the ability to transfer certification between participating states without having to be recertified. This makes your certification very portable and affords substance abuse counselors more freedom in changing jobs across state lines. One caveat to this is the difference between certification and licensure. As you browse the IC&RC's website and those of its participating states (and foreign countries), you may notice that some states issue a certification and other states a license. Texas, for example, issues its substance abuse counselor a license, while Kentucky has a certification and a license option. The difference is that those states with a licensure requirement prosecute ethical violations through their Attorney General's Office while those states with a certification requirement leave practice violations to be dealt with through the various certification boards.

COUNCIL ON SOCIAL WORK EDUCATION AND SOCIAL WORK LICENSING

The Council on Social Work Education (CSWE) is the accrediting body for undergraduate and graduate social work programs. Most state social work licensing boards require applicants to have graduated from a social work program that is accredited or under candidacy for accreditation by CSWE, however, this may vary from state to state. This ensures that applicants have met the competencies and associated practice behaviors required for social work practice. In addition, states with CSWE license requirements are eligible to accept licensing/certification reciprocity from other states with similar requirements. Baccalaureate social work students (BSW) are trained in generalist practice and many states have a license or certification at that level (e.g. LBSW; LSW). Master's social worker (MSW) graduates can have two or more levels of licensure. The first licensure level is available upon graduation with an MSW (e.g. LMSW). A clinical license usually requires two or more years of post-masters clinical practice under a board-approved clinical supervisor. Most boards require the supervisee to have the first-level MSW license and a supervisor contact and/or plan to ensure the supervision meets practice experience and hour requirements (for work and for supervision). Once these are met, the social worker is eligible to apply for the Licensed Clinical Social Worker (LCSW). These license levels require passing the associated test offered the Association of Social Work Boards (ASWB). The MSW is the "terminal degree" for social work, meaning that a doctorate (Ph.D. or D.S.W.) is not needed for clinical practice.

COUNCIL FOR ACCREDITATION OF COUNSELING AND RELATED EDUCATION PROGRAMS AND LICENSING FOR COUNSELORS

The CACREP is an accrediting body much like the CSWE. The council accredits colleges and universities master's and doctoral degree programs to assure that they meet a minimum level of educational and practice standards in their counseling program. Many states require a master's or doctoral degree from a CACREP-accredited institution in order to sit for licensure as a counselor in that state. State licenses vary, such as; Licensed Professional Counselor (LPC), Licensed Clinical Professional Counselor (LCPC), and Licensed Mental Health Counselor (LMHC), Licensure requires a masters-degreed mental health service provider and passage of the National Counselor Examination (NCE). Like with social workers, counselors must meet a minimum of supervised clinical experience hours and have two years to complete these hours. In addition, three federal agencies (Tri-Care, Veterans Administration, and Army Substance Abuse) require CACREP certification in order to practice with them (CACREP, 2009).

OTHER LICENSURES AND CERTIFICATIONS

Certainly IC&RC and CACREP are not the only national certifications available to the substance abuse counselor. Others include the National Association for Addiction Professionals (NAADAC) and the National Board for Certified Counselors (NBCC). Of course, for social workers, the National Association of Social Workers (NASW) is the long-standing and well-recognized organization that provides advocacy, information, and other benefits to its members. Another to consider is the American Society of Addiction Medicine (ASAM; a certification board for physicians who specialize in addiction). Although this organization is geared toward physicians, they do have an "Associate" status that allows a person to join and receive the benefits afforded to full membership. In addition, your state may have individual associations and credentialing organizations that are worth exploring.

RELATED WEBSITES

Here are the websites to contact the various certification boards and credentialing agencies just discussed:

International Credentialing and Reciprocity Consortium (IC&RC): www.
internationalcredentialing.org

The Council for Accreditation of Counseling and Educated Related Programs
(CACREP): http://www.cacrep.org/

The National Association for Addiction Professionals: http://www.naadac.
org/

The National Board for Certified Counselors: http://nbcc.org/

The National Association of Social Workers: http://socialworkers.org/

The American Society of Addiction Medicine: http://www.asam.org/

CONCLUSION

In today's world, credentials and expertise are almost synonymous. In order
to practice as a substance abuse counselor anywhere in the United States, a
person needs to be certified. In addition, gaining recognition on the national
level (through one of the many national organizations) lends more credence
to the professional's stature as a trained and well-qualified practitioner. This
chapter discusses just a few of the many organizations available to the substance
abuse counselor.

REFERENCES

Acion, L., Ramirez, M., Jorge, R., & Arndt, S. (2013). Increased risk of alcohol and drug use among children from deployed military families. *Addiction, 108*(8), 1418–1425.

Ahmadi, H., & Green, S. (2011). Screening, brief intervention, and referral to treatment for military spouses experiencing alcohol and substance use disorders: A literature review. *Journal of Clinical Psychology in Medical Settings, 18*(2), 129–136.

Akers, R., Krohn, M., Lanza-Kaduce, L., & Radosevich, M. (1979). Social learning and deviant behavior: A specific test of a general theory. *American Sociological Review, 44*(4), 636–655.

Alcoholics Anonymous. (2001). *Alcoholics Anonymous: The Story of How Many Thousands of Men and Women Have Recovered from Alcoholism* (4th edition). New York: Alcoholics Anonymous World Services.

Alcoholics Anonymous. (2012). *Twelve Steps and Twelve Traditions* (7th ed.). New York: A. A. World Services.

American Association of Community Psychiatrists (AACP). (2009). LOCUS: Level of care utilization system for psychiatric and addiction services (Adult Version, 2010). Retrieved from http://providersearch.mhnet.com/Portals/0/LOCUS.pdf.

American Psychiatric Association. (2013). *Diagnostic and Statistical Manual of Mental Disorders, Fifth edition*. Arlington, VA: American Psychiatric Association.

American Society of Addiction Medicine (ASAM). (2012). ASAM patient placement criteria (overview and revision). Retrieved from https://www.asam.org/docs/publications/asam_ppc_oversight_may_2011.

Anderson, D., Lundgren, J., Shapiro, J., & Paulosky, C. (2004). Assessment of eating disorders: Review and recommendations for clinical use. *Behavior Modification, 28*(6), 763–780. doi:10.1177/0145445503259851

Anthony, W (1993). Recovery From Mental Illness: The Guiding Vision of the Mental Health Service System in the 1990s. *Psychosocial Rehabilitation Journal, 16*(4), 11–23.

Arndt, S., Clayton, R., & Schultz, S. (2011). Trends in substance abuse treatment 1998–2008: Increasing older adult first-time admissions for illicit drugs. *The American Journal of Geriatric Psychiatry, 19*(8), 704–711.

Arnow, B., Kenardy, J., & Agras, W. (1995). The Emotional Eating Scale: The development of a measure to assess coping with negative affect by eating. *International Journal of Eating Disorders, 18*(1), 79–90.

Babor, T., & Grant, M. (1989). From clinical research to secondary prevention: International collaboration in the development of the Alcohol Use Disorders Identification Test (AUDIT). *Alcohol Health & Research World, 13*(3), 371–374.

Babor, T., Hofmann, M., DelBoca, F., Hesselbrock, V., Meyer, R., Dolinsky, Z., & Rounsaville, B. (1992). Types of alcoholics, I: Evidence for an empirically derived typology based on indicators of vulnerability and severity. *Archives of General Psychiatry, 49*(8), 599–608.

Bahr, S., Masters, A., & Taylor, B. (2012). What works in substance abuse treatment programs for offenders? *The Prison Journal, 92*(2), 251–271, doi:0032885512438836

Baillargeon, J., Penn, J., Knight, K., Harzke, A., Baillargeon, G., & Becker, E. (2010). Risk of reincarceration among prisoners with co-occurring severe mental illness and substance use disorders. *Administration and Policy in Mental Health and Mental Health Services Research, 37*(4), 367–374.

Baldwin, S., Christian, S., Berkeljon, A., & Shadish, W. (2012). The effects of family therapies for adolescent delinquency and substance abuse: A meta-analysis. *Journal of Marital and Family Therapy, 38*(1), 281–304.

Bandura, A. (1971). *Social Learning Theory: A Monograph.* New York: General Learning Press.

Bandura, A., Ross, D., & Ross, S. A. (1961). Transmission of aggression through imitation of aggressive models. *Journal of Abnormal and Social Psychology, 63*(3), 575.

Bartels, S., & Naslund, J. (2013). The underside of the silver tsunami—Older adults and mental health care. *New England Journal of Medicine, 368*(6), 493–496.

Bateson, G., Jackson, D., Haley, J., & Weakland, J. (1956). Toward a theory of schizophrenia. *Behavioral Science, 1*(4), 251–264.

Beardslee, W., Lester, P., Klosinski, L., Saltzman, W., Woodward, K., Nash, W., & Leskin, G. (2011). Family-centered preventive intervention for military families: Implications for implementation science. *Prevention Science, 12*(4), 339–348.

Beavers, W., Hampson, R., & Hulgus, Y. (1985). Commentary: The Beavers systems approach to family assessment. *Family Process, 24*(3), 398–405.

Bennett, G., Withers, J., Thomas, P., Higgins, D., Bailey, J., Parry, L., & Davies, E. (2005). A randomized trial of early warning signs relapse prevention training in the treatment of alcohol dependence. *Addictive Behaviors, 30*(6), 1111–1124.

Bernstein, E., Heeren, T., Winter, M., Ashong, D., Bliss, C., Madico, G., & Bernstein, J. (2012). Long-term follow-up after voluntary human immunodeficiency virus/ sexually transmitted infection counseling, point-of-service testing, and referral to substance abuse treatment from the emergency department. *Academic Emergency Medicine, 19*(4), 386–395.

Bini, E., Kritz, S., Brown, L., Jr., Robinson, J., Alderson, D., & Rotrosen, J. (2011). Barriers to providing health services for HIV/AIDS, hepatitis C virus infection and sexually transmitted infections in substance abuse treatment programs in the United States. *Journal of Addictive Diseases, 30*(2), 98–109.

Blank, K. (2009). Older adults and substance abuse: New data highlights concerns. *SAMHSA News, 17*(1), 1. http://www.samhsa.gov/SAMHSAnewsLetter/Volume_17_Number_1/OlderAdults.aspx

Bowden-Jones, H., & George, S. (2011). Gambling addiction. *British Medical Journal, 343.* doi:https://doi.org/10.1136/bmj.d7789

Bowen, M. (1974). Alcoholism as viewed through family systems theory and family psychotherapy. *Annals of the New York Academy of Sciences, 233*(1), 115–122.

Brannigan, R., Schackman, B., Falco, M., & Millman, R. (2004). The quality of highly regarded adolescent substance abuse treatment programs: Results of an in-depth national survey. *Archives of Pediatrics & Adolescent Medicine, 158*(9), 904–909.

Bray, R., Pemberton, M., Lane, M., Hourani, L., Mattiko, M., & Babeu, L. (2010). Substance use and mental health trends among US military active duty personnel: Key findings from the 2008 DOD Health Behavior Survey. *Military Medicine, 175*(6), 390–399.

Breunlin, D., Pinsof, W., & Russell, W. (2011). integrative problem-centered metaframeworks therapy I: Core concepts and hypothesizing. *Family Process, 50*(3), 293–313.

Brown, R. L., & Rounds, L. A. (1995). Conjoint screening questionnaires for alcohol and other drug abuse: Criterion validity in a primary care practice. *Wisconsin Medical Journal, 94*(3), 135–140.

Burke, C. (2010). Mindfulness-based approaches with children and adolescents: A preliminary review of current research in an emergent field. *Journal of Child and Family Studies, 19*(2), 133–144.

Budman, S., Soldz, S., Demby, A., Feldstein, M., Springer, T., & Davis, M. (1989). Cohesion, alliance and outcome in group psychotherapy. *Psychiatry, 52*(3), 339–350.

Burlingame, G., McClendon, D., & Alonso, J. (2011). Cohesion in group therapy. *Psychotherapy, 48*(1), 34–42. doi:10.1037/a0022063.

Burrow-Sanchez, J., Martinez, C., Jr., Hops, H., & Wrona, M. (2011). Cultural accommodation of substance abuse treatment for Latino adolescents *Journal of Ethnicity in Substance Abuse, 10*(3), 202–225.

Carnes, P. (2014). Patrick Carnes biography. Pine Grove Behavioral Health and Addictive Services. Retrieved from http://www.pinegrovetreatment.com/patrick-carnes.html

Centers for Disease Control and Prevention. (2011). Gay and bisexual men's health: Stigma and discrimination. Retrieved from http://www.cdc.gov/msmhealth/stigma-and-discrimination.htm

Center for Substance Abuse Treatment. (2006). Addiciton counseling competencies: The knowledge, skills, and attitudes of professional practice. Technical Assistance Publication (TAP) Series 21. HHS Publication No. (SMA) 14-4171. Rockville, MD: Substance Abuse and Mental Health Services Administration.

Council on Social Work Education. (2015). *Educational policies and accreditation standards for baccalaureate and naster's social work programs.* Retrieved from https://www.cswe.org/getattachment/Accreditation/Accreditation-Process/2015-EPAS/2015EPAS_Web_FINAL.pdf.aspx.

Chadwick, J., Andrade, L., Altice, F., & Petry, N. (2014). Correlates of having never been HIV tested among entrants to substance abuse treatment clinics: Empiric findings from real-world New England settings. *Journal of Psychoactive Drugs, 46*(3), 208–214.

Chan, Y., Dennis, M., & Funk, R. (2008). Prevalence and comorbidity of major internalizing and externalizing problems among adolescents and adults presenting to substance abuse treatment. *Journal of Substance Abuse Treatment, 34*(1), 14–24.

Chan, Y., Passetti, L., Garner, B., Lloyd, J., & Dennis, M. (2011). HIV risk behaviors: Risky sexual activities and needle use among adolescents in substance abuse treatment. *AIDS and Behavior, 15*(1), 114–124.

Cheung, M. (1997). Social construction theory and the Satir Model: Toward a synthesis. *American Journal of Family Therapy, 25*(4), 331–343.

Clarke, P., & Myers, J. (2012). Developmental counseling and therapy: A promising intervention for preventing relapse with substance-abusing clients. *Journal of Mental Health Counseling, 34*(4), 308–321.

Cloninger, C., Sigvardsson, S., & Bohman, M. (1996). Type I and type II alcoholism: An update. *Alcohol Health and Research World, 20*(1), 18–23.

Cohoon, B. (2011). Substance abuse and military families. *National Military Family Association,* Retreived from www.nationalacademies.org/hmd/~/media/60D7FD1 F25E340999718654FAFD61426.ashx

Colapinto, J. (1991). Structural family therapy. *Handbook of Family Therapy, 2,* 417–443.

Coll, J., Weiss, E., & Yarvis, J. (2011). No one leaves unchanged: insights for civilian mental health care professionals into the military experience and culture. *Social Work in Health Care, 50*(7), 487–500.

Code of Federal Regulation, Title 42, Part 2, (2017). *Confidentiality of Substance Use Disorder Patient Records,* Retrieved from https://www.gpo.gov/fdsys/pkg/CFR-2017-title42-vol1/xml/CFR-2017-title42-vol1-part2.xml#seqnum2.31

Cottrell, D., & Boston, P. (2002). Practitioner review: The effectiveness of systemic family therapy for children and adolescents. *Journal of Child Psychology and Psychiatry, 43*(5), 573–586.

Council for Accreditation of Counseling and Related Educational Programs. (2009). CACREP standards. Retrieved from http://www.cacrep.org/

Cranford, J., Nolen-Hoeksema, S., & Zucker, R. (2011). Alcohol involvement as a function of co-occurring alcohol use disorders and major depressive episode: Evidence from the national epidemiologic survey on alcohol and related conditions. *Drug and Alcohol Dependence, 117*(2), 145–151.

Dassanayake, T., Michie, P., Jones, A., Carter, G., Mallard, T., & Whyte, I. (2012). Cognitive impairment in patients clinically recovered from central nervous system depressant drug overdose. *Journal of Clinical Psychopharmacology, 32*(4), 503–510.

Dass-Brailsford, P., & Myrick, A. (2010). Psychological trauma and substance abuse: The need for an integrated approach. *Trauma, Violence, & Abuse, 11*(4), 202–213.

Deegan, P. (1996). Recovery as a journey of the heart. *Psychiatric Rehabilitation Journal, 19*(3), 91–97.

DeLorenze, G., Weisner, C., Tsai, A., Satre, D., & Quesenberry, C., Jr. (2011). Excess mortality among HIV-infected patients diagnosed with substance use dependence or abuse receiving care in a fully integrated medical care program. *Alcoholism: Clinical and Experimental Research, 35*(2), 203–210.

Dennis, L., & Hayes, R. (2013). Alcohol and prostate cancer.*Epidemiologic Reviews, 23*(1), 110–4.

Dewane, C. (2006). Use of self: A primer revisited. *Clinical Social Work Journal, 34*(4), 543–558. doi:10.1007/s10615-005-0021-5

Dodge, K., Krantz, B., Kenny, P., & Suciu, G. (2013). Substance abuse treatment modalities and outcomes in a naturalistic setting. *Addictive Disorders & Their Treatment, 12*(2), 76–90.

Donovan, D., Daley, D., Brigham, G., Hodgkins, C., Perl, H., Garrett, S., & Zammarelli, L. (2013). Stimulant abuser groups to engage in 12-Step: A multisite trial in the National Institute on Drug Abuse Clinical Trials Network. *Journal of Substance Abuse Treatment, 44*(1), 103–114.

Drake, R., Essock, S., Shaner, A., Carey, K., Minkoff, K., Kola, L., Lynde, D., Osher, F., Clark, R., Rickards, L. (2001). Implementing dual diagnosis services for clients with severe mental illness. *Psychiatric Services, 52*(4), 469–476.

Duppong Hurley, K., Lambert, M., Van Ryzin, M., Sullivan, J., & Stevens, A. (2013). Therapeutic alliance between youth and staff in residential group care: Psychometrics of the therapeutic alliance quality scale. *Children and Youth Services Review, 35*(1), 56–64.

Edwards, M., & Steinglass, P. (1995). Family therapy treatment outcomes for alcoholism. *Journal of Marital and Family Therapy, 21*(4), 475–509.

Ellis, A. (1995). Changing rational-emotive therapy (RET) to rational emotive behavior therapy (REBT). *Journal of Rational-Emotive & Cognitive-Behavior Therapy, 13*(2), 85–89.

Epstein, N., Baldwin, L., & Bishop, D. (1983). The McMaster family assessment device. *Journal of Marital and Family Therapy, 9*(2), 171–180.

Epstein, N., & Bishop, D. (1981). Problem centered systems therapy of the family. *Journal of Marital and Family Therapy, 7*(1), 23–31.

Falloon, I. R. H. (1991). Behavioral family therapy. In A. S. Gurman & D. P. Kniskern (Eds.), *Handbook of Family Therapy* (Vol. 2, pp. 65–95). Philadelphia, PA: Brunner/Mazel.

Faulkner, S. (2001). *Ropes course as an intervention: The impact on family cohesion and self-esteem for adolescents in therapeutic foster care and their foster families* (doctoral thesis). Retrieved from ProQuest Dissertations and Theses. (Order No. 3019517, The University of Texas at Arlington)

Faulkner, S., Faulkner, C., & Geurin, L. (2015). Substance abuse in rural Appalachia: Responding to community needs. *International journal of education and social science, 2*(8). Retrieved from www.ijessnet.com

Faulkner, S., & Faulkner, C. (2018). *Research Methods for Social Workers: A Practice-based Approach* (3rd ed.). New York, NY: Oxford University Press.

Fong, T. (2006). Understanding and managing compulsive sexual behaviors. *Psychiatry, 3*(11), 51–58.

Framo, J. (1976). Family of origin as a therapeutic resource for adults in marital and family therapy: You can and should go home again. *Family Process, 15*(2), 193–210.

Freud, A. (1937). *The Ego and the Mechanisms of Defence*. London: Hogarth Press and Institute of Psycho-Analysis. (Revised edition: 1966 (US), 1968 (UK))

Friedland, G. (2010). Infectious disease comorbidities adversely affecting substance users with HIV: Hepatitis C and tuberculosis. *Journal of Acquired Immune Deficiency Syndromes, 55*, S37–S42.

Friedlander, M., Escudero, V., Heatherington, L., & Diamond, G. (2011). Alliance in couple and family therapy. *Psychotherapy, 48*(1), 25.

Gamblers Anonymous. (2014). 12 steps for compulsive gamblers. Retrieved from http://www.gamblersanonymous.org/ga/content/recovery-program

Gardner, E., McLees, M., Steiner, J., del Rio, C., & Burman, W. (2011). The spectrum of engagement in HIV care and its relevance to test-and-treat strategies for prevention of HIV infection. *Clinical Infectious Diseases, 52*(6), 793–800.

Garner, D., Olmstead, M., & Polivy, J. (1983). Development and validation of a multidimensional eating disorder inventory for anorexia nervosa and bulimia. *International Journal of Eating Disorders, 2*(2), 15–34.

Gates, G. (2011). How many people are lesbian, gay, bisexual and transgender? *The Williams Institute;* University of California, Los Angeles. Retrieved from https://williamsinstitute.law.ucla.edu/wp-content/uploads/Gates-How-Many-People-LGBT-Apr-2011.pdf.

Gewirtz, A., Erbes, C., Polusny, M., Forgatch, M., & DeGarmo, D. (2011). Helping military families through the deployment process: Strategies to support parenting. *Professional Psychology: Research and Practice, 42*(1), 56.

Gilkerson, L. (2009). 12 step porn and addiction recovery groups – what are the differences? Defeat Lust and Pornography, personal blog. Retrieved from http://www.covenanteyes.com/2009/07/06/12-step-sex-addiction-recovery-groups-what-are-the-differences/

Ginter, W. (2012). Methadone anonymous and mutual support for medication-assisted recovery. *Journal of Groups in Addiction & Recovery, 7*(2-4), 189–201.

Gorski, T. (1990). The Cenaps model of relapse prevention: Basic principles and procedures. *Journal of Psychoactive Drugs, 22*(2), 125–133.

Gorski, T., & Miller, M. (1982). *Counseling for Relapse Prevention.* Independence MO: Herald House-Independent Press.

Gorski, T., & Miller, M. (1982). *Counseling for Relapse Prevention.* Independence, MO: Herald House/Independence Press.

Gorski, T. T. (2007). The GORSKI-CANAPS model: A comprehensive overview. Retrieved from https://terrygorski.com/2013/12/31/the-gorski-cenaps-model-a-comprehensive-overview/

Guerrero, E., Campos, M., Urada, D., & Yang, J. (2012). Do cultural and linguistic competence matter in Latinos' completion of mandated substance abuse treatment?. *Substance Abuse Treatment, Prevention, and Policy, 7*(1), 34.

Guerrero, E., & Cederbaum, J. (2011). Adoption and utilization of sexually transmitted infections testing in outpatient substance abuse treatment facilities serving high risk populations in the US. *International Journal of Drug Policy, 22*(1), 41–48.

Haas, A., Eliason, M., Mays, V., Mathy, R., Cochran, S., D'Augelli, A., & Clayton, P. (2010). Suicide and suicide risk in lesbian, gay, bisexual, and transgender populations: Review and recommendations. *Journal of Homosexuality, 58*(1), 10–51.

Hasin, D., Goodwin, R., Stinson, F., & Grant. B. (2005). Epidemiology of major depressive disorder: Results from the national epidemiological survey on alcoholism and related conditions. *Archives of General Psychiatry, 62*(10), 1097–1106.

Hawkins, J., & Catalano, R. (1985). Aftercare in drug abuse treatment. *International Journal of Addiction. 2*(6–7), 917–945.

Health IT.gov (n.d.). What is EHR interoperability and why is it important? Retrieved from https://www.healthit.gov/providers-professionals/faqs/what-ehr-interoperability-and-why-it-important

Henderson, M., & Freeman, C. (1987). A self-rating scale for bulimia. The 'BITE'. *The British Journal of Psychiatry, 150*(1), 18–24.

Hester, M., Williamson, E., Regan, L., Coulter, M., Chantler, K., Gangoli, G., & Green, L. (2012). *Exploring the service and support needs of male, lesbian, gay, bi-sexual and transgendered and black and other minority ethnic victims of domestic and sexual violence.* Report prepared for the Home Office. Bristol, UK: University of Bristol.

Hoagwood, K., Cavaleri, M., Olin, S., Burns, B., Slaton, E., Gruttadaro, D., & Hughes, R. (2010). Family support in children's mental health: A review and synthesis. *Clinical Child and Family Psychology Review, 13*(1), 1–45.

Hook, J., Hook, J., Davis, D., Worthington, E., & Penberthy, J. (2010). Measuring sexual addiction and compulsivity: A critical review of instruments. *Journal of Sex and Marital Therapy, 36*, 227–260. doi:10.1080/00926231003719673

Jellinek, E. M. (1960). *The Disease Concept of Alcoholism.* New Haven, CT: Hillhouse.

Johnson, E., Hammer, R., Nora, R., Tan, B., Eistenstein, N., & Englehart, C. (1988). The lie/bet questionnaire for screening pathological gamblers. *Psychological Reports, 80*, 83–88.

Johnson, P., Persad, G., & Sisti, D. (2014). The *Tarasoff* rule: The implications of inter-state variation and gaps in professional training. *Journal of the American Academy of Psychiatry Law, 42*(4), 469–477. Retrieved from http://www.jaapl.org/content/42/4/469.long

Joiner, T. E., Van Orden, K. A., Witte, T. K., & Rudd, M. D. (2009). *The Interpersonal Theory of Suicide: Guidance for Working with Suicidal Clients.* Washington, DC: American Psychological Association.

Kelly, J., Dow, S., Yeterian, J., & Kahler, C. (2010). Can 12-step group participation strengthen and extend the benefits of adolescent addiction treatment? A prospective analysis. *Drug and Alcohol Dependence, 110*(1), 117–125.

Kendler, K., Sundquist, K., Ohlsson, H., Palmér, K., Maes, H., Winkleby, M., & Sundquist, J. (2012). Genetic and familial environmental influences on the risk for drug abuse: A national Swedish adoption study. *Archives of General Psychiatry, 69*(7), 690–697.

Kreek, M., Levran, O., Reed, B., Schlussman, S., Zhou, Y., & Butelman, E. (2012). Opiate addiction and cocaine addiction: Underlying molecular neurobiology and genetics. *The Journal of Clinical Investigation, 122*(10), 3387–3393.

Lambert, M., & Barley, D. (2001). Research summary on the therapeutic relationship and psychotherapy outcome. *Psychotherapy: Theory, Research, Practice, Training, 38*(4), 357–361.

Lang, F., Floyd, M., & Beine, K. (2000). Clues to patients' explanations and concerns about their illnesses: A call for active listening. *Archives of Family Medicine, 9*(3), 222.

Lesieur, H., & Blume, S. (1992). Modifying the Addiction Severity Index for use with pathological gamblers. *The American Journal on Addictions, 1*(3), 240–247.

Lester, P., Mogil, C., Saltzman, W., Woodward, K., Nash, W., Leskin, G., & Beardslee, W. (2011). Families overcoming under stress: Implementing family-centered prevention for military families facing wartime deployments and combat operational stress. *Military Medicine, 176*(1), 19–25.

Liddle, H. A. (2009). Multidimensional family therapy: A science-based treatment system for adolescent drug and behavior problems. In J. Bray & M. Stanton (Eds.), *Blackwell Handbook of Family Psychology*. London: Blackwell.

Lin, J., Karno, M., Grella, C., Warda, U., Liao, D., Hu, P., & Moore, A. (2011). Alcohol, tobacco, and nonmedical drug use disorders in US adults aged 65 years and older: Data from the 2001–2002 National Epidemiologic Survey of Alcohol and Related Conditions. *The American Journal of Geriatric Psychiatry, 19*(3), 292–299.

Lincoln, A., Swift, E., & Shorteno-Fraser, M. (2008). Psychological adjustment and treatment of children and families with parents deployed in military combat. *Journal of Clinical Psychology, 64*(8), 984–992.

Lynch, S., DeHart, D., Belknap, J., Green, B., Dass-Brailsford, P., Johnson, K., & Whalley, E. (2014). A multisite study of the prevalence of serious mental illness, PTSD, and substance use disorders of women in jail. *Psychiatric Services, 65*(5), 670–674.

MacKinnon, L., & Miller, D. (1987). The new epistemology and the Milan approach: Feminist and sociopolitical considerations. *Journal of Marital and Family Therapy, 13*(2), 139–155.

Mat, F. (1994). Addressing the needs of cultural minorities in drug treatment. *Journal of Substance Abuse Treatment, 11*(4), 325–337.

Matheson, F., Doherty, S., & Grant, B. (2011). Community-based aftercare and return to custody in a national sample of substance-abusing women offenders. *American Journal of Public Health, 101*(6), 1126–1142.

Mayfield, D., McLeod, G., & Hall, P. (1974). The CAGE questionnaire: Validation of a new alcoholism screening instrument. *American Journal of Psychiatry, 131*(10), 1121–1123.

McCarty, D., Braude, L., Lyman, D., Dougherty, R., Daniels, A., Ghose, S., & Delphin-Rittmon, M. (2014). Substance abuse intensive outpatient programs: Assessing the evidence. *Psychiatric Services 65*(6), 717–726.

McClure, E., Acquavita, S., Harding, E., & Stitzer, M. (2013). Utilization of communication technology by patients enrolled in substance abuse treatment. *Drug and Alcohol Dependence, 129*(1), 145–150.

McLellan, A. T., Luborsky, L., Woody, G. E., & O'Brien, C. P. (1980). An improved diagnostic evaluation instrument for substance abuse patients: The Addiction Severity Index. *The Journal of Nervous and Mental Disease, 168*, 26–33.

McLeod, J. (2001). Developing a research tradition consistent with the practices and values of counselling and psychotherapy: Why counselling and psychotherapy research is necessary. *Counselling and Psychotherapy Research, 1*(1), 3–11.

McLeod, M., Goch, A., & Nowicki, S. (1986). Systemic family therapy. *Individual Psychology: Journal of Adlerian Theory, Research & Practice, 42*(4), 493–505.

Mericle, A., Ta Park, V., Holck, P., & Arria, A. (2012). Prevalence, patterns, and correlates of co-occurring substance use and mental disorders in the United States: variations by race/ethnicity. *Comprehensive Psychiatry, 53*(6), 657–665.

Messina, N., Grella, C., Cartier, J., & Torres, S. (2010). A randomized experimental study of gender-responsive substance abuse treatment for women in prison. *Journal of Substance Abuse Treatment, 38*(2), 97–107.

Mihalic, S., & Elliott, D. (1997). A social learning theory model of marital violence. *Journal of Family Violence, 12*(1), 21–47.

Milam, J. R., & Ketcham, K. (1984). *Under the Influence: A Guide to the Myths and Realities of Alcoholism.* New York: Random House.

Miller, G. A. (1985). *The Substance Abuse Subtle Screening Inventory (SASSI) Manual.* Springville, IN: SASSI Institute.

Miller, W. R., & Harris, R. J. (2000). A simple scale of Gorski's warning signs for relapse. *Journal of Studies on Alcohol, 61*(5), 759–765.

Minuchin, S. (1974). *Families and Family Therapy.* Cambridge, MA: Harvard University Press.

Minuchin, P. (1985). Families and individual development: Provocations from the field of family therapy. *Child Development, 56*(2), 289–302.

Morgan, J., Reid, F., & Lacey, J. (1999). The SCOFF questionnaire: Assessment of a new screening tool for eating disorders. *British Medical Journal, 319*(7223), 1467–1468.

Murphy, R., & Fairbank, J. (2013). Implementation and dissemination of military informed and evidence-based interventions for community dwelling military families. *Clinical Child and Family Psychology Review, 16*(4), 348–364.

Mustanski, B., Garofalo, R., & Emerson, E. (2010). Mental health disorders, psychological distress, and suicidality in a diverse sample of lesbian, gay, bisexual, and transgender youths. *American Journal of Public Health, 100*(12), 2426–2432.

National Alliance for Model State Drug Laws (NAMSDL). (2008). Prescription drug monitoring programs: A brief overview. Retrieved from http://www.namsdl.org/library/1BB774E2-1C23-D4F9-74387E4A023E5ED6/

National Alliance on Mental Illness. (2014). Dual diagnosis: Adolescents with co-occurring brain disorders and substance abuse disorders. Retrieved from http://www.nami.org/Content/ContentGroups/Illnesses/Dual_Diagnosis_Fact_Sheet.htm

National Association of Social Workers. (2008). *The Code of Ethics.* Washington, DC: NASW.

National Council of Social Service. (2007). *Documentation and Record Keeping: A Guide for Service Providers.* Singapore: Author.

National Institute of Alcohol Abuse and Alcoholism (NIAAA). (2005). Alcohol alert: Screening for alcohol use and alcohol related problems, Alert 65, National Institute of Health, National Institute of Alcohol Abuse and Alcoholism. Retrieved from http://pubs.niaaa.nih.gov/publications/aa65/AA65.pdf

National Institute on Drug Abuse. (2009). Hallucinogens: LSD, peyote, psilocybin and PCP. NIDA Info Facts, 1–7. Retrieved from https://www.drugabuse.gov/sites/default/files/hallucinogens09.pdf.

National Institute on Drug Abuse. (2011a). The science of drug abuse and addiction: How do opioids effect the brain and body? Research Report Series. Retrieved from http://www.drugabuse.gov/publications/research-reports/prescription-drugs/opioids/how-do-opioids-affect-brain-body

National Institute on Drug Abuse. (2011b). Topics in brief: Substance abuse among the military, veterans, and their families. Retrieved from http://www.drugabuse.gov/publications/topics-in-brief/substance-abuse-among-military-veterans-their-families

National Institute on Drug Abuse. (2012*a*). Drug facts: Spice. Retrieved from http://www.drugabuse.gov/publications/drugfacts/spice-synthetic-marijuana

National Institute on Drug Abuse. (2012*b*). Principles of drug addiction treatment: A research-based guide (3rd ed.). National Institute of Health, USA.Gov Retrieved from http://www.drugabuse.gov/publications/principles-drug-addiction-treatment-research-based-guide-third-edition/frequently-asked-questions/what-are-unique-needs-women-substance-use

National Institute on Drug Abuse. (2013). Drug facts: Cocaine. Retrieved from http://www.drugabuse.gov/publications/drugfacts/cocaine

Norcross, J., & Wampold, B. (2011). Evidence-based therapy relationships: Research conclusions and clinical practices. *Psychotherapy, 48*(1), 98.

Nutt, D., King, L., Saulsbury, W., & Blakemore, C. (2007). Development of a rational scale to assess the harm of drugs of potential misuse. *Lancet, 369*(9566), 1047–53.

O'Connor, E., Gaynes, B., Burda, B. U., Williams, C., & Whitlock, E. P. (2013). *Screening for Suicide Risk in Primary Care: A Systematic Evidence Review for the US Preventive Services Task Force.* Evidence Synthesis No. 103. AHRQ Publication No. 13-05188-EF-1. Rockville, MD: Agency for Healthcare Research and Quality.

Olson, D. (2011). FACES IV and the circumplex model: Validation study. *Journal of Marital and Family Therapy, 37*(1), 64–80.

Ouimette, P., Moos, R., & Finney, J. (1998). Influence of outpatient treatment and 12-step group involvement on one-year substance abuse treatment outcomes. *Journal of Studies on Alcohol, 59*(5), 513–522.

Overeaters Anonymous, Inc. (2018). The twelve steps of overeaters anonymous. Retrieved from http://www.oa.org/newcomers/twelve-steps/

Patrick, M., Schulenberg, J., O'malley, P., Johnston, L., & Bachman, J. (2011). Adolescents' reported reasons for alcohol and marijuana use as predictors of substance use and problems in adulthood. *Journal of Studies on Alcohol and Drugs, 72*(1), 106.

Patterson, G. R., Reid, R. B., Jones, R. R., & Conger, R. E. (1975). *A Social Learning Approach to Family Intervention: Vol. 1. Families with Aggressive Children.* Eugene, OR: Castalia.

Peele, S. (2001). Is gambling an addiction like drug and alcohol addiction? Developing realistic and useful conceptions of compulsive gambling. *Journal of Gambling Issues* (3). doi:10.4309/jgi.2001.3.2

Pinsof, W., Breunlin, D., Russell, W., & Lebow, J. (2011). Integrative problem-centered metaframeworks therapy II: Planning, conversing, and reading feedback. *Family Process, 50*(3), 314–336.

Ponzo, Z. (1976). Integrating techniques from five counseling theories. *The Personnel and Guidance Journal, 54*(8), 415–419.

Posner, K., Brown, G. K., Stanley, B., Brent, D. A., Yershova, K. V., Oquendo, M. A., . . . Mann, J. J. (2011). The Columbia-Suicide Severity Rating Scale: Initial validity and internal consistency findings from three multisite studies with adolescents and adults. *American Journal of Psychiatry, 168*(12):1266–1277. doi:10.1176/appi.ajp.2011.10111704

Pozzi, G., Martinotti, G., Reina, D., Dario, T., Frustaci, A., & Janiri, L. (2008). The assessment of post-detoxification anhedonia: Influence of clinical and psychosocial variables. *Substance Use & Misuse, 43*(5), 722–732.

Prendergast, M., Messina, N., Hall, E., & Warda, U. (2011). The relative effectiveness of women-only and mixed-gender treatment for substance-abusing women. *Journal of Substance Abuse Treatment, 40*(4), 336–348.

Prochaska, J. O., DiClemente, C. C., & Norcross, J. C. (1992). In search of how people change. Applications to addictive behaviors. *American Psychology, 47*(9), 1102–1114.

Redden, S., Tracy, S., & Shafer, M. (2013). A metaphor analysis of recovering substance abusers' sensemaking of medication-assisted treatment. *Qualitative Health Research, 23*(7), 951–962.

Reed, M., Evely, A., Cundill, G., Fazey, I., Glass, J., Laing, A., & Stringer, L. (2010). What is social learning? *Ecology and Society, 15*(4): r1. [online] URL: http://www.ecologyandsociety.org/vol15/iss4/resp1/

Rogers, C. (1957). The necessary and sufficient conditions of therapeutic personality change. *Journal of Consulting Psychology, 21*(2), 95.

Rogers, C., & Farson, R. (1957). *Active Listening [excerpts].* University of Chicago Industrial Relations Center, Chicago. Retrieved from http://www.gordontraining.com/free-workplace-articles/active-listening/.

Rollnick, S., & Miller, W. (1995). What is motivational interviewing? *Behavioural and Cognitive Psychotherapy, 23*(04), 325–334.

Ronksley, P., Brien, S., Turner, B., Mukamal, K., & Ghali, W. (2011). Association of alcohol consumption with selected cardiovascular disease outcomes: A systematic review and meta-analysis. *British Medical Journal, 342*:d671 doi:10.1136/bmj.d671. Retrieved from https://www.bmj.com/content/bmj/342/bmj.d671.full.pdf

Rosenbaum, C., Carreiro, S., & Babu, K. (2012). Here today, gone tomorrow and back again? A review of herbal marijuana alternaives (K2, Spice), synthetic cathinones (bath salts), kratom, Salvia divinorum, methoxetamine, and piperazines. *Journal of Medical Toxicology, 8*(1), 15–32.

Rubak, S., Sandbæk, A., Lauritzen, T., & Christensen, B. (2005). Motivational interviewing: A systematic review and meta-analysis. *British Journal of General Practice, 55*(513), 305–312.

Saltzman, W., Lester, P., Beardslee, W., Layne, C., Woodward, K., & Nash, W. (2011). Mechanisms of risk and resilience in military families: Theoretical and empirical basis of a family focused resilience enhancement program. *Clinical Child and Family Psychology Review, 14*(3), 213–230.

Sayers, S., Farrow, V., Ross, J., & Oslin, D. (2009). Family problems among recently returned military veterans referred for a mental health evaluation. *Journal of Clinical Psychiatry, 70*(2), 163.

Schonfeld, L., King-Kallimanis, B., Duchene, D., Etheridge, R., Herrera, J., Barry, K., & Lynn, N. (2010). Screening and brief intervention for substance misuse among older adults: The Florida BRITE project. *American Journal of Public Health, 100*(1), 108.

Screening for Mental Health, Inc. (SMH) and Suicide Prevention Resource Center (SPRC) (2009). *Suicide Assessment Five-Step Evaluation and Triage (SAFE-T).* Retrieved from https://www.sprc.org/resources-programs/suicide-assessment-five-step-evaluation-and-triage-safe-t-pocket-card.

Selvini-Palazzoli, M., Boscolo, L., Cecchin, G., & Prata, G. (1978). *Paradox and Counterparadox: A New Model in the Therapy of the family in Schizophrenic Transaction.* New York: Jason Aronson.

Selzer, M. L. (1971). The Michigan Alcohol Screening Test (MAST): The quest for a new diagnostic instrument. *American Journal of Psychiatry, 127*(12), 1653–1658.

Sheedy, C. K., &Whitter, M. (2009). *Guiding Principles and elements of Recovery-Oriented Systems Of Care: What Do We Know from the Research?* HHS Publication No. (SMA) 09-4439. Rockville, MD: Center for Substance Abuse Treatment, Substance Abuse and Mental Health Services Administration.

Shorey, R., Anderson, S., & Stuart, G. (2013). The relation between antisocial and borderline personality symptoms and early maladaptive schemas in a treatment seeking sample of male substance users. *Clinical Psychology & Psychotherapy, 21*(4), 341–351.

Sikharulidze, Z., Kapanadze, N., Otiashvili, D., Poole, S., & Woody, G. (2014). Desomorphine (crocodile) injection among in-treatment drug users in Tbilisi, Georgia. *Drug and Alcohol Dependence, 140*, 208.

Skinner, H. (1982). The drug abuse screening test. *Addictive Behavior, 7*(4), 363–371.

Skinner, H., Holt, H., Schuller, R., Roy, J., Israel, Y. (1884). Identification of alcohol abuse using laboratory tests and a history of trauma. *Annual of internal medicine, 101*(6), 847–851. doi:10.7326/0003-4819-101-6-847

Skinner, H., Steinhauer, P., & Santa-Barbara, J. (1983). The family assessment measure. *Canadian Journal of Community Mental Health, 2*(2), 91–103.

Sluzki, C. (1983). Process, structure and world views: Toward an integrated view of systemic models in family therapy. *Family Process, 22*(4), 469–476.

Smelson, D., Kalman, D., Losonczy, M., Kline, A., Sambamoorthi, U., Hill, L., & Ziedonis, D. (2012). A brief treatment engagement intervention for individuals with co-occurring mental illness and substance use disorders: Results of a randomized clinical trial. *Community Mental Health Journal, 48*(2), 127–132.

Stanley, B., & Brown, G. K. (2008). *Safety Plan Treatment Manual to Reduce Suicide Risk: Veteran Version.* Washington, DC: US Department of Veterans Affairs.

Stockton, R., Rohde, R., & Haughey, J. (1992). The Effects of Structured Group Exercises on Cohesion, Engagement, Avoidance, and Conflict. *Small Group Research, 23*(2), 155–168. doi:10.1177/1046496492232001.

Suarez, L., Belcher, H., Briggs, E., & Titus, J. (2012). Supporting the need for an integrated system of care for youth with co-occurring traumatic stress and substance abuse problems. *American Journal of Community Psychology, 49*(3-4), 430–440.

Substance Abuse and Mental Health Services Administration (SAMHSA). (1993). TIP 6: Screening for infectious diseases among substance abusers. Retrieved from http://www.ncbi.nlm.nih.gov/books/NBK64730/A25580

Substance Abuse and Mental Health Services Administration. (1998). Substance abuse among older adults, Treatment Improvement Protocol (TIP) Series, TIP 26 (HHS Publication No. SMA 12-3918). Rockville, MD: Author.

Substance Abuse and Mental Health Services Administration (SAMHSA). (1999). TIP 32: Treatment of adolescents with substance use disorders. Retrieved from http://store.samhsa.gov/product/TIP-32-Treatment-of-Adolescents-With-Substance-Use-Disorders/SMA12-4080

Substance Abuse and Mental Health Services Administration (SAMHSA). (2001). A provider's introduction to substance abuse treatment for lesbian, gay, bisexual, and transgender individuals. Retrieved from http://store.samhsa.gov/product/

A-Provider-s-Introduction-to-Substance-Abuse-Treatment-for-Lesbian-Gay-Bisexual-and-Transgender-Individuals/SMA12-4104

Substance Abuse and Mental Health Services Administration. (SAMHSA). (2004). TIP 39: Substance abuse treatment and family therapy. Retrieved from http://www.ncbi.nlm.nih.gov/books/NBK64265/pdf/TOC.pdf

Substance Abuse and Mental Health Services Administration (SAMHSA). (2005*a*). Brief counseling for marijuana dependence: A manual for treating adults. Retrieved from http://store.samhsa.gov/product/Brief-Counseling-for-Marijuana-Dependence-A-Manual-for-Treating-Adults/SMA12-4211

Substance Abuse and Mental Health Services Administration. (SAMHSA). (2005*b*). TIP 41: Substance abuse treatment: Group therapy. Retrieved from http://www.ncbi.nlm.nih.gov/books/NBK64220/

Substance Abuse and Mental Health Services Administration (SAMHSA). (2006*a*). Detoxification and substance abuse treatment: Quick guide for clinicians based on TIP 45. Retrieved from http://store.samhsa.gov/product/Detoxification-and-Substance-Abuse-Treatment/SMA06-4225

Substance Abuse and Mental Health Services Administration (SAMHSA). (2006*b*). TAP 19: Relapse prevention with chemically dependent criminal offenders, counselor's manual. Retrieved from http://store.samhsa.gov/product/TAP-19-Relapse-Prevention-with-Chemically-Dependent-Criminal-Offenders-Counselor-s-Manual/SMA06-4217

Substance Abuse and Mental Health Services Administration (SAMHSA). (2006*c*). TIP 46: Substance abuse: Administrative issues in outpatient treatment. Retrieved from http://www.ncbi.nlm.nih.gov/books/NBK64076/

Substance Abuse and Mental Health Services Administration (SAMHSA). (2007). The epidemiology of co-occurring substance use and mental disorders: Overview paper 8. Retrieved from http://store.samhsa.gov/product/The-Epidemiology-of-Co-Occurring-Substance-Use-and-Mental-Disorders/SMA07-4308

Substance Abuse and Mental Health Services Administration (SAMHSA). (2008*a*). An introduction to mutual support groups for alcohol and drug abuse. *Substance Abuse in Brief, 5*(1). Retrieved from http://store.samhsa.gov/product/An-Introduction-to-Mutual-Support-Groups-for-Alcohol-and-Drug-Abuse/SMA08-4336

Substance Abuse and Mental Health Services Administration (SAMHSA). (2008*b*). TAP 21: Addiction counseling competencies: The knowledge, skills and attitudes of professional practice. Retrieved from https://store.samhsa.gov/shin/content//SMA12-4171/SMA12-4171.pdf

Substance Abuse and Mental Health Services Administration (SAMHSA). (2008*c*). TIP 35: Enhancing motivation for change in substance abuse treatment. Retrieved from http://store.samhsa.gov/product/TIP-35-Enhancing-Motivation-for-Change-in-Substance-Abuse-Treatment/SMA13-4212

Substance Abuse and Mental Health Services Administration (SAMHSA). (2009*a*). TIP 31: Screening and assessing adolescents for substance abuse disorders. Retrieved from http://store.samhsa.gov/product/TIP-31-Screening-and-Assessing-Adolescents-for-Substance-Use-Disorders/SMA12-4079

Substance Abuse and Mental Health Services Administration (SAMHSA). (2009*b*). TIP 51: Substance abuse treatment: Addressing the specific needs of women. Retrieved from http://www.ncbi.nlm.nih.gov/books/NBK83256/tip51.ch1.s4

Substance Abuse and Mental Health Services Administration (SAMHSA). (2010*a*). SAMHSA's working definition of recovery. Retrieved from https://www.samhsa.gov/ recovery

Substance Abuse and Mental Health Services Administration (SAMHSA). (2010*b*). Substance abuse treatment news for the treatment field advisory: Protracted withdrawal, *9*(1), 1–8. Retrieved from http://store.samhsa.gov/shin/content//SMA10-4554/SMA10-4554.pdf

Substance Abuse and Mental Health Services Administration (SAMHSA). (2010*c*). Substance abuse treatment for persons with co-occurring disorders: Quick guide for mental health professionals based on TIP 42. Retrieved from http://store.samhsa. gov/product/Substance-Abuse-Treatment-for-Persons-With-Co-Occurring-Disorders/SMA10-4531

Substance Abuse and Mental Health Services Administration (SAMHSA). (2011). TIP 53: Addressing viral hepatitis in people with substance abuse disorders. Retrieved from http://www.ncbi.nlm.nih.gov/books/NBK92036/

Substance Abuse and Mental Health Services Administration (SAMHSA). (2012). Behavioral health issues among Afghanistan and Iraq US war veterans, *7*(1). Retrieved from http://store.samhsa.gov/shin/content//SMA12-4670/SMA12-4670.pdf

Substance Abuse and Mental Health Services Administration (SAMHSA). (2013). TAP 33: Screening, brief intervention and referral to treatment. Retrieved from http:// store.samhsa.gov/shin/content//SMA13-4741/TAP33.pdf

Substance Abuse and Mental Health Services Administration (SAMHSA). (2014). TIP 33: Improving Cultural Competence. Treatment Improvement Protocol. Retrieved from https://store.samhsa.gov/shin/content/SMA14-4849/SMA14-4849.pdf.

Tanner-Smith, E., Wilson, S., & Lipsey, M. (2013). The comparative effectiveness of outpatient treatment for adolescent substance abuse: A meta-analysis. *Journal of Substance Abuse Treatment, 44*(2), 145–158.

The International Service Organization International of SAA (2010). *The twelve steps of sex addict's anonymous.* In Group guide: Handbook for SAA groups, 7th ed., p 19. Retrieved from https://saa-recovery.org/wp-content/uploads/2016/07/SAA_ Group_Guide.pdf.

The White House, Office of the Press Secretary, (Nov 17, 2010). Executive Order: *Fundamental Principles and Policymaking Criteria for Partnerships with Faith-Based and Other Neighborhood Organizations.* Retrieved from https:// www.whitehouse.gov/the-press-office/2010/11/17/executive-order-fundamental-principles-and-policymaking-criteria-partner).

Tomlinson, K. L., & Brown, S. A. (2012). Self-medication or social learning? A comparison of models to predict early adolescent drinking. *Addictive Behaviors, 37*(2), 179–186.

Tuchman, E. (2010). Women and addiction: The importance of gender issues in substance abuse research. *Journal of Addictive Diseases, 29*(2), 127–138.

Tuckman, B. (1965). Developmental Sequence in Small Groups. *Psychological Bulletin, 63*(6), 384–499.

Tuckman, B., & Jensen, M. (1977). Stages of small-group development revisited. *Group and Organizational Studies 2*(4), 419–427.

United States. (2004). *The Health Insurance Portability and Accountability Act (HIPAA)*. Washington, DC: US Dept. of Labor, Employee Benefits Security Administration.

US Department of Health and Human Services. (1994). Women and drug abuse. *Department of Health and Human Services, Public Health Service,National Institutes of Health, National Institute on Drug Abuse*. NIH Publication No. 94-3732, 1994. http://archives.drugabuse.gov/WomenDrugs/Women-DrugAbuse3.html

US Department of Health and Human Services. (2012, September). *2012 National Strategy for Suicide Prevention: Goals and Objectives for Action*. Washington, DC: HHS. Retrieved from http://www.surgeongeneral.gov/library/reports/national-strategy-suicide-prevention/full_report-rev.pdf

US Department of Health and Human Services. (2015). *Connecting Health and Care for the Nation: A 10-Year Vision to Achieve an Interoperable Health IT Infrastructure*. Retrieved from http://www.healthit.gov/sites/default/files/ONC10yearInteroperabilityConceptPaper.pdf

US Public Health Service. (1999). Suicide: Risk and protective factors. Retrieved from https://www.cdc.gov/violenceprevention/suicide/riskprotectivefactors.html

Van Strien, T., Frijters, J., Bergers, G., & Defares, P. (1986). The Dutch eating behavior questionnaire (DEBQ) for assessment of restrained, emotional, and external eating behavior. *International Journal of Eating Disorders, 5*(2), 295–315.

Volkow, N. (2011). Substance abuse among older adults. *NIDA Notes: Nora's Blog*. Retrieved from http://www.drugabuse.gov/news-events/nida-notes/2011/12/substance-abuse-among-older-adults

Wang, Y., & Andrade, L. (2013). Epidemiology of alcohol and drug use in the elderly. *Current Opinion in Psychiatry, 26*(4), 343–348.

Whitaker, C., & Keith, D. (1981). Symbolic-experiential family therapy. *Handbook of Family Therapy, 1*, 187–225.

White, W. (2009). *Long-Term Strategies to Reduce the stigma attached to Addiction, Treatment, and Recovery Within the City of Philadelphia (with Particular Reference to Medication-Assisted Treatment/Recovery)*. Philadelphia, PA: Department of Behavioural Health and Mental Retardation Services.

Wilens, T., & Morrison, N. (2011). The intersection of attention-deficit/hyperactivity disorder and substance abuse. *Current Opinion in Psychiatry, 24*(4), 280.

Williams, R., & Chang, S. (2000). A comprehensive and comparative review of adolescent substance abuse treatment outcome. *Clinical Psychology: Science and Practice, 7*(2), 138–166.

Winters, K., Botzet, A., & Fahnhorst, T. (2011). Advances in adolescent substance abuse treatment. *Current Psychiatry Reports, 13*(5), 416–421.

Wise, B., Cuffe, S., & Fischer, T. (2001). Dual diagnosis and successful participation of adolescents in substance abuse treatment. *Journal of Substance Abuse Treatment, 21*(3), 161–165.

Woods, J., & Joseph, H. (2012). Reducing stigma through education to enhance medication-assisted recovery. *Journal of Addictive Diseases, 31*(3), 226–235.

World Health Organization. (2002). Self-directed violence. Retrieved from http://www.who.int/violence_injury_prevention/violence/world_report/factsheets/en/selfdirectedviolfacts.pdf

Yatchmenoff, D. K. (2005). Measuring client engagement from the client 's perspective in nonvoluntary child protective services. *Research on Social Work Practice, 15*(2), 84–96.

Zimmerman, G., Olsen, C., & Bosworth, M. (2000). A 'stages of change' approach to helping patients change behavior. *American Family Physician, 61*(5), 1409–1416.

Zweben, J., & Ashbrook, S. (2012). Mutual-help groups for people with co-occurring disorders. *Journal of Groups in Addiction & Recovery, 7*(2-4), 202–222.

INDEX

CPSIA information can be obtained
at www.ICGtesting.com
Printed in the USA
BVHW050149200723
667523BV00002B/3

9 780190 926854